DATE			

THE WRITINGS OF

CARLOS FUENTES

THE WRITINGS OF

CARLOS FUENTES

RAYMOND LESLIE WILLIAMS

UNIVERSITY OF TEXAS PRESS
AUSTIN

TEXAS PAN AMERICAN SERIES

Requests for permission to reproduce material from this work should be sent to Permissions, University of Texas Press, Box 7819, Austin, TX 78713-7819.

♾ The paper used in this publication meets the minimum requirements of American National Standard for Information Sciences—Permanence of Paper for Printed Library Materials, ANSI Z39.48–1984.

Library of Congress Cataloging-in-Publication Data

Williams, Raymond L.
    The writings of Carlos Fuentes / Raymond Leslie Williams. — 1st ed.
        p.   cm. — (Texas Pan American series)
    Includes bibliographical references (p.   ) and index.
    ISBN 0-292-79097-X (cloth : alk. paper)
    1. Fuentes, Carlos—Criticism and interpretation. 2. Fuentes, Carlos.
Terra nostra.   I. Title. II. Series.
PQ7297.F793Z94   1996   95-43526
863—dc20

For Héctor Aguilar Camín, Martín Caparrós, Juan Goytisolo, Héctor Libertella, Dante Medina, and Luis Rafael Sánchez

CONTENTS

Carlos Fuentes is one of the major writers of this century in Latin America. Smitten by the modernity of Miguel de Cervantes and Jorge Luis Borges at an early age, he has written extensively on the cultures of the Americas and those of other places in the world. His work includes more than a dozen novels, several volumes of short stories, numerous essays on literary, cultural, and political topics, and some theater. Just as Cervantes' father (a surgeon) took his son along on his travels throughout Castille during the reigns of Charles V and Philip II, giving the boy an early introduction to the politics and cultures of sixteenth-century Spain, Fuentes' father (a diplomat) took him along on his travels. Consequently, Fuentes received an early and broad education on the cultures and politics of the Americas. He has dedicated his lifetime to the further understanding, analysis, and explanation of these cultures and politics.

During the late 1980s and early 1990s, I spent several years teaching the writings of Fuentes and thinking about the possibility of writing this book. During that time, I offered three graduate seminars on the fiction of Fuentes and made several trips to Mexico to interview the author and carry out research there. I began writing the biographical chapter in 1989. The idea for the book in the present form, however, finally came together in July 1992 while I was engaged in a dialogue with Fuentes and Fuentes scholars in El Escorial, Spain.

A group of twenty writers and Fuentes scholars met that July to dedicate a week to discussions of Fuentes' work, with the author himself joining in. After a presentation on *Terra Nostra* by the Mexican writer and scholar Dante Medina, Fuentes and our group be-

THE WRITINGS OF **CARLOS FUENTES**

came involved in a discussion on Latin American identity. The Mexican writer Héctor Aguilar Camín pointed out that the official histories of Mexico include pre-Columbian Indian civilizations, underscoring the contributions of the Toltecs, the Olmecs, the Aztecs, and other Native American groups to Mexican culture, but these Mexican histories have systematically excluded Spanish contributions to Mexico. Fuentes, Aguilar Camín, Dante Medina, and a group of other participants spent the remainder of the afternoon in the lobby and on the veranda of our hotel discussing exactly what Latin America is: Indian? Spanish? Criollo? Fuentes and Aguilar Camín were particularly insistent in recognizing Spain along with the other cultures that have contributed to the makeup of the Americas.

These questions have been debated in Latin America, of course, for more than a century. The career of Carlos Fuentes has consisted of a lengthy meditation on this question. As I watched Fuentes' eyes light up over our discussion, I realized that, despite the age-old nature of this debate, the questions are as alive today as they were a century ago, when Domingo Faustino Sarmiento defined Latin American identity within the conceptual framework of the simple Manichaean dichotomy between civilization and barbarism.

The next afternoon, Fuentes, Aguilar Camín, the Argentine writers Héctor Libertella and Martín Caparrós, the Puerto Rican writer Luis Rafael Sánchez, and I had lunch together. Fuentes sat at the head of the table and tended to lead the discussion. The conversation was classic Fuentes: He spent two hours exploring Latin American cultural and political reality, questioning this group of Latin American intellectuals about the recent politics and literature of each of their countries. He moved systematically from one country to another, inquiring and then probing more deeply. This was quintessential Fuentes—the man of the Americas—exploring his Americas once again, from a hotel located above the Spanish town of El Escorial.

By the end of that five-day symposium, the multiple directions that this book could have taken had been refined. The two areas of Fuentes' writing and thought that most urgently required further consideration, I had been reminded, were the problems of Latin American culture and identity. From my reading and teaching of

Fuentes, I had already recognized those as prominent issues, but the experience in El Escorial confirmed their importance for this book.

At the end of the week, Spanish writer Juan Goytisolo appeared on the scene and delivered a closing lecture on the Fuentes story "Las dos orillas," which deals with the encounter between Europe and the Americas. Goytisolo stressed the importance of the Indian languages—Mayan, Aztec, etc.—in the new Spanish of the Americas. Fuentes, sitting next to Goytisolo during the lecture, spoke after his Spanish friend's remarks, commenting on the cultural diversity of Spain—its Arabic and Jewish contributions.

The sixteenth-century palace and monastery called El Escorial, constructed by Philip II and located in the town of the same name, evokes many of these issues. El Escorial is also a central image in *Terra Nostra* and a cornerstone of the present study. I will attempt to demonstrate how El Escorial was a mirror image of Latin America during its foundational centuries. I will show how this palace also synthesizes, in its architecture and its contents, as well as its ideology and discourse, Hispanic culture in the time of Philip II. Consequently, topics concerning the relationship between El Escorial and *Terra Nostra* appear throughout this study. These two works—El Escorial and *Terra Nostra*—are the basic texts I use for an understanding of Hispanic culture and identity, although I include others. Fuentes himself has referred to parallels between El Escorial and *Terra Nostra*. In an interview published in 1978, he stated: "*Terra Nostra* is this: it is a second nature. In many senses: in the sense that the verbal literary construction is very similar to the material of the narrated construction of El Escorial . . ." (Coddou, 1978).

By the 1990s, Fuentes' analysis of cultures of the Americas led him to coin the term "Indo-Afro-Ibero-America." For Fuentes (as for many others), other more commonly used terms create several problems. The terms "Hispanic" and "Spanish" America exclude numerous portions of the cultures of the Americas—most obviously Brazil and the Portuguese language (which, interestingly enough, was Fuentes' first spoken language). Fuentes has also pointed out that the term "Latin America" was invented by the French in the late nineteenth century in order to legitimize their growing colonial interests. Expanding rather than excluding (and also rejecting the colonial maneuvers of the French), Fuentes proposes the term "Indo-Afro-Ibero-

America" for references to the region of the Americas traditionally called Latin America. Following Fuentes' lead, I will use that term regularly in this study, falling back on "Latin American" and "the Americas" occasionally, but only for stylistic reasons (the main problem with the term "Indo-Afro-Ibero-America" is its stylistic clumsiness).

There is no extant book-length study on Carlos Fuentes, *Terra Nostra*, and the cultures of the Americas. Wendy Farris has published an introductory study of Fuentes' fiction up to 1983, titled *Carlos Fuentes* (1983). This useful work contains a fourteen-page biographical sketch of Fuentes, the most lengthy yet published in English, and a seventeen-page analysis of *Terra Nostra*. Robert Brody and Charles Rossman have compiled a volume of thirteen critical studies on Fuentes, *Carlos Fuentes: A Critical View* (1982), which includes incisive articles by some of the most insightful Latin Americanists who have written on Fuentes, among them Jaime Alazraki, John S. Brushwood, Frank Dauster, Gloria Durán, Merlin Forster, Roberto González Echevarría, Lanin Gyurko, Luis Leal, Richard Reeve, and Margaret Sayers Peden. Ana María Hernández de López has edited *La obra de Carlos Fuentes: Una visión múltiple* (1988), a volume that includes articles by some of these and other Fuentes scholars. A very informative and insightful book on *Terra Nostra* is *Realidad y ficción en* Terra Nostra *de Carlos Fuentes* (1989), by Ingrid Simson. Other books on Fuentes' fiction include *The Archetypes of Carlos Fuentes* (1980), by Gloria Durán, *El mito en la obra narrativa de Carlos Fuentes* (1987), by Francisco Javier Ordiz, *La narrativa de Carlos Fuentes* (1983), by Aida Elsa Ramírez Mattei, and *Nostalgia del futuro en la obra de Carlos Fuentes* (1974), by Liliana Befumo Boschi and Elsa Calabrese. The most incisive article-length studies on Terra Nostra have been published by Roberto González Echevarría, Djelal Kadir, Lucille Kerr, José Miguel Oviedo, and Catherine Swietliki.

I have divided this book into three parts. Part I, "An Intellectual Biography: The Journey to El Escorial and *Terra Nostra*," is a biography of Fuentes from his birth in 1928 to 1993. In this part, I make occasional reference to issues developed in the following chapters: Fuentes' individual works, the role of culture, the definitions and functions of history, and the formation of identity in Indo-Afro-Ibero-America. Part II, "Rereading *Terra Nostra*," begins with an analysis of El Escorial and then continues with other texts that are important to an understanding of *Terra Nostra,* texts ranging from *Don Quixote* to essays by José Ortega y Gasset and Octavio Paz. I draw parallels between El Escorial and *Terra Nostra.* Part III, "Rereading Fuentes," deals with Fuentes' other fiction and its relationship to *Terra Nostra.* I have organized Part III along the lines of Fuentes' own division of his total fiction into fourteen cycles that he has identified as "La Edad del Tiempo." In Appendix I, I have included an interview with Fuentes on the concept of "La Edad del Tiempo." Appendix II consists of the list of books in Fuentes' original idea for "La Edad del Tiempo" as it was first published in 1987, followed by his 1993 and 1994 revisions.

This study was supported with funds provided by various committees at the University of Colorado at Boulder and a leave provided by its Committee on Research and Creative Work. I am indebted to the friends and family of Fuentes, who were most helpful to me in my preparation of this book, particularly the biographical chapter: his mother Berta Fuentes, his sister Berta Fuentes, Gabriel García Márquez, William Styron, José Donoso, Juan Goytisolo, Pierre Schori, Sergio Pitol, R. H. Moreno-Durán, Héctor Libertella, Federico Patán, Luis Rafael Sánchez, Porfirio Muñoz Ledo, Víctor Flores Olea, Roberto Torretti, and José Campillo Sainz. I am also grateful to the colleagues and friends who read this manuscript in its different stages of development: John S. Brushwood, Howard Goldblatt, George McMurray, Warren Motte, and Donald Schmidt. I am particularly appreciative of the assistance provided by my wife, Pamela Williams, and by graduate assistants Michael Buzan, Tony Maul, and Jennifer Valko. Above all, I thank Carlos and Sylvia Fuentes, who were always gracious and helpful—from the beginning of this project in Mexico City in 1989 to its near-conclusion in El Escorial in 1992.

ABBREVIATIONS

AC	The Death of Artemio Cruz
B	Birthday
BM	The Buried Mirror
BW	Burnt Water
Campaign	The Campaign
Cantar	Cantar de ciegos
Cervantes	Cervantes o la crítica de la lectura
Constancia	Constancia and Other Stories for Virgins
CU	Christopher Unborn
DR	Distant Relations
GC	The Good Conscience
HH	Hydra Head
HP	Holy Place
LDE	Los días enmascarados
OG	Old Gringo
Orange	The Orange Tree
TN	Terra Nostra
Where	Where the Air Is Clear

THE WRITINGS OF

CARLOS FUENTES

An Intellectual Biography: The Journey to El Escorial and *Terra Nostra*

Yo soy yo y mi circunstancia.   — JOSÉ ORTEGA Y GASSET

Peoples cannot be sundered from their histories; they are not in any way "they *and* their history."   — AMÉRICO CASTRO

In the sixteenth century, the Spanish Crown spread its language, as well as its cultural and political practices, across the vast geographical stretch of the Americas identified today as Latin America. In the second half of the century, the Spanish King Philip II built El Escorial as a monument to God, to the Spanish Empire, to Spain, and, of course, to himself. Philip II was born in 1527. Almost exactly four centuries later, in 1928, the Mexican intellectual Carlos Fuentes was born in Panama City. He has dedicated a lifetime to the analysis and critique of the language, culture, and political practices inherited from Spain—as represented by El Escorial—as well as the other cultures that have been systematically excluded from Spanish tradition (Jewish and Arabic cultures), ignored by Spain (Anglo-American and other Northern European cultures), or dominated by Spain (the indigenous cultures of the Americas). A Mexican by nationality, Fuentes has been a consummate man of the Americas in search of an understanding of his cultural heritage, his history, and his identity as a citizen of the Americas.

Fuentes has explained his beginnings as follows:

> I was born on November 11, 1928, under the sign I would have chosen,
> Scorpio, and on a date shared with Dostoevsky, Crommelynck,
> and Vonnegut. My mother was rushed from a steaming-hot movie
> house in those days before Colonel Buendía took his son to dis-
> cover ice in the tropics. She was seeing King Vidor's version of *La
> Boheme* with John Gilbert and Lillian Gish. Perhaps the pangs of
> my birth were provoked by this anomaly: a silent screen version of
> Puccini's opera. Since then, the operatic and the cinematographic
> have had a tug-of-war with my words, as if expecting the Scorpio
> of fiction to rise from silent music and blind images. All this, let me
> add to clear up my biography, took place in the sweltering heat of
> Panama City, where my father was beginning his diplomatic ca-
> reer as an attaché to the Mexican legation.[1]

To be born in Panama City—the geographic center of the Americas—was, indeed, the most appropriate beginning for Fuentes. After
that, he lived his childhood in Mexico City, Washington, D.C., Rio
de Janeiro, Santiago, and Buenos Aires. He saw the remnants of the
Spanish cultural heritage throughout Indo-Afro-Ibero-America well
before ever laying eyes on El Escorial several decades later. Mexico
left the most definite mark on Fuentes; he spent all his summer vacations as a young child there, and it was there that he was formed
intellectually from adolescence through adulthood.

The Fuentes family lived in various cities because of the diplomatic career of Carlos' father, Rafael Fuentes Boettiger. Consequently, the history and politics of the Americas became part of the
young Carlos Fuentes' daily life. He calls Rafael Fuentes Boettiger a
jarocho, a colloquial term referring to his father's origins in the state
of Veracruz. He also had German family roots, and the discipline and
work ethic of the Fuentes family have been associated with this part
of their heritage. From the Veracruz lineage came the playful, jocular,
and open personality that, according to Mexican tradition, often dis-
tinguishes the Mexicans of the Caribbean region from their more
sober and introspective inland compatriots. Rafael Fuentes Boettiger
dreamed of becoming a movie actor, but his father (a banker in Vera-

cruz) would not allow that, so he pursued his diplomatic career. An atheist and a liberal at a time when most Mexicans tended to be Catholic and far more conservative, Rafael Fuentes Boettiger obviously was not a typical man of his times. He participated in the Mexican defense of the city of Veracruz in 1914 when U.S. Marines invaded it. The defense effort was a military failure and an experience that few Mexicans, including Fuentes, have ever forgotten.

The home atmosphere that Rafael established, according to his wife, Berta, was organized and disciplined. Rafael Fuentes Boettiger was known as a man of honesty and integrity who was staunchly loyal to his friends. His contemporaries viewed him as a fundamentally serious person who knew how to enjoy life. Well educated, he read a wide range of books, including North American best-sellers of the 1930s. (Consequently, Carlos Fuentes can discuss North American popular fiction of the 1930s in surprising detail.) His father's passion for the movies was one of the reasons Carlos saw so many movies from his early childhood on.

Rafael Fuentes Boettiger was twenty-five years old when he married the eighteen-year-old Berta Macías Rivas, a very attractive and intelligent young woman from Mazatlán. Her daughter describes Berta as fanatically Mexican, from a family that Mexicans in the northern region associated with President Alvaro Obregón (1920–1924). Obregón's northern Mexico was also famous during the 1920s for its exceptionally attractive women, and Berta fit that description. She was never as liberal-minded nor as spontaneous as Rafael Fuentes Boettiger, but she was a relatively open-minded and enlightened woman for her time and society. She lived elegantly during an epoch when life was indeed most privileged for the upper class in Mexico, and even in her eighties she still carried herself with grace and charm.[2]

When Fuentes was born in Panama City in 1928, Mexico was entering a period of exuberance and confidence. It was not an atmosphere exactly the same as the Roaring Twenties in the United States, for Mexico and its revolution were still being consolidated. A new nation was being forged out of the chaos of the revolution, and a new order was emerging. Mexico was laying the groundwork for its transformation into a modern state. After the revolution, Mexico was institutionalizing the recognition of the pre-Columbian roots of

Mexican culture, thus supporting, for example, the muralist movement that actively promoted Indian and mestizo culture.

Fuentes' initial visual images of Mexico, however, were of neither revolutionary generals nor Indian leaders. They were of two fas-
cinating physical spaces: the Hotel Garci-Crespo in the town of Te-
huacán and his grandparents' home in the genteel Colonia Roma of
Mexico City.[3] The Hotel Garci-Crespo was Mexico's 1930s version
of present-day Cancún—the trendy vacation spot for Mexico's upper
class and foreigners. Built in 1934, the Garci-Crespo was one of the
most beautiful tourist hotels in Mexico at the time and attracted
vacationers from throughout the Americas, although mostly from
Mexico, the United States, and Cuba. It was a palatial white stucco
two-story edifice sitting on several acres of land that served as a
playground for adults as well as children. While the nannies took
the guests' children to play in the pool or to go horseback riding, the
adults relaxed in thermal spas, played golf, or retired to one of the
gambling rooms.

"The Garci-Crespo filled my imagination," Fuentes has com-
mented on this example of a vanishing genre of hotels, now seen only
in a few Caribbean locations and in old Bogart movies.[4] Indeed, it
must have been as much a feast for the imagination for the seven-
year-old Carlos in 1935 as Disneyland is for children of the 1990s—
and as El Escorial was for Fuentes in 1967. Upon his arrival at
the hotel, he saw massive white stucco pillars at the entrance and
ten-foot-tall main doors with lathed spindles. He passed by leaded
stained-glass windows on each side and then faced a lobby fit for the
arrival of eighteenth-century French royalty: a spectacular fifty-foot-
high ceiling with finely lathed and stenciled wooden cross-beams
and a chandelier suspended from its center; richly painted enamel-
covered metal tiels four feet high along the walls, elegantly trimmed
in copper. Royal motifs adorned the lobby and the entire hotel, with
the royal family crests depicted throughout. Fuentes' first visual images of Mexico were of wealth, European elegance, and comfort: this
was the aristocratic Mexico first exported to the Americas from the
Spain of El Escorial; the images of royalty had been inherited from
Philip II generations before.

The elegant Guanajuato Street residence in the Colonia Roma
of Mexico City was the source of Fuentes' other first images of Mex-

ico, images from the 1930s, when his family lived in splendor. The area, a few blocks south of the historic center of Mexico City, was a wealthy and graceful neighborhood populated mostly by Mexico's upper middle class. Its turn-of-the-century stone residences and wide avenues projected an aura more of Paris than of a Third World city. In fact, many of its two- and three-story buildings were patterned after late-nineteenth-century French architectural models. To attend classes in the Escuela Franco-Español of the Colonia San Angel, Carlos took a trolley along the Avenida Alvaro Obregón, hardly different from a pleasant ride along the Boulevard Saint Michel in Paris at the time.

In 1989, Fuentes remembered well the herringbone design, located at a small child's eye level, on the stonework of the house on Guanajuato Street. He also recalled the boiler heater in the center of the home. This house was a typical two-story stone building of the neighborhood. The family of four stayed at their Guanajuato Street home during Christmas vacations, and Carlos also returned there for the summers after school ended each spring at the Cook School, a public school in Washington, D.C. On his parents' insistence, Carlos attended school during these summer vacations; year-round education between Washington and Mexico made him actively bilingual and bicultural from an early age. He remembers classes in Mexico where he heard his first lessons in Mexican history: as a young child he was already learning the names of the Aztec and Toltec gods, from Huitzilopochti to Tlaloc—the same gods that appeared decades later in *Terra Nostra.*

For the young Carlos, one of the most gratifying experiences of the summer vacations in the Colonia Roma was the movies. His parents or his grandmother strolled with him and his younger sister the five blocks down the Avenida Alvaro Obregón to a grand movie house called the Balmori, the first in Mexico to feature sound films. They saw Greta Garbo, Rita Hayworth, Humphrey Bogart, and many other North American movie stars who were as idolized by Fuentes and his generation of Latin American writers as they were by moviegoers in the United States. The names of many of these Hollywood stars appeared later in novels such as *Holy Place* and *A Change of Skin.*

Beyond Mexico, two important moments from Fuentes' early

childhood remained in his memory as an adult. One was of Alfonso Reyes in 1931 in Brazil, when Carlos was still a three-year-old boy. Fuentes has often said that he learned literature from the lap of Alfonso Reyes, one of Mexico's major twentieth-century writers, and this affirmation has its origins in the Brazilian experience. From those days, Carlos remembers Reyes as his most cherished mentor. The author of more than thirty volumes of essays and creative works, Reyes lived in the same world of books and discipline that eventually became Fuentes' daily regimen.

The other memorable childhood experience took place at the Cook School in Washington, D.C., where Fuentes attended grade school from 1934 to 1940. In his early years there, Carlos had been a well-liked leader among his classmates; he was popular—or, in the parlance of the time, "regular" (*Myself,* 7). He organized little plays, assigning his friends their parts while he directed. On March 18, 1938, however, he suddenly lost his status as a regular: the president of Mexico, Lázaro Cárdenas, nationalized the oil owned by North American companies, and overnight, Mexicans in Washington were the object of scorn. "Instantly, suprisingly, I became a pariah in my school. Cold shoulders, aggressive stares, epithets, and sometimes blows" (*Myself,* 7).

Cárdenas, who was president from 1934 to 1940, headed one of the most progressive governments in Mexican history. In addition to nationalizing the oil, he aggressively promoted land reform, parceling out portions of agricultural land to the dispossessed. His was also Mexico's most nationalistic government of the century. Fuentes has always been an admirer of Cárdenas, whom he has considered a genuine voice of the revolution that most governments of the Institutional Revolutionary Party (PRI) have reduced to empty rhetoric. In an essay published in the 1960s, Fuentes wrote of Cárdenas with great admiration, maintaining that this leader still served as a great model for Mexicans in the 1960s.

Despite the disappointing experiences of his final year at the Cook School, Fuentes' early childhood was generally rich and fulfilling. His mother, Berta, insisted that the family's home always be essentially Mexican, no matter where they lived: they spoke only Spanish at home (even during the stay in Washington), and they played popular Mexican music on the old 78 rpm records. According to her, even during the years in Washington, Fuentes "never felt unconnected to Mexico." Indeed, in 1939 his father took him to see a film, *Man of Conquest,* at the old RKO-Keith in Washington, and when the protagonist proclaimed the secession of the Republic of Texas from Mexico, the eleven-year-old Carlos jumped up on the theater seat and proclaimed, "Viva México! Death to the gringos!" (*Myself,* 9). It was a declaration of citizenship perhaps even more convincing than his diplomatic passport.

The young Carlos could hardly have enjoyed a better family life: He, his parents, and his sister represented an exceptionally close family unit that functioned in a surprisingly democratic fashion for 1930s Mexico. They always dined together, and the children had the right to express their opinions at the dinner table—certainly not a common practice in Mexican society at that time. Carlos was encouraged to develop his own independent mind. The parents even upheld a family tradition of calling a *mesa redonda,* or "round table," meeting when important decisions were to be made. They often participated in social and cultural events together—concerts, opera, and film being their preferences. Consequently, at a young age Carlos became exceptionally knowlegeable about film and music from the United States and Mexico.

Early Adolescence: 1941–1944

Fuentes spent his early adolescence, ages twelve to fifteen, in the two most European countries of South America, Chile and Argentina. Unlike his life in Washington, he now lived the Spanish language fully, and his Southern Cone experience in these two countries marked his cultural and political formation for a lifetime. He was living in two countries where the populace was intensely politicized. It was an experience that provided Fuentes with his initiation into a lifetime involvement with progressive politics. During these years, he also encountered the cultural legacy of Spain outside Mexico for the first time: it was an initial glimpse of the culture and ideology propagated from El Escorial several centuries before. During his stay in the Southern Cone, the young Carlos began writing and published his first story in a school magazine.

When the Fuentes family arrived in Santiago in 1941, Chile was experiencing the democratic revolution of the Popular Front, which had been in power from 1938 to the end of 1941. Three decades later, Fuentes remembered one of the chief politicians and spokespersons for the Socialists, Oscar Schnake, as well as the leader Marmaduke Grove. He also recalled the political satire magazine that ridiculed Schnake most severely, *Topaze*. The electrified political atmosphere and Marxist ideas in the air offered a marked contrast to his recent experience in Washington. Indeed, Fuentes was living in one of the most politicized nations of the Americas.

While in Chile, Fuentes studied in two of Santiago's better private schools: the Cambridge School and the Grange School. "I'm half Aztec," the adolescent Carlos enjoyed telling his classmates at the Grange School—his latest imaginative method of articulating the Mexican identity he had first declared publicly in the movie theater in Washington, D.C. Children of diplomats and foreigners, and mostly white upper class, the boys at the school had no reason to doubt the proud young Mexican's story. This was only one of numerous imaginative ventures in which Fuentes was engaged during the year at the Grange School, for he also wrote stories and even coauthored a novel with his best friend at the school, Roberto Torretti. Fuentes still remembers that one of his teachers in Chile, Alejandro Tarragó, told him, "You have to be a writer," and that Fuentes took his advice to heart. Several of the boys at the Grange School wrote fiction, but the one story their teacher Julio Durán selected for publication in the magazine of another high school had been penned by Fuentes. In addition, Fuentes and Torretti, avid readers of Dumas, decided to write their own adventure novel; the result was a two-hundred-page manuscript, a historical novel, but projected into the future. (Years later, Fuentes-the-professional-writer frequently admonished his readers to "imagine the past and remember the future," and he wrote a novel projecting into the future, *Christopher Unborn*.) Fuentes and Torretti divided their novel into two parts. The first part of the novel, "The Cycle and the Hammer," took place from 1945 forward and dealt with a young French boy's experience in a postwar France entirely dominated by the Soviet Union, for Fuentes and Torretti hypothesized that Europe after the war would be communist and in the hands of the Soviets. Torretti said that the story, however, "seemed very boring to us," so they wrote a second part, which took place in approximately 1980 and in which the Soviet bloc was disintegrating. (This was the first of several remarkably accurate political prophecies that Fuentes has made.) The second part was more playful, perhaps more like Dumas, with adventure and royalty. Fuentes made drawings of the faces of the main characters.[5]

Fuentes' life in 1943 was centered on the Grange School, a private secondary school (grades seven through twelve) founded in 1936 by John Jackson, a Chilean of British background who, despite being born in Chile, spoke Spanish with a heavy British accent and who was the school's headmaster. Located just on the north of Santiago with a superb view of the *cordillera* of the Andes mountains, the Grange School of 1943 was outside the city of Santiago, on the grounds of the Prince of Wales Country Club. It was a school for Chile's upper class, its foreign diplomats, and its foreign businessmen. The institution's basic entrance requirements were a knowlege of English and the financial ability to pay tuition. Consequently, the Grange School tended to draw students from a social rather than intellectual elite. The curriculum at the school was originally taught half in English and half in Spanish, but by the time Fuentes enrolled in 1943, the nationalist government of the Popular Front required that all the classes be taught in Spanish. Students attended school for a full day Monday through Friday, and half a day on Saturday. A typical school day for Fuentes began with an inspection of all the students and a brief Anglican religious service (in English), followed by a morning of classes and lunch. After lunch, the students were free for an hour of recess on the school's ample grounds. Carlos and Roberto Torretti were in the third year of secondary school (the equivalent of ninth grade in a high school in the United States) in 1943. The school stressed academics less than some of the other private secondary schools because of its promotion of sports—cricket, rugby, and soccer. Rather than emphasizing academics exclusively (as did the best French lycées in Chile), the Grange School's program was intended to build "character" in the Anglo-American tradition. Its unofficial agenda was to make its students Europeans—Brits of good character.

"We were enormously pretentious," Roberto Torretti has explained, describing the attitudes of the young Carlos and the group at the Grange School.[6] Torretti himself was already reading Dosto-evski at age thirteen, and Fuentes was no more modest in his literary undertakings. As already cosmopolitan and multilingual young men, they exuded confidence. What they lacked as athletes at the Grange School (neither Fuentes nor Torretti performed well in sports), they more than compensated for with their ambitious and sometimes pre-tentious intellectual activities. They were already imagining the pos-sibility of being the formidable intellectuals that they were indeed to become: Torretti is an internationally recognized philosopher on the faculty of the University of Puerto Rico in Río Piedras, and he has had books published in both Latin America and the United States.[7]

The political scenario that the Fuentes family participated in had been set in motion in 1938 when the Chileans elected Pedro Aguirre Cerda, leader of the Popular Front, as president. The most powerful in this alliance of leftist parties was the Socialist Party, led by Oscar Schnake and Marmaduke Grove. Aguirre Cerda actually represented the Radical Party in this fragile conglomeration of the Left. Nevertheless, with the support of the verbose Grove, who ac-companied him during his campaign, Aguirre Cerda was elected in December 1938. The Popular Front became "a symbol of union in the minds of the masses, union against oppression."[8] Despite this seemingly mystical feeling of support among the masses, Aguirre Cerda was unable to carry out most of his progressive agenda, for he was under attack from the opposition parties as well as those within his own Popular Front. Oscar Schnake, now the minister of devel-opment, was under severe attack by the communists. By late 1941, when the Fuentes family arrived in Santiago, the Popular Front was in crisis and Aguirre Cerda was about to die.

Fuentes remembered the situation in Chile for many years, and the Chilean experience was a significant stage in the development of a political vision that would later question authoritarian politics and, more specifically, the ideology of El Escorial. Above all, Fuentes viv-idly remembered Oscar Schnake, the former secretary general of the Socialist Party and the minister of development who revolutionized the workers' union in Chile. He and Marmaduke Grove headed the left wing of the Socialist Party, frequently intimidating Chile's tra-ditional upper class. Fuentes saw both of them lead the opposition against President-elect Juan Antonio Ríos, who represented a center/conservative alliance.

Fuentes was a precocious and acute critic of international politics. He and his friends invented and played a game of international political intrigue in which each of the players assumed the role of a country. Moreover, in 1944 and 1945, when he was sixteen and seventeen years old, Fuentes maintained a correspondence with Torretti that dealt mostly with national and international politics. From early adolescence, then, Fuentes was an informed and shrewd observer of international politics. He tended to be more interested in the international scenario—the grand narrative—than local situations. During his correspondence with Torretti, Fuentes also met censorship for the first time: his letters to Torretti, written during World War II, were frequently intercepted and opened in Panama by U.S. authorities. Testing the accuracy of the censors, Fuentes and Torretti purposely wrote political commentary, only to find these lines blotted out of their letters by the authorities.

Near the end of the year in Chile, Rafael Fuentes Boettiger called a family "round table" meeting and proposed the idea of moving to Buenos Aires. The family reached an agreement to relocate, and in October 1943, they crossed the Andes to Buenos Aires, to reside in an apartment on the corner of Callao and Quintana in the center of the Argentine capital. The military governed Argentina, and Juan Perón was an increasingly visible minister of labor. The Fuentes family was not at all pleased with the conservative curriculum offered in the public schools under the direction of the right-wing Gustavo Adolfo Martínez Zuviría (who wrote novels under the pen name of "Hugo Wast"). Consequently, Fuentes' parents allowed him a vacation from school in Argentina, so he explored Buenos Aires for several months, an experience that included following tango orchestras and reading the new Argentine comic books—*Billiken* and *Patarozú*. Despite these pleasures, life in the Argentina of the 1940s was always strained: Nazism was fervent and quite tangible in the streets of Buenos Aires. According to Fuentes' sister, Berta, the Argentine citizens' reputation for being the most snobbish people of Latin America was well justified.[9] Nevertheless, Fuentes himself has fond memories of his year in Buenos Aires, including the discovery of Borges and his first sexual experience—Fuentes had an affair with a beautiful thirty-year-old Czech woman.

Fuentes' ongoing discovery of the cultural heritage of the Americas now involved Argentine literature, too. He had read Argentine letters from gaucho poems to Domingo Faustino Sarmiento's *Memories of Provincial Life* to Miguel Cané's *Juvenilia* and Ricardo Güiraldes' *Don Segundo Sombra*. Most important, he discovered the writer who was at the forefront of the Argentine avant-garde and who was promoting modern literature in Argentina in general: Jorge Luis Borges. The discovery of Borges was essential to the formation of Fuentes-the-modern-writer.

After a year in Argentina, Fuentes requested a family "round table" and asked to return to Mexico. The family agreed to split up temporarily so that Carlos could live in his homeland. His father remained in Buenos Aires in his diplomatic position, and his mother and sister returned with Carlos to Mexico City. The trip from Buenos Aires was a memorable weeklong adventure: They traveled on a Pan American Airways flight full of soldiers that, for security reasons, landed every afternoon and took six days to fly from Buenos Aires to Miami. Fuentes remembers well reading Borges' *Ficciones* on that flight. This volume of now classic Borges narratives, so important to several generations of Latin American writers, appeared in print in the year of Fuentes' return to Mexico City. With *Ficciones,* Latin American writers of Fuentes' generation discovered a freedom to invent as never before. Borges undermined many of the assumptions of the realist-naturalist tradition.

From Miami, the three members of the Fuentes family flew directly to Mexico City, where they moved into the home of Carlos' maternal grandmother at Calle Montes de Oca No. 37 in the Colonia Condesa, a comfortable two-story house located in one of the most charming neighborhoods in the Mexico City of the 1940s.

The Formative Years: 1944–1952

When the sixteen-year-old Carlos Fuentes arrived in Mexico in 1944, his country was experiencing what the international business com-

munity later called the "Mexican Miracle." Under the presidency of
Manuel Avila Camacho (1940–1946), the revolution of Cárdenas was
attenuated, and Mexico underwent a period of industrialization and
modernization. The nationalism of the 1930s was still extant, but it
was affected by an increasingly international vision: muralists Diego
Rivera, José Clemente Orozco, and David Siqueiros were losing
popularity to the new universal painting of Rufino Tamayo and Juan
Soriano.[10] The cosmopolitan and universal Alfonso Reyes, an unorthodox voice of diversity in the 1930s, became a major presence of
the new establishment of the 1940s. His was the voice of the grand
narrative—Mexican adaptations of Western canonical literature.
Fuentes was in Mexico during all these formative years except 1950,
when he was studying in Geneva. He finished his secondary education in Mexico, began studying law at the Universidad Nacional Autónoma de México (UNAM), and wrote his first stories. During the
1940s, Reyes had a significant influence on Fuentes: Reyes believed
firmly in the value of cultural traditions in all societies, and first
Reyes and later Fuentes worked toward defining these cultural values
for Indo-Afro-Ibero-American society.

In the 1940s, Mexico City was a small town in the process of
being transformed into a city. As Fuentes' sister, Berta, remembers,
it still seemed "very provincial" to the family when they returned
from cosmopolitan Buenos Aires.[11] These were golden years in the
capital, a city in which the wealthy drove their sleek Packards, Lin-
colns, and Cadillacs. President Avila Camacho's strategy was to gain
the confidence of investors and use the second European war as an
opportunity to industrialize. He loosened many of the nationalistic
policies of the Cárdenas government, including the law against private religious education. Consequently, the children of the upper
class could attend schools operated by the Marists, the Jesuits, and
other religious groups.

Mexico was institutionalizing a culture that was nationalistic
while attempting to be universal. Consequently, Mexican muralists
were institutionalized during the 1930s and 1940s. The writers Samuel Ramos and José Vasconcelos attempted to define a Mexican
identity in a universal context, and their works were amply read—
indeed, they were best-sellers—during the 1940s. Fuentes inherited

the problem of identity as a central issue for Latin American intellectuals of the 1940s and a matter of particular interest in a rapidly transforming Mexico.

During these years, the Fuentes family inhabited three residences in Mexico City, corresponding to different periods in Fuentes' intellectual development. Upon their arrival, as mentioned, they lived with their grandparents in the Colonia Condesa. When Rafael Fuentes Boettiger returned from Argentina, they moved into a strikingly contemporary home in what the Mexicans call "California Style," with smooth lines, ample open space and light, located at Calle Louisiana No. 10, in the Colonia Nápoles, where they lived from 1945 to 1948. Then they moved to the Colonia Roma, where they occupied a more traditional gray stone two-story home at Calle Tíber No. 10 until 1955. Carlos Fuentes' friends from the university, such as Víctor Flores Olea, visited him on Tíber, where he hosted his very first cultural activities (frequently poetry readings) and wrote the stories appearing in the volume *Los días enmascarados*. Flores Olea remembers the home on Tíber as one where Fuentes organized *tertulias* to create dialogue among the future intellectuals of their generation. Fuentes' friends also remember him during this period as the gracious host who generously offered drinks from an always well-stocked liquor cabinet.

From 1944 to 1946 Fuentes attended the Colegio México (not to be confused with the Colegio de México, an institution of higher education), a secondary school operated by Marists that received well-prepared students from the middle and upper-middle sectors of Mexican society. Fuentes' sister described Carlos as "very sociable" during this period and "always very involved." His *inquietud* was expressed in his voracious desire for knowledge: in high school he was constantly reading and writing, always enthusiastic about learning everything from European literature to the neighborhoods in Mexico City. He usually rode public transportation to school, rubbing shoulders with the people on the street and hearing the Spanish language as it was spoken by his compatriots of all social classes.

He often visited his old family friend and now mentor, the venerable Alfonso Reyes. Fuentes and future writer Sergio Pitol would meet at the home library of Reyes, listening to his opinions and advice on a wide range of subjects. Don Alfonso exercised a regular regimen, writing from 5:00 a.m. to 8:00 a.m. daily. The rigid discipline of Reyes and Rafael Fuentes Boettinger explains much of Fuentes' arduous work schedule and remarkable productivity. Reyes also left his intellectual mark on Fuentes, as the latter has explained: "He taught me that culture had a smile, that the intellectual tradition of the whole world was ours by birthright, and that Mexican litera- ture was important because it was literature, not because it was Mexi- can" (*Myself,* 19).

During the years from 1947 to 1953 Fuentes became an intellec- tual. He read literature, continued writing, studied law, and made some of his lifelong literary friends. He attended a college prepara- tory school, the Colegio Francés, studied in Geneva in 1950, and from there made trips to Paris and other parts of Europe. Fuentes enjoyed an active social life, dividing his time between his friends and his family. Mexico's upper class lived a genteel life of concerts, operas, and parties, to which the men wore tuxedos and the women the latest fashions from the United States and Europe. Social and moral mores were rigidly conservative and notably ceremonial. These were the years when Fuentes' closest friends from the UNAM, such as Víctor Flores Olea, were making the rounds in Mexico City, be- coming acquainted with the setting later fictionalized in *Where the Air Is Clear.*

During his years as a high school and law student, Fuentes did not yet have any real presence on the Mexican cultural scene. The most influential cultural organ for the reading public, the Sunday cultural supplement of the newspaper *Novedades* ("México en la Cul- tura"), dedicated its weekly pieces to established writers, such as Al- fonso Reyes and Mariano Azuela. The youngest Mexican to appear with any regularity was Octavio Paz, then in his thirties, a decade older than Fuentes. For the most part, however, *Novedades* dealt with the latest trends in foreign art, pre-Columbian art and culture, and the established men of letters. Young writers in Mexico were virtually ignored.

Fuentes' intellectual life at the university and with friends, nev- ertheless, was stimulating and intense. These were important years of literary apprenticeship, and he dedicated much time to writing. Even though he was still unpublished and unknown as a writer, his family and friends were well aware of his creative activity and his aspirations to be a professional writer. For example, the Mexican diplomat and writer Mario Moya Palencia, who also studied at the Colegio México, has told how, as a high school student, he anonymously submitted a short story for a contest. When the prizes were announced and the names of the anonymous contestants revealed, Moya Palencia received nothing and Carlos Fuentes was named as the winner of the first, second, and third prizes.

Fuentes belongs to a generation of intellectuals that called itself the "Generation of *Medio Siglo*." As young students in the early 1950s, they felt destined to play a major role in Mexico's cultural and political future. They were the Mexicans who could have been equated in some ways with what was once called "the best and the brightest" in the United States, and they were well aware of their privileged status. Fuentes became acquainted with them in 1951 upon returning from Switzerland. The group consisted of Víctor Flores Olea (who became an astute political analyst, and later a diplomat as well as a political and cultural figure in Mexico), Sergio Pitol (who became one of Mexico's major novelists), Porfirio Muñoz Ledo (subsequently a political leader in the PRI and then in the opposition to the PRI), Miguel de la Madrid (president of Mexico, 1982–1988), and others who have led successful professional and political careers in Mexico, such as Javier Wimer and Enrique González Pedrero. All these young men were progressive and cosmopolitan, politically sophisticated, and fluent in several languages. Many of them had completed their high school studies at the Colegio México. One of their former law professors from the UNAM, José Campillo Sainz, looking back forty years later, described the group as "exceptionally intelligent and motivated" and spoke of Fuentes as an "excellent student." [12] They were groomed to become Mexico's leaders.

The generation of *Medio Siglo* was politically well educated, informed by readings from Machiavelli to Erasmus, from the Enlightenment of David Hume to Rousseau, and in Marxism from Marx to Lukacs. (Fuentes, in fact, has been citing Machiavelli, Erasmus, and the rest throughout his life.) They were admirers of the last Mexican president to practice revolutionary ideals, Cárdenas, and later were strongly affected by the Cuban Revolution. Reared and educated in a world polarized by the Iron Curtain, they never accepted the Manichaean dichotomy of only two political alternatives. [13]

In Fuentes' case, it is important to keep in mind his formative political experiences: the New Deal in Washington, the Mexican Revolution as promoted by the progressive Cárdenas, and the Popular Front in Chile. The educational background of the generation of *Medio Siglo,* as well as the experience with these governments, explain much of Fuentes' always-progressive political vision.

Fuentes was the catalyst for one project that brought his generation together when they were students—the publication of a magazine called *Medio Siglo.* The idea for *Medio Siglo* had come from their professor Mario de la Cueva, and it was soon in the hands of two of the most capable youths of the group, Carlos Fuentes and Porfirio Muñoz Ledo. Others who worked closely with them in 1952 and 1953 were Salvador Elizondo, Sergio Pitol, Víctor Flores Olea, and Javier Wimer. The magazine described itself as "the expression of the law students" and covered a broad range of cultural and political topics. The intellectual horizons and quality of *Medio Siglo* were remarkably high for a student magazine. For example, Salvador Elizondo and Víctor Flores Olea published an incisive article titled "The Idea of Man in the Contemporary Novel," which included commentary on Hesse, Huxley, Faulkner, Kafka, Joyce, and others. Fuentes served as the president of the editorial board. The magazine had two groups: one headed by Fuentes and Flores Olea, and the other led by Muñoz Ledo and Wimer. The latter were more radical in their politics than Fuentes and Flores Olea were, according to Muñoz Ledo.[14] Fuentes' own contributions to *Medio Siglo* included both cultural and political topics. He published essays on José Clemente Orozco and on Mexico within the Latin American political scenario, and reviews of recent books of literary and political interest. With the publication of *Medio Siglo,* Fuentes and his friends were announcing their generation's presence in Mexico.

Another unifying factor for Fuentes and the group was the intellectual and social life they shared. They were great admirers of several of their outstanding professors, particularly Manuel Pedroso, José Campillo Sainz, and Mario de la Cueva. Pedroso, a Spanish exile and former diplomat, was a brilliant liberal humanist—a twentieth-century Renaissance man who mentored the group. His students often approached him after class for informal discussions that turned out to be Pedroso's monologues on a multiplicity of issues. Sergio

Pitol recalls that once Fuentes arrived from Switzerland and joined the group, the level of the discourse in these conversations was immediately raised.[15] Pedroso recommended many readings that Carlos and the group diligently undertook. In the early 1950s, the law school of the UNAM was still located in the heart of Mexico City, on Calle San Ildefonso, and the discussions with Professor Pedroso often drifted out of the classroom, down San Ildefonso, and into nearby cafés. With mentors such as Reyes and Pedroso, Fuentes was under the tutelage of the most prominent teachers in Mexico at the time. He adored Pedroso and often spoke of him later in essays and interviews. Like Reyes, Pedroso believed in the crucial role of culture and the intellectuals in the political process.

Fuentes and this group socialized regularly, and one of their most memorable rituals was the dinners they enjoyed together approximately once a month at the Restaurante Bavaria near the corner of Insurgentes Sur and Pennsylvania Street in the Colonia Nápoles of Mexico City. In the early 1950s, the Colonia Nápoles was one of the chic areas of the city, and the Restaurante Bavaria was a congenial place to drink beer, eat, and talk endlessly about politics, the university, literature, and the like.[16] An L-shaped restaurant with a capacity for approximately two hundred people, the Bavaria was an informal meeting place where the group could pull tables together for ten or twelve in one of the corners and hold forth until the management finally put the chairs on the remaining empty tables and turned off the lights—which they frequently needed to do to get Fuentes and his friends to leave at closing time.[17] Usually a dozen of them met at the Bavaria, including Professor Campillo Sainz, who maintains that what unified them was their spirit of young *inquietos.* When closing time came at the Bavaria, Campillo Sainz, who was thirty years old and married, returned home to his family, and Fuentes and his friends departed to explore the city. More than one member of the group has described Fuentes in his early twenties as "friendly," "pleasant," and quite entertaining with his exceptional ability to mimic.

"Carlos has been a lover of Mexico City," Campillo Sainz has explained, and nightlife was indeed a significant part of Fuentes' ongoing love affair with that city. The typical student with his class background met with friends at Sanborns Restaurante (Sanborns de los Azulejos) and might frequent the better restaurants in the Colonia Roma and Colonia Nápoles. In Mexico City, Fuentes accepted few limits, however, for he and his friends ventured everywhere, from the most chic nightclubs to the most down-and-out flophouses. "We would go to a whorehouse oddly called El Buen Tono, choose a poor Mexican girl who usually said her name was Gladys and she came from Guadalajara, and go to our respective rooms" (*Myself,* 21).

Mexico City in the early 1950s offered a vital and exciting urban center for these energetic and inquisitive young intellectuals in their twenties, and their experience provided Fuentes with much of the anecdotal material that appeared later in *Where the Air Is Clear.* "These were the years we lived *Where the Air Is Clear,*" his friend Flores Olea (his most frequent companion) explained years later when evoking the early 1950s.[18] These were also the years when they discovered the writings of D. H. Lawrence, Aldous Huxley, James Joyce, André Gide, T. S. Eliot, and Thomas Mann—usually on the recommendation of Professor Pedroso. These readings, after Cervantes and Borges, were keys to the formation of Fuentes-the-modern-writer. By the time he was writing *Where the Air Is Clear* in the mid-1950s, Fuentes had assimilated many of the narrative strategies of the modernists that he had read as an adolescent.

During the period from 1946 to 1952, the other important facet of Fuentes' social life was his family. The Fuentes family sometimes appeared in the social pages of the newspapers, with Rafael Fuentes Boettiger and Carlos Fuentes smartly dressed in black tuxedos. Fuentes loved the opera, and his sister, Berta, remembers that he was an accomplished mimic of the opera singers.[19] In 1948, Fuentes appeared in a newspaper in his first tuxedo—a handsome, heavyset, long-haired twenty-year-old with black-rimmed glasses.[20] He was also shown in pictures with family and friends of the family in such places as the private home of his cousins the Romandía family in 1948 and at a party in the Chilean Embassy in 1949. In the spring of 1950, his picture was published in the newspaper for his farewell party as he boarded the plane for his trip to Switzerland.

On the flight to Switzerland, Fuentes stopped in Paris, where he met Octavio Paz—then a young poet and a budding author, with *The Labyrinth of Solitude* already published—for the first time. Fuentes recalls, "I remember Paz in the so-called existentialist nightclubs of the time in Paris, in discussion with the very animated and handsome Albert Camus, who alternated philosophy and the boogie-woogie in La Rose Rouge" (*Myself,* 22). He also remembers Paz in a gallery on the Place Vendome, reflecting on Max Ernst's postwar painting *Europe after the Rain.* Paz treated Fuentes kindly, and they immediately became friends, attending the opening of Ernst's exhibition together and dedicating a week to incessant conversation about books and art. Paz was clearly influential in Fuentes' early intellectual formation, particularly in the promotion and defense of literary modernism in Mexico. Writing in the mid-1980s, Fuentes explained the importance of Paz for him: "In the generous friendship of Octavio Paz, I learned that there were no privileged centers of culture, race, or politics; that nothing should be left out of literature, because our time is a time of deadly reduction" (*Myself,* 22). This important lesson would later represent a foundation for Fuentes' aesthetics and politics, culminating in the novel that questions privileged centers of culture, *Terra Nostra.*

Fuentes' trip to Europe in 1950 was also his introduction to the Great Britain of Prime Minister Clement R. Attlee and the postwar devastation and deprivation of London. Fuentes was particularly impressed with the sense of solidarity among the British, despite the difficult postwar living conditions.[21] When the twenty-two-year-old Fuentes arrived at the magnificent Regent Palace Hotel in London, it was a memorable multicultural experience for him, for he took as much note of the East Indians—the first time he had ever seen Indians wearing turbans—as of the splendid structure with its neoclassic motifs. He was located near the square of Piccadilly Circus, in the heart of London's vibrant theater district. Access to the fine European theater of the time was one of the most memorable cultural experiences of his first trip to Great Britain.[22] He was also excited about the discovery of Foyles' bookstore (Foyle W. & G. Ltd.) on Charing Cross Road, a massive edifice of four floors well stocked with books.

Fuentes spent the year in Geneva studying at the Institut des Hautes Etudes Internationales and living in a garret overlooking the beautiful square of the Bourg-du-Four, with its many coffeehouses and old bookstores. He frequently took a book to read on Jean-Jacques Rousseau Island, where Lake Geneva meets the Rhone River. The time spent reading Western canonical literature was accompanied by reflections on his own possibilities, as a Mexican, of writing literature and traveling the road of Don Quixote. Above all, it was an important year in the formation of Fuentes-the-modern-writer, for he read many of the modern classics, from Cervantes to Faulkner. Reflecting on that period and on the adventurous path offered by Cervantes, Fuentes explains: "In my way, this is the road I wanted to travel. I read Rousseau, or the adventures of the I; Joyce and Faulkner, or the adventures of the We; Cervantes, or the adventures of the You he calls the Idle, the Amiable Reader: you. And I read, in shower of fire and in the lightning of enthusiasm, Rimbaud" (*Myself,* 24).

The climax of Fuentes' first European experience came in the summer of 1950 at a dinner with some Mexican friends in the Baur-au-Lac Hotel on Lake Zurich. He noticed three ladies sitting in the restaurant with a gentleman in his seventies, and suddenly realized that the solitary man was Thomas Mann. As he studied Mann, Fuentes came to the realization that "Thomas Mann had managed, out of his solitude, to find the affinity between the personal destiny of the author and that of his contemporaries in general" (*Myself,* 25–26). Seeing Mann that evening and reflecting upon him were important experiences for Fuentes: "I shall always thank him for silently teaching me that, in literature, you know only what you imagine" (*Myself,* 26). Fuentes' belief in the role of imagination, indeed, became a doctrine of a lifetime, a lesson learned not only from Mann but also from Cervantes and Borges.

The Search for Identity: 1953–1957

Fuentes' career as a professional writer blossomed from 1953 to 1957, and he became a well-known literary figure in Mexico. Before the publication of his first book, the story "Chac Mool" had appeared in the prestigious *Revista de la Universidad de México,* and by the end of the year, *Los días enmascarados,* his first volume of stories, was circulating in Mexico City. He also cofounded a prominent literary journal in Mexico, *Revista Mexicana de Literatura,* in 1955. Like many young Mexican intellectuals of the 1950s who were writing under the shadow of Paz's powerful *Labyrinth of Solitude,* Fuentes was searching for a concept of Mexican identity. This was a symbolic beginning along the path to El Escorial and the eventual writing of *Terra Nostra*.

Fuentes' active social life with his family in Mexico City ended in 1953, for on November 3 of that year his family left for Panama, where Rafael Fuentes Boettiger accepted his first position as ambassador, given to him under the government of President Adolfo Ruiz Cortines. Engaged in the completion of the stories for *Los días enmascarados,* Fuentes decided to remain in Mexico, where he lived in the family's apartment on Rubén Darío Street, overlooking Chapultepec Park, and wrote *Where the Air Is Clear.*

During these years, Ruiz Cortines (president of Mexico from 1952 to 1958) continued many of the policies and programs of Manuel Avila Camacho (1940–1946) and Miguel Alemán (1946–1952). Ruiz Cortines developed a similar program of industrialization, coupled with a strategy of encouraging foreign investment, exports, and tourism. Mexico's political leaders systematically used their power to move into related personal economic investments. Consequently, as one scholar explained, "the country has enjoyed rapid industrialization but at the cost of high levels of official corruption." [23] In the 1950s, the expanding economy was able to absorb the increased production of large-scale products. Mexico also continued its trend toward political and economic centralization, which had been initiated in the 1940s. The growth of a centralized government meant the expansion of the bureaucracy, which, in turn, attracted people to the mushrooming metropolis of Mexico City.

These were the years when Octavio Paz rose to prominence in Mexico and in the central intellectual debate focused on Mexican identity. Paz's *Labyrinth of Solitude* set the tone for many of these discussions. Some of his ideas actually had their origins in well-known concepts of Mexican character and Mexican identity that had been set forth by Samuel Ramos in the 1930s. Indeed, both Ramos and Paz enhanced Fuentes' understanding, as evidenced particularly in *Los días enmascarados* and *Where the Air Is Clear.*

In December 1954 a small, innocuous note appeared at the bottom of the second page of the Sunday cultural supplement of *Novedades* announcing the publication of a volume of short stories by Carlos Fuentes, titled *Los días enmascarados*—his first book. Next to the note was a one-by-two-inch black-and-white reproduction of the new book's cover. To the left of that was a similar commentary and picture announcing a book by Juan José Arreola, and to the right appeared announcements of books by the young Mexican writers Tomás Segovia and Elena Poniatowska. The very brief and anonymous commmentary on Fuentes described him as an "excellent writer."[24] Despite the laudatory tone of these few sentences, the comment was certainly an inauspicious beginning for a major writer. Nevertheless, it marked the real birth of his literary career, for when *Los días enmascarados* appeared in print, Fuentes committed himself to a lifetime of writing, even though in the 1950s no one in Mexico made a living from publishing fiction.

Fuentes had made an agreement with his father that he would study law if he could dedicate himself to writing afterward.[25] In the interim, between finishing law school and launching his career as a professional writer, he held various positions. During 1954 he worked as assistant press secretary of the Ministry of Foreign Affairs, but his primary intellectual activity in the mid-1950s was writing *Where the Air Is Clear* from his home on Rubén Darío Street.

Fuentes and Emmanuel Carballo cofounded the journal *Revista Mexicana de Literatura,* which, according to one knowledgeable critic, "promoted Mexican literature while maintaining an awareness of writing in other countries."[26] With this journal, Fuentes clearly put into practice one of the lessons he had learned from Alfonso Reyes—that Mexican literature was important because it was literature, not because it was Mexican. Adhering to this universal message inherited from Reyes, the *Revista Mexicana de Literatura* served the cosmopolitan function of magazines that appeared throughout Latin America in the 1950s: in Colombia, the equivalent publication was *Mito,* which was also founded in 1955, in Cuba it was *Orígenes,* and in Venezuela it was *Sardio.* Like them, the *Revista Mexicana de Literatura* brought modern European and North American cultural practices to Latin America, from the T. S. Eliot generation to Jean-Paul Sartre and Albert Camus, who were in vogue in the 1950s. The journal was a combination of modernist aesthetics and social commitment; Sartre was extraordinarily influential in Mexico and the remainder of the Americas in the 1950s, and his idea of the *engagé* writer became virtually sacred. Some other writers whose names graced the pages of the *Revista Mexicana de Literatura* included Leonora Carrington, Mariano Picón Salas, and Juan Rulfo. Following the cosmopolitan line that Paz, Octavio G. Barreda, Alí Chumacero, Xavier Villaurrutia, Gilberto Owen, and others had established with their magazine *El hijo pródigo,* the *Revista Mexicana de Literatura* represented an attempt to universalize the Mexican literary vision. In this context, "universalization" also meant modernization; the readings of Fuentes and his generation of the Western modernists had its impact as Fuentes popularized modern literature in Mexico. Evidence of his work on *Where the Air Is Clear* during his editorship of the *Revista Mexicana de Literatura* was the publication of "Fragment of a Novel" in 1956.[27]

Los días enmascarados was very well received in Mexico, although it was published by a small press, Los Presentes, founded by Juan José Arreola. The publications of this press were not accessible enough to the general reading public in Mexico in 1954 and 1955 to sell in great volume. The best-seller of the year 1955, in fact, was a scandalous novel of political muckraking, Luis Spota's *Casi el paraíso.* Spota earned money; Fuentes earned the respect of Mexico's intellectuals. Sergio Pitol, who began writing at the same time, remembers *Los días enmascarados* as a seminal book for Mexican literature at the time it appeared, for its use of fantasy and innovative narrative technique was a relative anomaly compared to the fiction in vogue. Fuentes' underrepresented kind of writing was known and read by a small group of Mexican intellectuals who were also reading Borges and Arreola.[28]

Indeed, *Los días enmascarados* represented a substantial innovation in Mexican literature, although Arreola, Agustín Yáñez, and Julio Torri had already begun to explore some of the possibilities of the fantastic in the late 1940s and early 1950s. Mexican fiction in the 1950s was still predominantly rural and quite traditional, even though literary historians can point to selected cases of (relatively ignored) modernist novels ranging from 1920s avant-garde fiction—such as that of Jaime Torres Bodet—to Agustín Yáñez's *Al filo del agua,* published in 1947. Nevertheless, *Al filo del agua* was not widely read in Mexico in the early 1950s.[29]

Los días enmascarados consists of six stories, all of which contain some element of fantasy. Three of the stories are inventive Borgesian games of pure fantasy: "En defensa de la Trigolibia," "Letanía de la orquídea," and "El que inventó la pólvora." "En defensa de la Trigolibia" is one of those games that functions as an autonomous verbal construct, a fictional world of "Nusitanios" who speak an invented language called Trigolibia. It is a game of language invention, full of neologisms. In "Letanía de la Orquídea," a character sprouts an orchid from his body, while in "El que inventó la pólvora," the material world melts away. The three other stories also have some fantastic elements, but they are set in Mexico and have fantasy interwoven with Mexican history and indigenous cultural traditions. "Chac Mool" is a fantasy constructed around a plot involving a Mexican pre-Columbian rain god. Fuentes returns to Mexican history and the story of the Empress Carlota in Mexico in "Tlactocatzine, del Jardín de Flandes," a precursor of *Terra Nostra*. "Por la boca de los dioses," like "Chac Mool," uses a pre-Columbian deity, as well as fantasy, to develop a story dealing with power and control. Fuentes' *Los días enmascarados,* along with Arreola's *Confabulario,* brought to Mexican fiction the inventive possibilities that Borges had initially explored in his *Ficciones*: the spirit of modernity. In these stories, Borges pioneered such "classic" Borgesian concepts as the universe as a library, all books as one book, and the death of the author, concepts treated by numerous theorists and later fictionalized by Fuentes in *Terra Nostra*.

With the rise of Fuentes and the *Revista Mexicana de Literatura,* the group of writers and artists of the generation of *Medio Siglo* began establishing themselves in Mexico as a cultural force. The fiction writers of this generation were Sergio Pitol, Elena Poniatowska, Sergio Galindo, Juan García Ponce, Rosario Castellanos, Inés Arredondo, Josefina Vicens, Vicente Leñero, Juan Vicente Melo, José de la Colina, and Emilio Carballido. They have all become recognized modern writers in Mexico, and the fiction of Castellanos, Poniatowska, Pitol, and García Ponce is well respected throughout the Hispanic world and beyond. Equally recognized as poets of what Fuentes has called "mi generación" were José Emilio Pacheco, Alí Chumacero, Jaime Sabines, Jaime García Terrés, Rubén Bonifaz Nuño, and Montes de Oca. The painter José Luis Cuevas, about whom Fuentes has occasionally written, also was part of the generation. They were all thoroughly modern; they were the generation that first popularized and then even institutionalized modern literature in Mexico.

This rebellious group was ripe for a radical change in the Mexican cultural scene when a fictional revolution arrived in the form of *Where the Air Is Clear.* They were also searching for new ways of defining themselves. By the mid-1950s, their leaders had fully discovered their modernity: "For my generation in Mexico, the problem did not consist in discovering our modernity but in discovering our tradition," Fuentes has explained (*Myself,* 23). After Paz's *Labyrinth of Solitude,* the major statement to be made about both Mexican tradition and identity was to be found in *Where the Air Is Clear.*

The Years of the Boom: 1958–1971

When *Where the Air Is Clear* appeared in April 1958, Fuentes ceased being just another of Mexico's promising young intellectuals and became one of its major novelists. He also became an instant celebrity, even though the initial reception of the book was quite negative. From that time through the 1960s, as his books and articles appeared, his star continued to rise in Mexico as well as in the remainder of Indo-Afro-Ibero-America: having gained celebrity status in Mexico in the late 1950s, in the early 1960s he attained similar status in all of the Hispanic world; by the late 1960s his fame had spread to Europe and the United States. These were the years when he pursued some of the issues set forth in *Where the Air Is Clear, The Death of Artemio Cruz* (1962), *Aura* (1962), and *A Change of Skin* (1967). They were also the years of the Cuban Revolution and of the internationally recognized boom of the Latin American novel. During this period he married Mexican actress Rita Macedo, and in 1967 he was honored with one of the major literary prizes in the Hispanic world, the Biblioteca Breve Prize, which resulted in his first trip to Spain and El Escorial. The encounter with El Escorial, in turn, was followed by a twenty-year meditation on Hispanic culture.

During these years, Mexico was led by PRI presidents Adolfo López Mateos (1958–1964) and Gustavo Díaz Ordaz (1964–1970).

The nation's economic "miracle" continued with moderate inflation (less than 3 percent in the 1960s), but Mexico had one of the most unequal income distributions in Latin America. In 1969, the bottom half of the population received 15 percent of the national income and the top 20 percent received 64 percent.[30] The shift from an agricultural economy to an industrial one continued. In 1940, agriculture occupied 67 percent of the population and represented 18 percent of the gross national product; in 1970, 50 percent of the population worked in agriculture, and it constituted 11 percent of the GNP. International prestige was signaled by the selling of Mexican bonds on the United States and European markets for the first time since the nineteenth century. Mexico City's being awarded the opportunity to host the 1968 Olympics was also viewed as an internationally prestigious event.

The late 1950s and the 1960s in Mexico were characterized by labor strikes and peasant unrest. Genaro Vásquez and Lucio Cabañas led an armed revolt in the southwestern state of Guerrero; tens of thousands of army troops eliminated the rebels. The government also subdued an urban guerrilla movement. President Díaz Ordaz fired the reform-minded president of the PRI, Carlos Madrazo, soon after he attempted to democratize the selection of PRI candidates at the local level in 1965.

Fuentes and Rita Macedo met in 1958 on a double date with Octavio Paz and Maka Tchernicha to see Camus' play *Requiem for a Nun,* based on Faulkner. When they married later that year, the newlyweds moved into a penthouse in the chic Zona Rosa area of downtown Mexico City, on the fifth floor of a shiny glass and metal building at Liverpool No. 170, near the corner of Liverpool and Florencia Streets.

During the first week of April 1958, the imminent appearance of *Where the Air Is Clear* was publicized in articles in *Novedades,* announcing that it would be available in bookstores throughout the nation on Monday, April 7. The novel instantly became the focus of national polemics; at age thirty, Fuentes was at the center of the Mexican cultural scene. One of the Sunday issues of *Novedades* was particularly notable, for in the left-hand column of the page was a picture of Alfonso Reyes with an accompanying article about him; a picture of identical size of Fuentes appeared, also with an article, in the right-hand column. Obviously, *Novedades* was portraying visually the past and the future of Mexican letters.

Where the Air Is Clear is a lengthy novel dealing with many subjects: it was Fuentes' novelistic response to Paz's *Labyrinth of Solitude* and the question of identity in Mexico; it was his novel about Mexico City; it was his technical tour de force, using the narrative strategies of *Manhattan Transfer* and *Berlin Alexanderplatz*. Fuentes' first novel portrays a panorama of Mexico's social classes and tells the story of several Mexican families in their class settings. Above all, it was Fuentes' first critique of the nationally institutionalized modernization and industrialization project that had been developing in Mexico since the 1940s. In addition, *Where the Air Is Clear* began to introduce some of the themes of *Terra Nostra*.

The years from 1958 to 1961, when Carlos and Rita lived on Liverpool Street, were intellectually active ones. He received the full impact of *Where the Air Is Clear:* the praise, the negative reviews, the defenses written of the book, the sales of the novel, and the like. They were also the most exhilarating and polemical years of the Cuban Revolution. Next, Fuentes wrote *The Good Conscience* and then began *The Death of Artemio Cruz*. He also frequented the French Institute's Cine Club to see the latest European and American films. With respect to politics, Fuentes was one of the most prominent Indo-Afro-Ibero-American intellectuals to support the Cuban Revolution immediately. In fact, he was among the very first foreign intellectuals to arrive in Cuba when the revolution triumphed: on January 2, 1959, Fuentes, Fernando Benítez, and Manuel Becerra Acosta were on a Mexicana Airlines flight for Havana at the same time that Fidel Castro rode triumphantly in a jeep from Santiago to the Cuban capital. Fuentes, upon arriving, found a "great jubilation" in Havana, as the populace celebrated the revolution. The three Mexicans experienced an intense week of the Cuban Revolution, watching the celebrations and festivities, meeting with Fidel Castro, and lending their support.

In the early stages of the Cuban Revolution, Fuentes was one of its most energetic defenders and proponents, his affirmative voice resonating from Mexico to Chile. The Chilean writer José Donoso has related how Fuentes strongly influenced the political awareness of his generation of writers, who had been relatively uninformed of

Latin American politics beyond their respective home countries. When in 1962 Fuentes went to the Congreso de Intelectuales de la Universidad de Concepción in Chile, and spoke fervently in favor of the revolution, this political discourse and political commitment was, in fact, a revelation for Donoso.[31] Before the Boom, according to Donoso, Latin American writers were isolated geographically, culturally, and politically. The Cuban Revolution served as a rallying point for many Latin American intellectuals, and Fuentes was the principal catalyst for their political awakening.

The late 1950s and early 1960s were the most politically radical period of Fuentes' intellectual life. He, Flores Olea, and the others of the generation of *Medio Siglo* all had been trained with ideas ranging from Rousseau to Marx, and many of them were firmly aligned with the international Left from the 1950s. Fuentes published some of his most radical political essays during the late 1950s and early 1960s, and he dedicated his novel *The Death of Artemio Cruz* to the Marxist scholar C. Wright Mills.

Most of Fuentes' political essays of this period appeared in the Mexican magazines *El Espectador* and *La Política*. In 1959, a group of young intellectuals sympathetic to the political Left had established *El Espectador,* urging the creation of "a new left that was undogmatic, cultured, informed." [32] The collaborators, in addition to Fuentes, were Víctor Flores Olea, Enrique González Pedrero, Jaime García Terrés, Francisco López Cámara, and Luis Villoro. *El Espectador* was short-lived, but some of the same group, along with several others, founded another political magazine, *La Política*. It appeared from 1961 to 1967, with collaborations from Fuentes, Alonso Aguilar, Fernando Benítez, Fernando Carmona, José de la Colina, Vicente Lombardo Toledano, Salvador Novo, Emilio Uranga, Víctor Rico Galán, Víctor Flores Olea, Alejandro Gómez Arias, Enrique González Pedrero, David Alfaro Siqueiros, and Angel Bassols Batalla. They all supported the Cuban Revolution in its early years and were stridently critical of the Mexican political establishment. Fuentes has remained consistently on the Left throughout his life; his politics were those of a radical democrat in the 1980s and early 1990s.[33] Whether it be Nicaragua or any other nation, Fuentes insisted on the right to national sovereignty and the democratic process. In the 1980s and 1990s, then, Fuentes became critical of the Cuban regime of

Fidel Castro because of the lack of human rights, freedom of speech, and democratic processes.[34]

To understand fully this generation's politics, it is useful to keep in mind, first, that their mentors, Manuel Pedroso and Mario de la Cueva, were progressive social democrats. In the case of Fuentes, in particular, an important factor was his father, Rafael Fuentes Boettiger—an atheist, a political progressive, and an enthusiastic supporter of Lázaro Cárdenas. The other key to understanding Fuentes' political vision is that during his formative years he lived with three very progressive governments: the Mexico of Lázaro Cárdenas, the United States of the New Deal, and Chile in the wake of the Popular Front.

Fuentes' second novel, *The Good Conscience* (1959), an explicitly political work, is deeply historical, with a strong sense of class history. It is a traditional family story, written in the realist mode, that relates how the nineteenth-century oligarchy in Guanajuato exercised its economic and political power. The Ceballos family allies itself with local governors and ministers through several generations. The protagonist, Jaime Ceballos, suffers the repressive atmosphere and hypocrisy of Guanajuato. A sensitive young man, he grows in social conscience, religious faith, and sensuality as he experiences the contradictions of traditional upper-class life there. In the end, nevertheless, he conforms to the expectations of his family and class.

The cultural and political revolution of the 1960s in the West began for Fuentes in the early years of the decade. Energetic and vital in his early thirties, he was as enthralled with film and fiction writing as he was with revolutionary politics and rock and roll music. (During the 1960s, he usually wrote with rock and roll blasting in the background.) According to Gabriel García Márquez, he and Fuentes "made the Zona Rosa a cultural center" in Mexico City, starting *tertulias,* or literary soirées, in two cafés, one called El Tirol and the other the Kineret.[35] These *tertulias* not only were a stimulus for the intellectual life of Fuentes and García Márquez but also contributed to the creation of an entirely new film movement in Mexico.

García Márquez and Fuentes had met in 1962 when they began collaborating on the dialogue for the film *El Gallo de Oro,* a work by Juan Rulfo. García Márquez had written the original dialogue for this film, but the language was too Colombian for a Mexican audience. Consequently, the director, Manuel Barbachano, suggested to García Márquez that he work with Fuentes, who was returning from Europe, in order to Mexicanize the language. The two writers thought initially that they would be able to revise the script in a few days, but they worked together every night for three months. According to García Márquez, suffering together through this process created a strong bond between the two. A very private person, García Márquez has considered Fuentes a respected and close friend ever since.[36]

The Death of Artemio Cruz, Fuentes' critique of the Mexican Revolution and one of his most important novels, appeared in Mexico in 1962. It reflected his assimilation of the modern novel in the West; his use of narrative points of view was typical of William Faulkner and John Dos Passos, who had been so important to him. It was also a portrayal and condemnation of the new ruling class in Mexico, the upper-middle class that fought in the Mexican Revolution and built the new modern capitalistic state that was being formed in the 1940s precisely when the Fuentes family arrived in Mexico City from Buenos Aires. The strident politics of this novel corresponded to Fuentes' political writings since the Cuban Revolution.

The reaction to *The Death of Artemio Cruz* was swift and strong; this novel had more international impact than *Where the Air Is Clear. The Death of Artemio Cruz* drew immediate international attention as one of the early masterpieces of the Boom. It is one of the best-selling books ever printed by the Fondo de Cultura Económica in Mexico and has been published in more than twenty languages. During the same year, Fuentes' novella *Aura* appeared; consequently, from 1958 to 1962 Fuentes published a substantial body of work: four novels. With this narrative corpus, he had established at least four of the important constants in his fictional work: a strong historical vision of reality, a portrayal of pre-Hispanic myth, a commitment to critique and social change, and innovation in narrative strategies. This was the Fuentes of the grand narrative; the broad scope and deep historical consciousness, among other factors, made him a major modern writer of the Americas.

In *Aura,* Fuentes turns to the world of another reality, one in which mysterious forces lead to a supernatural denouement. The protagonist, a young historian named Felipe Montero, answers an advertisement to edit the papers of the deceased husband of an elderly woman, Consuelo. Montero receives a good salary, as well as room and board, for his work. Once in the home, he falls in love with Aura, Consuelo's niece. As Montero reads the love letters that General Llorente wrote to Consuelo when she was fifteen, he associates Aura with Consuelo. He also discovers himself in General Llorente. At the end of the novel, as Felipe holds Aura in his arms, she is transformed into Consuelo.[37]

Two years after the publication of *Aura,* Fuentes published a volume of short stories titled *Cantar de ciegos,* whose seven cosmopolitan fictions are set in Mexico City. One of the most successful was "Las dos Elenas," a story dedicated to José Luis Cuevas that deals with the triangular relationship between a young and hip married couple and the wife's mother, who has an affair with her son-in-law. The triangular relationship and the symbolic incest prefigure *Terra Nostra.* The other stories also deal with human relationships within the spatial limits of "small-screen fiction."[38]

The social, the purely intellectual, and the cultural in general reached notable levels of interaction for Fuentes and the intellectuals of his generation in Mexico during the late 1960s. He was surrounded by a group of key individuals on the cultural scene whom outsiders in Mexico began to call "la Mafia." They included Fernando Benítez, Carlos Monsivais, Octavio Paz, Emmanuel Carballo, Juan García Ponce, José Luis Cuevas, Jaime García Terrés, Huberto Batis, Juan Vicente Melo, Sergio Pitol, and Salvador Elizondo. They seemed to control all the most influential literary and cultural organs, among them *Siempre, Plural,* and *Novedades.* The nonmember Vicente Leñero protested that writers excluded from La Mafia found it difficult to survive in Mexico. Fuentes and the rest of La Mafia did indeed exercise a virtual hegemony over Mexican literary culture during the late 1960s. And there were some talented writers, besides Leñero, who were excluded. Nevertheless, La Mafia sometimes incorporated Mexico's most promising young writers, such as José Emilio Pacheco, Carlos Monsivais, and Gustavo Sainz, who gained considerable access to Mexican cultural organs during the 1960s.

One center of cultural life in Mexico City during this period was Fuentes' second home in the wealthy Colonia San Angel on the south side of Mexico City, a Spanish Colonial–style home located at Segunda Cerrada de Galeana No. 16. For several years, Fuentes and Rita Macedo hosted social gatherings that have been described by intellectuals as literary soirées or *tertulias* and that often ended as lively parties. Rarely did an international celebrity—writer or actor—pass through Mexico City without a visit to the Fuentes home in San Angel on Sunday afternoon.[39] This Sunday ritual began in 1964, when Carlos and Rita moved from his first house in San Angel to this residence and invited García Márquez and his wife, Mercedes, for tea one Sunday. After a few Sundays with the four of them, Fuentes began inviting others, and the soirées became progressively larger.[40] Luis Buñuel and Rodman Rockefeller were among the numerous celebrities whom Fuentes hosted.

For many foreign artists and writers, the most vivid memory of their first trip to Mexico was a party at the Fuentes home in San Angel. In 1992, William Styron remembered well when he first met Fuentes in 1964 and was invited to a swinging sixties party in San Angel—with many celebrities and "beautiful people." One of these guests was the painter José Luis Cuevas. Styron described the Fuentes of 1964 as "very much like he is now [in 1992]. Very outgoing, expansive, engaging, very vital, filled with ideas." [41] Styron and Fuentes had corresponded before meeting and, on the basis of this correspondence and having read each other's work, had formed a "mutual admiration society," according to Styron.[42]

The Boom of the Latin American novel in the 1960s was a result of numerous institutions, individuals, and circumstances, among them the Cuban Revolution (which bonded Latin American intellectuals), Harper and Row Publishing Company in the United States, the Spanish literary agent Carmen Balcells, the Spanish publishing firm Seix Barral, the rise of international Latin Americanism as an academic discipline, the publication of the magazine *Mundo Nuevo* in Paris by Emir Rodríguez Monegal beginning in the mid-1960s, and the appearance on the scene of a brilliant translator, Gregory Rabassa. As José Donoso documents in his *Historia personal del Boom,* however, Fuentes was central to making all these factors work together; he brought together many of the different strands. Most of the writers of the Boom were even guests at the Fuentes home in San

Angel, including Mario Vargas Llosa and José Donoso. The latter, in fact, lived in a bungalow in Fuentes' backyard, writing there for three years in the early 1960s.

Fuentes followed closely and supported the writing of one of the major novels of the Boom, Gabriel García Márquez's *One Hundred Years of Solitude*. García Márquez liked to chat about his work when it was in progress, and he found in Fuentes the ideal dialogic friend while he was writing the novel in 1965 and 1966, the same period when he was joining in the Sunday soirées in San Angel. Fuentes was also one of the few individuals to read the manuscript before its publication, prompting him to write an article of considerable impact in the principal Spanish-language literary organ of the Boom, *Mundo Nuevo*.

The year 1967 was an important one for Fuentes for several reasons. He published the novels *A Change of Skin* and *Holy Place*, received the prestigious Spanish prize Biblioteca Breve, and made his first trip to Spain, when he first visited El Escorial. This visit to the enormous monument to Philip II's genius, ambition, and religious faith opened the door to the writing of *Terra Nostra*. Fuentes had been interested for years in the relationship between Spain and Indo-Afro-Ibero-America, but the austere structure of El Escorial, about which Luis Buñuel had spoken so much to Fuentes, was a key experience for Fuentes with respect to Spain and *Terra Nostra*. From Spain he went to Venice, Paris, and London in 1967. Once in London, he moved into a home in Hampstead Hills Gardens, from which he took the tube daily to the British Museum, working in the Reading Room to do research for *Terra Nostra*. In the domed Reading Room, a treasury of Western civilization, Fuentes relived the world of Renaissance Europe, researching medieval esoteric religious practices, sixteenth-century hunting customs, Italian Renaissance art, and the like.

Holy Place was a short and intense psychological novel narrated by its protagonist, Guillermo, who has sexual desire for his mother, a movie actress. Experimental in structure and style, this entire novel is an interior monologue directed to the mother. Guillermo attends the best schools in Switzerland, spends time in Mexico City, and near the end of the novel follows his mother to Italy. As in *Terra Nostra*, many of the scenes are possible scenarios rather than "facts." At the

end, Guillermo is apparently transformed into a dog, thus prefiguring the multiple transformations in *Terra Nostra.*

In *A Change of Skin,* Fuentes continued with the experimenta-
tion of *Holy Place.* The novel deals with the car trip of the four main
characters—Javier, Elizabeth, Franz, and Isabel—from Mexico City
to Veracruz. They spend the night in a small hotel in the town of
Cholula when their car breaks down. During the night, the couples
switch partners, but then they return to their original partners. They
also explore an ancient Aztec pyramid. The novel delves into the
pasts of the four characters, describing key scenes of their respective
lives. Through interior monologues and dialogues that function as
flashbacks, the reader learns that Franz was a Nazi, that Elizabeth and
Javier met in New York, and that Javier teaches at a university. Different strands of the novel's plot are more possibilities than real ac-
counts of actions, as is the case for the "events" of *Terra Nostra.* As
one critic has pointed out, "Here, even more than in Fuentes' earlier
novels, rules of temporal logic do not apply."[43]

Fuentes' main work in the late 1960s and early 1970s was *Terra
Nostra.* He continued working on this book in London in 1968, and
his first published product was a short text titled "Nowhere," an early
version of a section of *Terra Nostra* that appeared in print in his volume *Cuerpos y ofrendas* in 1972. In the spring of 1968, Fuentes went
to Paris, where he continued work on *Terra Nostra.*

Fuentes experienced two important upheavals in 1968. He wit-
nessed the May 1968 uprising on the streets of Paris and wrote of that
Parisian spring in a short book, *París: O la revolución de mayo* (1968),
offering Latin American readers journalistic impressions of a writer's
experience in the strife-torn French capital.

Mexico City also was the setting for a historic uprising on the
streets in 1968, and no Mexican intellectual, including Fuentes,
would be exactly the same after the momentous events of that October, a watershed period in the history of modern Mexico. In September and October 1968 students and other groups critical of the
government organized sporadic protests that had begun, in fact, in
July. As the 1968 Olympic Games approached and tensions grew,
several intellectuals, including Octavio Paz (who was then serving as
ambassador to India), recommended to President Díaz Ordaz that he
find a solution in conciliation and compromise. Paz's letter to Díaz

Ordaz pointed out that some aspects of the criticism directed toward the government, as well as some of the demands, had validity and were grounds for dialogue and understanding. The government chose not to listen, however, and when the students organized a massive protest in October, government soldiers killed hundreds of Mexican citizens. Fuentes returned from Europe to Mexico in November 1968 to face the crisis there. Large portions of the Mexican populace, including most of its intellectuals, had lost confidence in the government. Octavio Paz resigned his ambassadorial post, and numerous intellectuals who were associated with the Left, including Fuentes, José Emilio Pacheco, and Carlos Monsivais, publicly defended Paz's position. From that moment, students and intellectuals in Mexico, including Fuentes, have had a different and more difficult relationship with the state—ranging from discreetly ambiguous at best to overtly antagonistic at worst.

The late 1960s and early 1970s were agitated and unstable years for Mexico, and for Fuentes as well, for he separated from Rita Macedo and was engaged in a wide range of literary and political activities. In February 1969 he went to Cuernavaca, where he wrote the novel *Birthday* (1969) and the essay *La nueva novela hispanoamericana. Birthday,* one of the most radical experiments in his fiction, placed Fuentes momentarily in the postmodern camp. *La nueva novela hispanoamericana* deals with Julio Cortázar, García Márquez, Vargas Llosa, Donoso, and others. Fuentes was at the forefront of a search for a new critical language with which to read the novels of the Boom. This essay, which appeared in six editions from 1969 to 1980, provided much of the language used through the following decade; it became, moreover, a seminal book for critics and scholars of the Indo-Afro-Ibero-American novel, for in it Fuentes provided new criteria for reading the contemporary novel. He set forth the oft-mentioned concept of the "novel of language" used by numerous critics of Latin American literature after 1969. And in it he also emphasized the role of myth in this fiction. Without this book and Luis Harss's *Into the Mainstream,* it would have been difficult to sustain the Boom of the Latin American novel.

For the most part, Fuentes was in Mexico writing from 1969 to 1971, the years when the Boom was at its zenith and the personal relationships among Fuentes, García Márquez, Vargas Llosa, Cortázar, and Donoso were at their best. García Márquez, Vargas Llosa, and Donoso lived primarily in Barcelona, and Fuentes frequently visited them there. In December 1968, García Márquez, Cortázar, and Fuentes boarded a train in Paris for Prague and then toured several countries of the former Soviet bloc. As well as close friends, they were a united front politically and aesthetically. This was an intensely creative period for the writers of the Boom, as demonstrated by their landmark novels: *One Hundred Years of Solitude* (1967) by García Márquez, *A Change of Skin* (1967) by Fuentes, *62: A Model Kit* (1968) by Cortázar, *Conversation in the Cathedral* (1969) by Vargas Llosa, and *The Obscene Bird of the Night* (1970) by Donoso.

Despite the friendships, schisms among the writers of the Boom began to surface, for both political and personal reasons. The first major public forum over which political differences appeared was Cuba and the celebrated case of the poet Heberto Padilla. When Padilla was arrested for writing poetry that the Cuban government considered unacceptable, several of Latin America's most prominent intellectuals protested. Fuentes, Vargas Llosa, Donoso, and others signed a letter directed to Castro demanding the release of Padilla. Over the ensuing years, García Márquez and Cortázar remained firmly aligned with Fidel Castro; Fuentes, Donoso, and Vargas Llosa have been more distanced and occasionally critical.

The last time the writers of the Boom were all together, in fact, was in 1970 in France. A theater festival in Avignon included a presentation of Fuentes' play *El tuerto es rey.* Julio Cortázar owned a home near Avignon, in the small town of Saignon, so Fuentes, García Márquez, Vargas Llosa, and Donoso, along with the Spanish writer Juan Goytisolo, stayed together there. In Avignon the six writers made plans for the critical quarterly magazine *Libre.* Goytisolo was the editor of this journal, which, according to him, "should have welded us together [but] became, in fact, for a series of imponderable reasons, a weapon pitting us against each other, till in the end we were enemies." [44] Goytisolo explains how the Padilla affair produced feelings of doubt, mistrust, and even outright hostility in place of the old warmth and camaraderie among these friends. *Libre* was financed by a millionaire, Albina de Boisrourray, a young, beautiful woman with a passion for literature and cinema. She offered to fund the magazine if Goytisolo would serve as editor. When Goytisolo met with Fuentes and the other writers of the Boom in Avignon, he intended to publish a magazine that would support the Cuban regime from the outside and also strengthen the position of intellectuals who, like Padilla, were struggling from the inside for freedom of expression and real democracy. But *Libre* soon resulted in further divisions among the writers of the Boom. Since then, the friendships and alliances among Latin American writers have been defined, to a large extent, by positions in favor of or against the Cuban government.[45]

Fuentes' last novel of the 1958–1971 Boom years was *Birthday* (1969), a work pointing more to his postmodern projects of the 1970s and 1980s than to his grand narrative schemes of the 1960s. It follows the experimental mode of *A Change of Skin,* with little concern for chronological order, causality, or the rational development of plot. The contradictions that subvert the already established characters and events of the plot multiply beyond those of *A Change of Skin* and prefigure the contradictions and subversion of *Terra Nostra. Birthday* opens with George and Emily (husband and wife) entering their son George's room to sing "Happy Birthday." Then follows a series of ambiguous scenes with an old man, a boy, and a woman. George and Georgie function as doubles in the novel, and, as in *Terra Nostra,* characters merge and exchange places. Farris points out that "the fluid narrative force that snakes in and out of characters who in turn are also fluid, like those in *A Change of Skin* and *Terra Nostra,* illustrates Fuentes' theory of 'de-I-ification'—the disappearance of a defined narrator."[46]

Terra Nostra: 1971–1992

During the period from 1971 to 1992, Fuentes returned to the lifestyle of an international itinerant that had characterized his youth before he settled in Mexico City in 1944. He dedicated most of the year 1971 to working on *Terra Nostra* in Mexico. On November 20, 1970, he had met the Mexican journalist Sylvia Lemus, and after a yearlong romance, they were married on January 24, 1972, in Mexico City. From 1972 to 1992 they lived in twenty-two different homes, mostly in Mexico, France, Great Britain, and the United States. During this time, Fuentes was as productive as during the earlier period, publishing the major novel of his career, *Terra Nostra,* as well as *Hydra Head* (1978), *Distant Relations* (1981), *Old Gringo* (1985), *Christopher Unborn* (1987), *The Campaign* (1991), and two volumes of short fiction. Recognition of his work took many forms, including two of the most prestigious awards in the Hispanic world, the Rómulo Gallegos Prize, which he received in Caracas in 1975, and the Cervantes Prize, which he accepted in Madrid in 1987. In addition to his constant writing during this period, he served as ambassador to France from 1975 to 1977 and taught on the faculty of several universities, including Harvard and Cambridge. He continued with some of his modern and utopian grand narratives, but the Fuentes of the 1970s and 1980s was also affected by postmodern culture.

After their marriage in Mexico City, Carlos and Sylvia moved to Paris (8, rue de Bievre), where he continued working on *Terra Nostra.* He had begun the actual writing of the novel in London in 1967 and continued it in London and Paris the following year and in Mexico City in 1969. He also dedicated a considerable amount of time in the early 1970s, in Paris and Barcelona, to working on *Terra Nostra.* In 1973, Sylvia gave birth to their son, Carlos Rafael. The family then moved to McLean, Virginia, and Fuentes commuted daily to the Woodrow Wilson International Center for Scholars in Washington, D.C., where he continued his novel project. He recalls that it was an exhilarating year, with *Terra Nostra* in its final stages.[47] When completed in early 1975, *Terra Nostra* represented Fuentes' major opus on the cultures and history of the Americas and the culmination of his lifelong meditation on the history and identity of Indo-Afro-Ibero-America. He had fictionalized the architecture and ideology of El Escorial. He also published a book that complemented his major statements to date on the cultures of Indo-Afro-Ibero-America: *Cervantes o la crítica de la lectura.*

Fuentes accepted President Luis Echeverría's offer of the Mexican ambassadorship to France in 1975, and in February of that year he and Sylvia arrived in Paris to assume the post. Fuentes took the position in a ceremony in which he was wearing the suit of his father, Rafael Fuentes Boettiger, who had died in 1971. During the twenty-six-month stay in Paris, Fuentes took some rest from the intensity of writing *Terra Nostra* and engaged in a variety of cultural and political activities. The Fuentes family lived quite well in Paris; William Styron recalls a sumptuous dinner at the Mexican Embassy in Paris one Christmas in the mid-1970s, graciously hosted by Carlos and Sylvia.[48]

After the Parisian diplomatic residency, Fuentes returned to academic life. The year 1977 was a transition between his life in France and the next stage, in the Americas. Leaving Paris in April 1977, he then lectured at the Colegio Nacional in Mexico City, at Cambridge University, and at Barnard College. He also served on the jury at the Cannes film festival, but the most important event of the year for him was receiving the Rómulo Gallegos Novel Prize in Caracas for *Terra Nostra*. Among his predecessors for this prestigious award were Gabriel García Márquez and Mario Vargas Llosa.

In 1978 the Fuentes family began a decade-long residence in the Americas, North and South, living until 1989 mostly in Mexico and the United States. They moved to New Jersey in July 1978. That year, Fuentes taught at Columbia University and the University of Pennsylvania, and his novel *Hydra Head* appeared in print. Although not considered one of his major novels by some critics, this excursion into the genre of the spy thriller did receive a positive critical reception in several languages. Clearly less ambitious than any of his previous novels, *Hydra Head* is nevertheless one of his most entertaining works. Returning to the games of international political intrigue that he had played with Roberto Torretti and his other adolescent friends in Chile, Fuentes in this novel deals with the struggle of Arabs and Israelis to obtain knowledge and control of Mexico's oil reserves. A character named Timon of Athens works in favor of Mexico's interests. Fuentes explained the novel as follows: "The characters' names and actions are verbs. The verb and the action have a protagonistic quality in this genre . . . so I tried to write this novel based on characters who are nothing but their names and actions which are nothing but verbs."[49]

From 1979 through 1983, Fuentes' principal residence was Princeton, New Jersey, although he and his family traveled regularly to Mexico City and elsewhere. For example, they spent the spring semester of 1981 at Dartmouth College and the fall of 1983 (September through December) in Mexico City. During these years, Fuentes published the novel *Distant Relations* (1980) and the short story collection *Burnt Water* (1981). In *Distant Relations,* Fuentes returned to interests exploited in *Terra Nostra:* identity and its relationship to the past and history. Like *Aura* and *Birthday, Distant Relations* contains characters who have parallel lives or seem to function as reincarnations. When the story begins, Fuentes-as-narrator meets his old friend Count Branly in Paris, and Branly recounts his family history. Branly's recollections involve encounters with Hugo Heredia, a Mexican archeologist, and Hugo's son Víctor. At the end of the novel, a double figure pursues Fuentes, just as some doubles have followed the Heredia family. *Burnt Water* is a narrative quartet that returns to a more traditional use of narrative technique. The four stories evoke something of *The Good Conscience,* Fuentes' previous treatment of the old order in Mexico. The main characters represent the old aristocracy from the days of Porfirio Díaz.

The winter of 1981 at Dartmouth College was a most stimulating and productive experience for Fuentes. On the one hand, he thoroughly enjoyed working on his playful and satirical novel *Christopher Unborn* there. On the other, it was during this highly creative period that he conceived his plan for his total work as "La Edad del Tiempo." When he published *Cristóbal nonato* in 1987, it included a page titled "La Edad del Tiempo," with his total fictional work— past and future—divided into fourteen cycles. His subsequent books have also included a page with the plan for "La Edad del Tiempo," with minor revisions to the original plan.[50]

Fuentes spent the spring of 1984 as the Lewin Visiting Professor in the Humanities at Washington University in St. Louis, where he offered an undergraduate seminar on Latin American literature. His weekly lecture in that seminar was open to the public; these lectures eventually became the material for the collection of essays titled *Valiente mundo nuevo* (1990). In the essays, Fuentes reviews Latin American literature (which he identifies as Indo-Afro-Ibero-American literature) from the Colonial writer Bernal Díaz del Castillo to Gabriel García Márquez and Julio Cortázar.

The Fuentes family spent the autumns of 1984 and 1985 in Cambridge, Massachusetts, where Carlos lectured in the Department of Comparative Literature at Harvard University. During these two years, he also lectured regularly at universities in the United States and, in addition, did stints in Mexico City. In 1985 he published *The Old Gringo,* the novel that deals most directly with the relationship between the United States and Mexico and with the clichés and stereotypes that Mexicans hold of Americans and vice versa. The novel and many of its clichés were made into a less-than-successful film of the same title, with Fuentes' friend Jane Fonda in a lead role opposite Gregory Peck.

After a semester at Cornell University during the spring of 1986, the Fuentes family moved to Cambridge, Great Britain, where they lived for a year in the elegant Merton House in St. John's College of Cambridge University. Carlos gave weekly public lectures on a broad range of cultural topics, thoroughly enjoyed the intellectual ambience and architectural splendor of Cambridge University, and wrote the stories he later published as *Constancia and Other Stories for Virgins* (1989). Like *Burnt Water*, these stories represented a return to many of Fuentes' storytelling strategies of the early 1960s.

After staying for a few months in Washington, D.C., and Mexico City in 1988 and 1989, the Fuentes family moved to London in January 1990, where they remained through 1992. Fuentes dedicated most of his time in London to the book and BBC program titled *The Buried Mirror*, yet another chapter of his ongoing analysis of the cultures of the Americas and Spain. Both the book and the program appeared in 1992; before that, he had published the novel *The Campaign*, the first volume in a series of novels on the history of the Americas. This series is a continuation of many of the issues of *Terra Nostra: Terra Nostra* deals with the origins of the cultures and history of the Americas; *The Campaign* begins the history of the Americas from the independence in the Southern Cone and can be read as a parody of a nineteenth-century historical novel.

In February, March, and April of 1992, Fuentes was featured in the Mexican media with regularity because of a conflict with his longtime friend Octavio Paz. Tensions had been growing between these two giants of contemporary Mexican literature since the late 1980s. The Mexican Enrique Krauze, a historian and close collaborator with Paz in the publication of Paz's magazine *Vuelta*, had published an attack on Fuentes in the form of an article that appeared in *Vuelta* and *The New Republic* in 1988.[51] The essence of his critique was that Krauze believed Fuentes was not a very good historian in his novels. Fuentes did not respond. In 1990 Paz organized an international symposium in Mexico City, inviting economic and political figures who defended the neoliberal political and economic programs that were sweeping Eastern Europe and Latin America as a reaction against Marxism and the Left. (He declined to invite Fuentes or García Márquez on the grounds that they were "novelists" and not "thinkers.") In February 1992, Víctor Flores Olea (then director of the Consejo Nacional para las Artes y la Cultura) and José Sarakaún (then chancellor of the National University, or UNAM) organized an international symposium, "Coloquio de Invierno," with keynote speakers on the Left, such as Fuentes, Gabriel García Márquez, William Styron, Sergio Ramírez from Nicaragua, and a host of other distinguished participants. Octavio Paz was not invited initially, so he protested—and then received his official letter of invitation, which he promptly refused to accept. The day before the symposium opened, Paz denounced it publicly on the basis that government funds were being used to support a conference dedicated exclusively to the Left, thus excluding the opposition. For the remainder of the two-week conference, the debate continued between the supporters of Paz (the Mexican center-to-Right) and the supporters of Fuentes (the Mexican center-to-Left).

The conflict between Paz and Fuentes was amply covered by the national media for three months, finally resulting in the inevitable split between Mexico's two major living intellectual figures. In 1992, for the first time since they became friends in Paris in 1950, Fuentes and Paz no longer spoke to each other as friends. For several months, *Vuelta* dedicated considerable space to denouncing the "Coloquio de Invierno" and criticizing Fuentes.[52] The conflicts between Paz and Fuentes, which were articulated primarily by the followers of the two in Mexico, were covered by the Mexican media regularly from February through April 1992.

After 1992

Despite the polemics in Mexico, Fuentes continued his intense writing program into the 1990s. One of his most successful works, *The Orange Tree,* appeared in 1993. In this book, Fuentes returned to some of the foundational issues originally explored in *Terra Nostra:* the book's central image, the orange, represents Spanish identity.

Fuentes finished this book in the fall of 1992, when the relationship between Spain and the Americas was foremost in the minds of many intellectuals of the Americas; some of it was actually written in the town of El Escorial in the summer of 1992.

In the 1990s, the Fuentes family has divided its time between Mexico City and London, usually living approximately half of the year in Mexico City and the other half in Great Britain. Fuentes owns a flat in London and a home in the Colonia San Jerónimo of Mexico City. (He has also frequently gone on lecture tours in the United States, once each autumn and once each spring.) In addition to his lifelong discipline of writing daily, Fuentes enjoys the opera and theater of London and finds that attending theater often stimulates his own writing.[53] In the 1990s, he has also traveled regularly to Argentina and Colombia, usually visiting each country once or twice a year, always maintaining contact with the different regions of the Americas.

Imagining the Past and Remembering the Future

Historical understanding of the cultures of the Americas and the identity of the citizen of Indo-Afro-Ibero-America, both of which have their roots in medieval Spain, have been the constant interests of Carlos Fuentes. In this sense, Fuentes' literary career has been a continual writing and rewriting of *Terra Nostra*. This ongoing project has been a lifelong search for the historical origins and identity of Mexico in particular and Indo-Afro-Ibero-America in general. Their expression in his work relates closely to his political vision, which has been progressive and fully committed to social change and to multiculturalism.

Fuentes' writing affirms the belief that high culture can contribute to the improvement of society. This liberal humanism in general and his firm conviction in the role of culture were inherited from his mentors Alfonso Reyes and Manuel Pedroso, who, in turn, were strongly influenced by Ortega y Gasset and Américo Castro. In the early years of his writing, Octavio Paz also exerted considerable influence on Fuentes; Fuentes undertook Paz's search for identity in Mexican terms and as a part of an affirmation of Mexico's modernity.

Under the tutelage of Reyes and Pedroso, Fuentes gained respect for the powerful role a cultural heritage can play, be it Spanish, Mexican, Indo-Afro-Ibero-American, or "universal." A fundamental difference between the generation of Reyes and the generation of Fuentes is the latter's more progressive political vision, again, tempered by influences such as the New Deal, Lázaro Cárdenas, the Chilean Popular Front, and the Cuban Revolution.

In firm solidarity with Cervantes and Borges, Fuentes has stood consistently in defense of imagination as the quintessential agent of transformation. In this sense, he is as utopian as the men of the Renaissance who came to the Americas in search of El Dorado. Fuentes' sense of the geopolitics of the Americas is vastly more sophisticated than that of these first Europeans in the Americas. Nevertheless, they were perhaps the first Europeans to follow Fuentes' admonition to imagine the past and remember the future. Through his interpretation and critique of the images of El Escorial, through his lifelong meditation on Hispanic culture, and through his writing and rewriting of *Terra Nostra,* Fuentes has dedicated a lifetime to imagining the past and remembering the future.

Rereading *Terra Nostra*

Las creencias constituyen el estrato básico, el más profundo de la arquitectura de nuestra vida. — JOSÉ ORTEGA Y GASSET

En suma, que el hombre no tiene naturaleza, *sino que tiene . . . historia.* — JOSÉ ORTEGA Y GASSET

Asumma of three decades of Carlos Fuentes' writing career, *Terra Nostra* was born in the mid-sixties, even though references in his previous work, from as early as *Los días enmascarados* and *Where the Air Is Clear,* allude to some of the concerns of *Terra Nostra.*[1] This novel represents the culmination of his modern project, begun with *Los días enmascarados* and offering his exhaustive readings of the culture and history of the Americas. At the same time, *Terra Nostra* is a postmodern exercise, for this novel holds relationships with both modern and postmodern writing. Above all, *Terra Nostra* bears an intimate relationship to the cultural and political object that served as its catalyst—El Escorial. Fuentes rewrites the medieval, Renaissance, and neoclassic architecture of El Escorial in *Terra Nostra,* in addition to fictionalizing a series of cultural and political issues related to the Spain of El Escorial.

Fuentes states at the beginning of his essay on Cervantes, *Cervantes o la crítica de la lectura,* that the relationship between Spain and the Americas has been ambiguous at best and antagonistic at worst. *Terra Nostra* is Fuentes' most elaborate and complex treatment of the interaction among the cultures of Spain and the cultures of the Americas. Here he considers the historical origins of Indo-Afro-Ibero-American culture, looking back to Greco-Roman culture and to the cultural and religious practices of the Middle Ages. Rethinking Spain's historical legacy of domination and rule during the sixteenth and seventeenth centuries, Fuentes inquires what Spain's other options might have been, had she pursued different political and cultural alternatives. His concerns include the Spanish Crown's decision to isolate Spain and its colonies from cultural difference and from the other political entities of Europe. Following the model of Borges (who also imagined the future), near the end of the novel Fuentes imagines a future without the expulsion of the Arabs and Jews in 1492, a future without the politics of the Spanish Inquisition, and the like.

After placing this novel in its historical setting and providing a reading of the cultural artifact with which it holds an intertextual relationship—El Escorial—I will demonstrate how and what *Terra Nostra* contributes to a historical understanding of Hispanic culture. Similarly, I am interested in how *Terra Nostra* embodies numerous cultural contradictions of the official culture of Spain in the sixteenth century, when it promulgated Hispanic culture throughout the Americas. I will analyze the function of narrating and seeing in this novel. Finally, I will reconsider these problems within the context of the modern and postmodern. In the context of the postmodern, I will explore Fuentes' postmodern rewriting of the architecture of El Escorial.

Before *Terra Nostra*: El Escorial

El Escorial is a complex architectural construct, replete with elaborate religious, political, and military imagery. Its medieval and Renaissance architectural motifs were most consistently neoclassical; its architectural plan was based on the medieval monastery and hospital, most prominently, monasteries in Tarragona, Yuste, and Granada.[2] El Escorial is a multicultural object that embodies and reflects the heterogeneous cultural forces in play in sixteenth-century Spain, from traditional Arabic to traditional Roman, from sixteenth-century Italian to sixteenth-century Flemish. A wide array of other cultural traditions, such as those from Castille, are also evident. Philip II claimed to have built El Escorial in order to provide a monastery for monks to pray for the salvation of the kings and for the benefits the royalty received. According to Charles V, El Escorial was to be "a dwelling place for God." The setting was ostensibly a monastery, and El Escorial did indeed serve this function, but it was much more: a royal palace, a military fortress, a government center, a medieval city, a university, and a library. In imagery and function, El Escorial was a synthesis of Hispanic culture of the sixteenth century, the same contradictory and heterogeneous Hispanic culture exported to the Spanish colonies for more than three centuries.

In addition to monasteries, several medieval villas and palaces project visual images similar to that of El Escorial. Notable precedents to El Escorial were the Palazzo Vecchio in Florence, the Monastery of St. Gall in Switzerland, and the Diocletian Palace in Spalato.[3]

The historical setting for *Terra Nostra* and the construction of El Escorial encompassed the sixteenth-century Spain of Philip II (king 1556–1598), the Inquisition, the European Renaissance, the Reformation, and the conquest of the Americas. When Charles V abdicated as king of Spain in January 1556, transferring his possessions and powers to his son Philip II, the Iberian Peninsula still was not referred to as "Spain," because it was a conglomeration of heretofore relatively autonomous economic and political entities that had alliances with the Spanish Crown. (It was not until the 1590s that the Castilians began to use the term "Spanish Empire.")

The important European cultural and political events corresponding to Philip II's reign were the invention of the printing press, Martin Luther's rebellion and the Reformation, the writings of Erasmus, and the Spanish Inquisition. Well known to Fuentes, Erasmus was an influential thinker whose *In Praise of Folly* circulated widely in Europe during the sixteenth century. Fuentes points out that Erasmus promoted a new culture of humanism: now everything had several meanings. According to Fuentes, neither reason nor faith exhausted reality (*BM,* 174). Charles V had demonstrated relatively little interest in the Inquisition, officially launched in 1478, although he did use it to arrest the growth of Illuminism in the 1520s and Erasmianism in the 1530s.[4]

The eldest son of Charles V and Isabella of Portugal, Philip II was born in 1527. Educated in his youth by Martínez Siliceo and Bartolomé de Carranza, he was particularly attracted to mathematics and architecture but had little ability in foreign languages. His limitations in foreign languages were perhaps one reason why he preferred to enclose himself in Spain, never traveling outside his homeland after 1559. He also liked painting, acquiring works by Bosch, Brueghel, Titian, and other masters for display in El Escorial. Philip II had four wives: María of Portugal, who died giving birth to a son (who also died before becoming king); Mary Tudor, who died childless; Elizabeth of Valois, who bore him two daughters; and Anne of Austria, who gave birth to Don Philip.

When Philip II assumed power in 1556, his state faced the serious financial crisis that characterized the remainder of the century. He also encountered the threat of numerous religious groups whose members held beliefs that differed from those of orthodox Catholicism. Charles V had been monitoring the Jews and Moors, and he actively countered the challenge posed by the Erasmians and the Lutherans. Philip's religious position was forthright, for he stated irrevocably: "I do not propose nor desire to be the ruler of heretics."[5] Consequently, the Inquisition harassed mystics and humanists; even the mystic poet Fray Luis de León was imprisoned in 1572 for five years.

Philip II exhibited little tolerance for those he perceived as different—the other. His government attempted to exclude all groups that did not conform to his universal design. As one scholar has indicated: "Most men believed God held a design for the universe, and Spaniards were certain they were appointed by their superior culture, language, faith, and wealth to fulfill it."[6] Philip II also believed in *limpieza de sangre* (clean blood), and his government made rigorous inquiries into the ethnic backgrounds of many groups. He controlled the circulation of books with great care, systematically censoring any text that might contain even the slightest heretical reference. Philip II's third inquisitor-general, Gaspar de Quiroga, prohibited the circulation of 33,000 books, mostly foreign classical texts, including the work of writers as canonical today as Rabelais, Machiavelli, and Dante.

One of the most notable characteristics of the dominant ideology was the contradiction between the professed superiority of things Spanish—its culture, its language, its faith—and the fact that the Spanish Empire was in fact held together loosely by patently multicultural groups that consisted of Europeans and inhabitants of the Americas. The Arabs and Jews had exercised enormous influence in Spain in the centuries leading up to Philip's reign. Numerous other cultural groups also had a significant preserve in Spain. As one scholar of the period has pointed out, "Phillip's *monarquía* was far-flung and basically indefensible, only held together by the collective will of Genovese merchants, Flemish bankers, Italian and German soldiers, Portuguese and Italian sailors, American miners, and Spanish officials."[7] Consequently, the very concept of a pure, well-defined, and homogeneous "Spanish" culture was most questionable in sixteenth-century Spain.

Philip II built El Escorial as an imposing medieval, Renaissance, and neoclassical monument with a basic structure typical of medieval monasteries and hospitals. The edifice itself consists of a 101-by-261-meter granite rectangular building constructed in the shape of a grill, located 1,000 meters above sea level in the foothills of the Guadarrama Mountains. The walls rise six stories on the exterior, with towers at each of the four corners reaching above these walls; the towers have spires bearing crosses at the top. A basilica near the center of the structure also towers high above the walls. The enormous dimensions and complexity of the building can be appreciated by taking into account its 2,600 windows (including 296 exterior windows), 1,200 doors, 459 towers, 88 fountains, 86 staircases, 16 patios, 15 cloisters, and 9 towers.

In the mid-sixteenth century, Philip II began contemplating the construction of such an edifice. In 1558 he initiated the search for a site, declaring, "It should be a healthy place, with good air and water, isolated in the country; a place for contemplation, and distant from Madrid, but not too far away."[8] In 1562 he located the site, and the construction began soon thereafter. El Escorial's architectural precedents were the Monasterio de San Isidro de León, from the twelfth century, the Monasterio de Poblet in Tarragona, the Monasterio Jerónimo de Yuste (where Charles V retired and was buried in 1558), the Hospital de Granada (the west half of El Escorial is a near replica of this edifice), and the Hospital de Santa Cruz de Toledo. Certain areas of the Alcázar in Toledo, designed by Francisco de Villalpando, also served as models for El Escorial.

The architectural concept for El Escorial developed over the years, and the present configuration includes many constructions built after the original plans were conceived, well into the eighteenth century. The main designers of El Escorial, however, were two of the most renowned architects in Spain during the sixteenth century: Juan Bautista de Toledo and Juan de Herrera.

Juan Bautista de Toledo, who had worked under Michelangelo in the Vatican, drew the plans for the main body of El Escorial and most of the related designs. His "universal design," as he and his contemporaries identified his plan, actually referred to the "universal" because Bautista drew from architecture of both Italy and Spain. The cross-shaped floor plans in El Escorial imitated fifteenth-century Italian and Spanish hospitals, as well as medieval monasteries.

Juan de Herrera worked as an assistant to Juan Bautista de Toledo. A reader and follower of the celebrated sixteenth-century humanists, Herrera served in the army of Charles V before assisting Juan Bautista in the designing of El Escorial. Herrera worked with Bautista until the latter's death in 1567; then he was responsible for the completion of the complex, including several parts that had not yet been designed by his master. He was interested in the work of the Italian architect Vitruvio and influenced by the Italian Renaissance masters. According to Kubler, Herrera had been contracted as "an outsider who would be a humanist and theorist of the fine art of architecture, rather than a builder from the ranks of artisans and contractors."[9]

The models for El Escorial included medieval monasteries, and El Escorial has indeed functioned as a monastery. The monastery area was almost complete by 1571; in 1572 work began on the king's area. The basilica was begun in 1574, and the last stone was placed in the basilica in 1584 but was not consecrated until 1594. Philip II resided in El Escorial most spring and summer months, beginning in 1576.

Reading El Escorial

As a complex multicultural artifact of sixteenth-century Spain, El Escorial offers a multiplicity of readings. On its most literal level, El Escorial can be interpreted as a religious text of the Catholic Church's official discourse. The building also contains a political and military discourse articulated in an ecclesiastic and military language that was characteristically medieval. In addition, El Escorial exhibits contradictions between the ecclesiastic and the civil, as well as between the forces of exclusion and inclusion.

As a religious text of official discourse, El Escorial did fulfill its function as a setting for the monks of the Order of San Jerónimo to pray and serve God. The ceilings in numerous spaces—the king's office, the sacristy, the basilica, several ceilings in the monastery— were painted with motifs of angels, saints, and other biblical figures. The enclosed configuration of the space, along with the paintings of biblical motifs on the notably high ceilings, created the illusion of a space that was indeed, as defined by Philip II, "a dwelling place for God": enclosed in El Escorial, Philip II believed he was near heaven, and the murals on the high ceilings enhanced this sensation.

Representation in El Escorial was a form of imitation and repetition. Michel Foucault has pointed out that until the end of the sixteenth century (precisely when El Escorial was being built), resemblance played a constructive role in the knowledge of Western culture. During that period, painting imitated space and was posited as a form of repetition, be it the theater of life or the mirror of nature.[10] Perched comfortably on the Guadarrama Mountains, El Escorial imitated nature and the heavens, as represented in the Bible and other religious writings. El Escorial's forms of imitation— architectural topoi of the period—repeated themselves throughout the building. The walls, the towers, the doors, and the windows, among numerous other forms, appear and reappear, in different sizes, throughout El Escorial.

Foucault also notes that in the sixteenth century, rhetorical strategies such as *convenientia, acumultio,* and *sympathy* told how the world had to fold upon itself, duplicate itself, reflect itself, or form a chain with itself so that things could resemble one another.[11] As each wall or corner of El Escorial duplicates another, the building folds upon itself in the fashion typical of the sixteenth-century world. One of the paintings there, *San Jerónimo y San Agustín,* by Alonso Sánchez Coello (1531–1588), illustrates well the tendency of El Escorial to reflect itself. In this painting, a godlike Saint Augustine holds in his right hand a building with the architectural lines of El Escorial. This mini-Escorial duplicates the building in which the observer stands while observing this replica of *civitas Dei.*

Images of Philip II and the religious order of San Jerónimo monks were also reproduced on the walls of El Escorial. Portraits of Philip II, such as the one by Juan Pantoja de la Cruz (1551–1608), adorn these walls. These paintings of Philip II and other Spanish monarchs turn the politics of El Escorial upon themselves in constant repetition. The San Jerónimo monks saw themselves duplicated daily in the numerous paintings of their martyr San Jerónimo suffering.

Seen from the outside, this "great lyrical stone" (as El Escorial was once described by Miguel de Unamuno) projects multiple and duplicating images of a military fortress: the massive granite walls, with towers in each of the four corners of the rectangular building, mirror the imposing military fortresses constructed in the Americas in the sixteenth and seventeenth centuries, such as the fortress of San Felipe in Cartagena de las Indias in Colombia, the fortress of San Juan de Ulúa in Veracruz, Mexico, the fortress of Azare on the coast of Venezuela, and the equally grandiose and architecturally similar fortresses that protected Havana in Cuba, San Juan in Puerto Rico, and Santo Domingo in the Dominican Republic.[12] In the case of Cartagena de las Indias, the combination of the San Felipe military fortress, the walls that surround the city with its towers (architecturally identical to the towers of El Escorial), and the Basilica of San Pedro Claver (located inside the walled city of Cartagena de las Indias) produces architectural structures and spaces quite similar to the exterior imagery of El Escorial. A comparison between El Escorial and San Felipe is not gratuitous, for the Colombian historian Eduardo Lemaitre has documented the orders that Philip II gave for the construction of a "fortaleza grandiosa" when San Felipe was built:

Pero después de aquellos primeros asaltos, sobre todo la toma, cuasi destrucción y costoso rescate de la ciudad, causados por el inglés

> Sir Francis Drake, la Corona escuchó al fin los clamores de los
> cartageneros y Felipe II ordenó llevar a cabo un pionero y gran-
> dioso plan de defensas de todos sus dominios de Ultramar.[13]

To match the grandiose plans for "a dwelling place for God," then,
Philip II also ordered the construction of grandiose military fortresses
in his colonies. As Lemaitre explains, San Felipe was "a great project
of grandiose fortresses with four corner towers."[14]

Seen from the outside, El Escorial is stark in its uniformity and
lack of ornamentation. Juan Bautista had not originally planned for
such extreme uniformity. According to his plan, the western part of
the building was to have one floor less than the finished product
does, and towers in the centers of the northern and southern facades
were to provide it with much more height. When Philip decided to
double the number of monks in the monastery (from fifty to one
hundred), the entire building was raised to four floors. The extreme
uniformity of El Escorial, then, was shaped according to the desires
of Philip II.

The space from the main entrance, passing through the door-
way and entering the Patio de los Reyes, brings to bear issues of exclusion and inclusion. The very presence of this massive main entrance as a barrier to the basilica located beyond the Patio de los
Reyes communicates exclusion: the general populace did not have
ready access to the space of the Catholic mass hidden beyond these
imposing doors. Upon entering the Patio de los Reyes, the observer's
glance is directed upward, following the lines of the six Greek columns that undergird the statues of the six kings of Judea: Josafat,
Ezequias, David, Salomon, Josias, and Manasés. The presence of
these biblical kings produces yet another confluence between the religious and the political and serves to legitimate the presence of
Philip II in the divine order of El Escorial. The general populace, in
order to pass through the doors to the basilica from the Patio de los
Reyes, needed the assistance of the hierarchy, for the heavy metal
doors had to be opened in advance; an individual from the outside
would not be able to open them. These barred doors, in fact, give
the structure the physical appearance of a prison with bars, producing a sense of exclusion of the general populace rather than inclusion:
access is possible only after passing under the statues of the six kings

of Judea and through the imposing door entrance. Thus, the implicit message of these large, heavy, metal doors was that access to the church and God was possible only through the divine intervention of the king of Spain.

This imposing main entrance, with San Lorenzo standing at the top and center, between two Greek columns on his right and two others on his left, brings to bear some of the central issues underlying the ideology of El Escorial. The statue of San Lorenzo, four meters high, simultaneously evokes the religious and the military. The religious is emphasized by the representation in the statue of a serene and meek saint (with face and hands of marble) standing with a Bible in his left hand and a staff in his right. Beyond this meek and religious surface, however, is the military, for San Lorenzo was the saint selected for the naming of the edifice (Monasterio de San Lorenzo El Real de El Escorial) to celebrate the military victory achieved on his birthday. A personalized political symbol is located below the statue of San Lorenzo: the royal arms of Philip II. The exterior entrance to El Escorial, then, calls to mind major institutions of power in Spain.

As one enters El Escorial, passing the granite walls, the marble floors, and the carved wood rafters, the architectural and painted imagery inside the building also emphasizes the political and military mission of Philip II; the confluence of religious and political discourses reveals the multiplicity of functions of this ostensibly religious construct. One of the most visually remarkable incursions of the political text occurs in the basilica, where the bronze statues of the standard religious figures found in Catholic churches—saints and apostles—are accompanied by cenotaphs of the kings themselves. The most stunning confluence of religious and political discourse, however, is the presence of the king of Spain, Philip II: he appears as a bronze gilded figure to the right of the altar, praying alongside his three former wives and his son. Appearing in the basilica this way, the political figure legitimates his role (and the role of other Spanish kings) as the most distinguished occupant of this "dwelling place for God" and as the ruler of Spain and its colonies.

The confluence of religious and political imagery is particularly acute in the basilica. Philip II designed the basilica and his bedroom to assure direct visual access to the basilica's altar. The king could therefore observe the priest and the entire mass from his privileged position of voyeur, lying comfortably on his bed. He could also observe the figures of Christ, the Virgin Mary, and all the saints occupying their appropriate spaces (all gold-gilded statues), as well as *his own figure.* This remarkable juxtaposition of religious and political imagery in the same sacred space reproduces the above-mentioned political strategies with respect to the murals, while revealing the political unconscious of the "dwelling place for God."[15]

Several of the murals also reveal a confluence of the religious and the political, yet another sign that El Escorial was much more ideologically complex than is signaled by its explicit function as "a dwelling place for God." In the Gallery of Battles, a lengthy mural, painted in bright colors, is testimony to the irrefutable political function of El Escorial. Titled *The Battle of Higuerela* (the victory of Juan II of Castille over the Granadinos in 1431), the mural lauds the military accomplishments of the Spanish Crown and also celebrates the triumph of Hispanic over Arabic values. Mural painters Fabrizio Zastello, Onazio Cambiasso, and Lazzaro Tavarone portrayed distinguished-looking, white-bearded Spaniards of imposing physical appearance beneath their armor, battling dark-faced and menacing Arabs wearing turbans. Philip II's strategy was to associate himself (and his campaign for European hegemony) with the campaigns of the Spanish Christian monarchs of the Middle Ages. He made this connection in the Gallery of Battles by depicting two of his campaigns, the Battle of San Quintín and the clashes with the English in the Azores, on the walls facing *The Battle of Higuerela.*

The politics of another mural, *The Story of the Redemption,* which tells the Jesus narrative, are equally indicative. In the last section of the mural, Jesus is killed not by Romans but by Arabs, an anachronism of several centuries that served the political strategies of the Spanish Crown. The ideology of these two murals justified Unamuno's observation that "there should not be any Spaniard—with an historical awareness of his Spanishness—who does not visit it some time in his life, just as the pious Moslems visit their Mecca."[16]

From the sixteenth-century chronicler of El Escorial, Fray José de la Sigüenza, to the twentieth-century philosophers Unamuno and Ortega y Gasset, no one has questioned the *españolidad* of this cultural object identified as El Escorial. Nevertheless, this Spanish "dwelling place for God" was actually a multicultural object influenced by Arabic and other traditions and containing a diverse collection of some four thousand Arabic manuscripts along with other heterodox texts. With respect to its cultural politics, then, El Escorial contains numerous internal contradictions.

Architectural imagery from a wide range of cultures, both European and Arabic, permeates El Escorial. The Patio of Masks is overshadowed by signs of Philip II's Catholicism and Spanishness: the facade of the Catholic Church. The patio is surrounded by porticos formed by a semicircled configuration of arches on Tuscan columns, contributing to its generally Italian design. Flemish influence can also be noted in the roofs and chimney tops. Philip II insisted on bringing two wooden inlaid doors, carved in Germany, for the king's chamber. And Hans de Evalo, also German, constructed a miniature "watchtower" for the table in the king's study.

The political contradictions of Philip II's regime are fully evident in the ideology and discourse of El Escorial. Both the contents and the functions of the edifice point to a dominant regime that contradicted its own official ideology. For example, this regime banned most foreign classics. Nevertheless, the library of El Escorial contained more than 40,000 volumes, including a large number of Latin and Greek manuscripts, as well as other texts that, strictly speaking, should have been considered heterodox. (The finely elaborated Doric bookcases in the library were designed by Juan de Herrera and built by José Flecha.) With respect to the library collection, Philip II himself promoted the cultural contradictions inherent in his Escorial: "He is known to have acquired more than 200 books on magic, kept a horoscope prepared by Mathias Hacus, received frequent advice from astrologers, ordered all extant works by medieval Marjocan philosopher Ramón Lull to be brought to the Escorial, and patronised alchemists like Diego de Santiago." [17] Lull, in turn, was a poet whose writing was a palimpsest of Arabic tradition. The multicultural forces in sixteenth-century Spain and Europe were too strong for even Philip II to suppress, although his official political objectives were to do so. The contradictions inherent in El Escorial and the cultural possibilities of which Philip II was obviously aware but refused to recognize are one important subject of *Terra Nostra*. El Escorial is a patently multicultural object that was denied its multiethnic makeup by Philip II; similarly, he and his heirs denied the multicultural composition of Indo-Afro-Ibero-American society.

In addition to containing elements of the medieval, the Renaissance, and the neoclassical, the architecture of El Escorial shares with the postmodern the unresolved ambiguity created by the juxtaposition of different styles.[18] (An attempt to describe El Escorial as postmodern, nevertheless, would be an anachronistic and questionable exercise.) It does share with the postmodern juxtapositions that create contradictions, one of the most visible and obvious being the neoclassical Greek columns at the entrance and the austere and massive walls surrounding them. These juxtapositions and unresolved contradictions, as well as the architectural complexity of El Escorial, all contribute to an understanding of Fuentes' choice of this edifice as the setting for *Terra Nostra*.

Representation in El Escorial, then, consists of imitation, repetition, and duplication—the typical sixteenth-century pattern. Fuentes uses the pattern in El Escorial as a point of departure in *Terra Nostra*. As a microcosm of sixteenth-century Spanish society, its duplicating patterns provided the assurance that everything will find its mirror and its macrocosmic justification on another, larger scale. This use of the microcosm, according to Foucault, was also typical of the sixteenth century.[19] Despite the rigidity of Philip and El Escorial, this edifice is a patently multicultural object. Its political, military, and religious functions are evidenced in its architecture. This center of sixteenth-century political, military, and ecclesiastical power serves as a foundation for Fuentes, the place from which he narrates *Terra Nostra*.

The Pre-Texts: *Terra Nostra* and Related Texts by Fuentes

El Escorial was one of the major texts that eventually generated *Terra Nostra*. Fuentes published three texts closely related to this central work, one preceding the publication of the novel, one appearing simultaneously with it, and one appearing later. These three texts—a fragment of fiction titled "Nowhere," the essay *Cervantes or the Critique of Reading*, and the book *Buried Mirror*—are the works most closely related to the central themes of El Escorial and *Terra Nostra*.

The text that preceded the publication of *Terra Nostra,* "Nowhere," is a set of twenty-two short pieces that appeared in Spain in 1972 as the last part of the short fictions published under the title *Cuerpos y ofrendas.* The first of these twenty-two texts is titled "El Señor visita sus tierras" and the last, "Discurso exhortatorio." They are almost identical to twenty-two sections in Part I of *Terra Nostra* that begin and end with the same titles. They confirm that Fuentes was relatively advanced in *Terra Nostra* by the early 1970s, for he made no substantive changes from this version; he made only relatively insignificant changes in word selection or phraseology. The theological student Ludovico from the novel appears as "Alonso" in "Nowhere," and the section titled "No hay tal lugar" in *Cuerpos y ofrendas* appears under the title of "Nowhere" in *Terra Nostra.* Despite these minor changes, the "Nowhere" of *Cuerpos y ofrendas* represents an advanced stage in the writing of *Terra Nostra.* In *Cuerpos y ofrendas,* the "Nowhere" sections consist of thirty-seven pages of narrative that bring to bear some of the major issues of *Terra Nostra.* They narrate the excesses and abuses of El Señor ("El Señor visita sus tierras"), the issues of authority and theology debated during the sixteenth century ("El halcón y la paloma"), Felipe's desire for women ("Las Castellanas"), El Señor's rape of a peasant girl ("Jus prima noctis"), the abuses of the Inquisition ("El pequeño inquisidor"), the abuse of the citizens ("El rostro de Simón"), the dreams and discussions of an ideal world and utopia ("La ciudad del sol" and "No hay tal lugar"), dreams of a better society ("El sueño de Alonso"), a rebellion of millenarians ("Aquí y ahora"), the killing of rebels by the king ("El premio"), and the oppressive and repressive discourse of power ("Discurso exhortativo"). These "pre-texts" of *Terra Nostra* represent a substantive portion of Part I of the novel.

Cervantes or the Critique of Reading is Fuentes' 110-page essay on *Don Quixote* and the Spanish literary and political context around the creation of this Spanish classic; it was written during the year he was completing *Terra Nostra.* Fuentes himself has explained how *Terra Nostra* and this essay on Cervantes are related: "In a certain way, the present essay is a branch of the novel that has occupied me for the past six years, *Terra Nostra.* The three dates that constitute the temporal references of the novel help establish the temporal frame of Cervantes and *Don Quixote:* 1492, 1521, and 1598."[20] According to Fuentes, although the central issue of this essay is Cervantes and his work, it is also a review of diverse aspects of life in Spain during the period from 1499 to 1598, which covers the main construction of El Escorial or, literarily, from the publication of *La Celestina* in 1499 to that of *Don Quixote* in 1605. In his essay, Fuentes presents his vision of a multicultural Spain, inhabited by Jews, Moors, and Spaniards in medieval and Renaissance times. Drawing upon the work of Américo Castro, José Ortega y Gasset, and other scholars, Fuentes is particularly concerned with understanding how, beneath the veneer of orthodoxy, Spain was a vibrant world of heterodoxy, even during the Middle Ages. (This is the contradictory orthodoxy and heterodoxy observed in my previous reading of El Escorial.) At one point, Fuentes even confesses his (politically incorrect) admiration for medieval cultural achievements: "Perhaps I should clarify at this point that I do not possess the progressive arrogance necessary to negate the magnificent cultural flourishing that took place in Europe between the eleventh and fifteenth centuries" (*Cervantes*, 20–21). Fuentes' admiration for the Middle Ages, however, should not be associated with the orthodox, Catholic world of papal hierarchy. Rather, through readings of the scholarly writings of Américo Castro and other primary texts, Fuentes exalts the Arabic erotic literature of the Middle Ages and the Spanish literature that draws on these rich non-Hispanic traditions, such as *The Book of Good Love* and *La Celestina.*

When Fuentes wrote *Cervantes or the Critique of Reading* in the 1970s, the term "multiculturalism" had not yet been popularized, nor does he use that term. In referring to Américo Castro's observations on the cultural complexity of medieval Spain, Fuentes speaks of "cultural complex"—an early expression of his later vision of multiculturalism.

In his book on Cervantes, Fuentes also sets forth his vision of the novel, a concept that can be seen, in retrospect, as a Bakhtinian and Foucauldian concept of the genre. Although Fuentes was not yet citing Bakhtin in the mid-1970s, his regular insistence on the multiple languages of the novel relates directly to the concept of heteroglossia—or "other languages"—promoted by Bakhtin. (Later, in the 1980s, Fuentes began citing Bakhtin directly.) Using some ideas from *Les mots et les choses,* Fuentes states in *Cervantes or the Critique of Reading:* "And it is in the Medieval period in which an order is inscribed in which words and things only do coincide, but all reading is, in the end, the reading of the divine word" (*Cervantes,* 18). Here Fuentes paraphrases Foucault's idea that in the medieval world, words and things coincided, and then he adds his own observation: All reading in the medieval period is of the divine word. An understanding of this medieval conception of the word and of reading is important for an understanding of Cervantes because he lived and wrote during the Counter-Reformation—with all the rigidity and orthodoxy of the medieval period and none of its merits. (Built during the Reformation and Counter-Reformation, El Escorial attempts to exude the same rigidity and orthodoxy.)

In *Cervantes or the Critique of Reading,* Fuentes also proposes that Cervantes creates a new role for the reader—the writer who reads himself while he is reading the novel. This special awareness of a new role for the reader also reverts to Ortega y Gasset, who had made a similar point in *Historia como sistema,* speaking of a reader who has the choice of making himself or not making himself in the act of reading. Ortega states: "Man is the novelist of himself, original or plagiarist."[21] Numerous basic ideas in Fuentes' book on Cervantes as well as *Terra Nostra,* in fact, directly evoke Ortega y Gasset's return to fifteenth- and sixteenth-century Spain in *Historia como sistema.* Fuentes, like Ortega y Gasset, envisions sixteenth-century Spain as a nation in wrenching *inquietud* and crisis. Ortega y Gasset also questioned the modern faith in science and reason. Like Fuentes, this Spanish philosopher saw pure reason in crisis. Ortega y Gasset set forth an idea fundamental for Fuentes when he stated in *Historia como sistema:* "Let us happily and courageously renounce the comfort to presume that thought is real and logical." For Fuentes, too, the West's faith in exclusively scientific thought needs to be questioned. Since the 1960s, Fuentes has spoken of the tendency in the West to conceive of reality and thought in terms of Manichaean polarities. Ortega y Gasset's interest in the reader, as well as his conception of man, are quite similar to Fuentes' reader and man as described in *Cervantes* and *Terra Nostra.* Ortega y Gasset states: "Man gradually accumulates his being—the past: he makes a being in the dialectical

process of his experiences." [22] The idea that man is his past is fundamental to Fuentes' conception of the characters in *Terra Nostra,* for
several of them seem to be the reincarnation, of sorts, of characters
already seen in the novel. This is the case, for example, of the numerous characters that appear with six toes and a cross on their backs.
Ortega y Gasset also states: "I am the past," exactly as the characters
function in *Terra Nostra.*

The Buried Mirror: Reflections on Spain and the New World
(1992) is a more recent book-length consideration of the relationship
between Spain and the New World, and thus a reconsideration of
central issues in *Terra Nostra.* Fuentes' Spain—like Philip II's El Escorial—is multicultural: Fuentes emphasizes how Christian, Arab,
Jewish, Greek, Carthaginian, Roman, Gothic, and Gypsy roots can
all be found in the Iberian Peninsula. With these multiple cultures
already intact in Spain, and the sixteenth-century encounter with
Arawaks, Aztecs, Quechuas, and other groups indigenous to the
Americas, Philip II of Spain faced what Fuentes describes as "the
challenge of the Other" (*BM,* 34). The courts of Charles V and
Philip II faced this challenge at a time when the European spirit of
the Renaissance was alive, a spirit fomented by the writers Juan Ruiz,
Fernando de Rojas, Erasmus, and the Italian Marsilio Ficino, who
affirmed that "all is possible." Despite occasional incursions of the
Renaissance spirit into Spain, it remained hidden in the "night of El
Escorial," according to Fuentes, rather than reappearing in the sun-
light of the Enlightenment (*BM,* 216). In this way, El Escorial became for Fuentes a key metaphor for the directions that Spain took
in the sixteenth, seventeenth, and eighteenth centuries, directions
that prevented the spirit of the Renaissance or the Enlightenment
from flourishing in the Americas.

What future does Fuentes find for the Americas led by a medieval Spain enclosed in "the night of El Escorial?" From its rich
multicultural traditions, Spain has left a cultural heritage that Fuentes believes offers hope for both the present and the future of the
Americas. Echoing Ortega y Gasset once again, a consistent note in
The Buried Mirror is Fuentes' return to cultural heritage and cultural
values as important resources. As he states in his introduction: "A
rediscovery of cultural values can give us, with luck and effort, the
necessary vision of cultural, economic and political convergences.

Perhaps this is our mission in the coming century" (*Buried Mirror*, 10). This firm belief in cultural values is Fuentes' rewriting of Ortega y Gasset and Alfonso Reyes. The different political and cultural alternatives present for Spain and Hispanic culture are issues that Fuentes explores in *Terra Nostra*.

Cervantes or the Critique of Reading and *The Buried Mirror* thus offer many of the ideas on the culture of the Americas and on the novel fictionalized and elaborated in *Terra Nostra*.

Terra Nostra and Its Intertexts

Terra Nostra is self-consciously laden with texts, and in this sense it emerges as a Borgesian and Foucauldian project implying that all books are one. In addition to El Escorial, the most notable of these numerous texts are *The Book of Good Love, La Celestina, El burlador de Sevilla, In Praise of Folly, Don Quixote,* the fiction of Borges, and Joyce's *Ulysses.* In addition, three of the most prominent essayists present in *Terra Nostra* are Américo Castro, José Ortega y Gasset, and Octavio Paz. Fuentes' debts to Ortega y Gasset and Américo Castro are substantial. Ortega y Gasset had already influenced an entire generation of thinkers and essayists of the Hispanic world, writers who shared his reaction against the natural sciences and human reason, privileging rather the value of culture, the human spirit, and *creencias* or "beliefs." Ortega y Gasset had affirmed in 1941 in *Historia como sistema* that "beliefs are what truly constitute the state of man." [23] In addition, Fuentes draws from a wealth of other texts in *Terra Nostra,* from the Kaballah to the letters of Cortés, from the Bible to *Les Misérables,* from the letters of Columbus to Kafka's *The Metamorphosis.*

In *Les Mots et les Choses* (a book that Fuentes discovered when he was in the early stages of *Terra Nostra*), Foucault not only has a chapter on *Don Quixote* with a discussion of *Las Meninas* and Borges but he also uses some language that could well have its origins in Ortega y Gasset too. In speaking of beliefs, for example, Ortega y Gasset stated: "This means that, among other things, they possess an architecture and act in architecture." [24]

Ortega y Gasset's emphasis on "things," "architecture," and

"hierarchy" as seen here all becomes the critical language later, of course, of Foucault. In his *Historia como sistema,* Ortega y Gasset also speaks of "orders," making this book a forerunner of *Les Mots et les Choses.* Thus Fuentes had the precedent of Foucauldian concepts in Ortega y Gasset, as well as *Les Mots et les Choses,* when he began *Terra Nostra* in 1967. In the context of Fuentes, the important commonality between Foucault and Ortega y Gasset was a new sense of history and, more specifically, a sense that human history is not a matter of immutable truths but of human constructs in constant transformation. Ortega y Gasset had asserted in the 1940s, "Life is a job," believing that the individual makes his or her own reality through a series of acts. Foucault believed modern historians were responsible for having changed the old idea of a fixed and immutable history, a belief conveyed by his statement that "historians see the emergence, as though before their very eyes, of an opposition between those who believe in the immobility of nature—in the manner of Tournefort and, above all, Linnaens—and those who, with Bonnet, Renost de Maillet, and Diderot, already have a presentiment of life's creative powers, of its inexhaustible power of transformation, of its plasticity, and of that movement by means of which no one is master." [25] This philosopher's sense of transforming history is a basic concept of *Terra Nostra.*

In the bibliography of his book on Cervantes, Fuentes includes three of Américo Castro's studies: *El pensamiento de Cervantes, España en su historia,* and *La realidad histórica de España.* As Roberto González Echevarría has pointed out, an ideological underpinning of Fuentes' construct on Hispanic culture and history is Américo Castro's theory of Spanish history. Castro had promulgated the idea that the historical conflicts among Jews, Arabs, and Christians resulted in a fragmented Hispanic culture in which the Catholic victors violently suppressed the Jews and the Arabs. According to Castro, the fragmentation of the cultures of Spain is replicated in the fragmentation of cultures in Latin America. According to González Echevarría, Fuentes blends these ideas of Castro with others of Foucault in order to render Castro's fragmentation as Foucault's separation of words and things. [26]

In his book on Cervantes, Fuentes refers to Castro as the scholar who proposed that "the most original and universal part of the Hispanic genius has its origins in the forms of life constructed during the 900 years of the Christian-Islamic-Jewish blending" (*Cervantes*, 4). Thus, González Echevarría is correct in tracing Fuentes' concept of Hispanic culture back to Américo Castro. The roots of Fuentes' multiculturalism are also to be found in Castro. In citing Castro's *España en su historia,* Fuentes notes that the Spanish thinker described the history of Spain as "the history of an insecurity." Spain's historical insecurity emerges as yet another concern of *Terra Nostra* when, for example, Fuentes proposes historical alternatives that Spain lacked the courage to pursue.

With respect to Paz, Fuentes includes *El arco y la lira* in the bibliography of *Cervantes or the Critique of Reading,* but Paz's seminal essay, *The Labyrinth of Solitude* (1950), is also central. González Echevarría has delineated the relationship between *The Labyrinth of Solitude* and *Terra Nostra:*

> In a sense, *Terra Nostra* is still a reaction to Paz's 1950 book. If in *El laberinto* Paz spoke of a schism at the core of the Mexican soul, torn by his scorn of a whorish mother (Malinche) and his admiring hate for a violent father (Cortés), Fuentes attempts a reconciliation in *Terra Nostra*—a reconciliation that would include not only an acceptance of the liberal Spain whose tradition Paz already claimed, but also of the dark, violent and retrograde Spain that most Latin Americans and Spaniards abhor.[27]

Fuentes was unquestionably marked by *The Labyrinth of Solitude,* as were many writers of his generation, and Paz's mark is obvious in *Los días enmascarados* and *Where the Air Is Clear.* Moreover, many of the lifetime concerns of Paz and Fuentes are thematic material of *Terra Nostra.* The latter work, however, carries these issues in a conceptual framework so far beyond *The Labyrinth of Solitude* that González Echevarría is exaggerating Paz's importance on Fuentes during the 1970s. It is also questionable that Fuentes suggests the "acceptance" of "the dark, violent and retrograde Spain." Rather, Fuentes depicts a heterogeneous and multicultural Spain of the Middle Ages that was denied by Philip II and other Spanish kings.

The intertextual relationship between *Terra Nostra* and certain well-known canonical texts functions in a variety of ways.[28] Texts of

Juan Ruiz, Fernando de Rojas, Tirso de Molina, Cervantes, and Joyce appear in *Terra Nostra* not as influences or sources in the traditional sense but rather, as the term "intertextuality" was originally proposed by Kristeva and later developed by Culler, as part of a sign system.[29] Juan Ruiz's *The Book of Good Love* (1330) is one of the texts that most subtly and indirectly appears in *Terra Nostra*, in contrast to *El burlador de Sevilla, La Celestina,* and *Don Quixote,* which have major characters in the novel. *The Book of Good Love,* a song to the pleasures of the body, is absorbed and transformed in *Terra Nostra* as the literary presence of the Califato de Córdoba. The acts of transgressive eroticism that take place inside the walls of Fuentes' El Escorial—called El Palacio—are transformations from *The Book of Good Love,* which, in turn, was a product stemming from Arabic culture. The Andalusian poet Ibn Haz's *El collar de la paloma,* written in 1022, was an erotic autobiography assimilated into *The Book of Good Love,* according to María Rosa Lida and Américo Castro (*Cervantes,* 43). The Arabic spaces and Arabic culture in *Terra Nostra* frequently represent a momentary sexual liberation within a Catholic and Hispanic ambience of repression. In the narrative segment titled "El primer niño" (*TN,* 522–524), for example, Felipe, Celestina, and Ludovico, who had suffered the oppression and persecution of El Señor earlier in the novel, engage in an unorthodox (and liberating) ménage a trois. Using an Arabic reference, the narrator states: "The castle was the place where everything they had dreamed was becoming reality" (*TN,* 515).

The character Celestina, from *La Celestina* (1499), by Fernando de Rojas, is a major presence in *Terra Nostra,* appearing throughout the novel. Rojas, a descendant of converted Jews, wrote *La Celestina* as a humanistic alternative to the growing orthodoxy of Spain. It is a story of characters like some of those in *Terra Nostra:* an old go-between, her female pupils, two young lovers, and their servants. In *La Celestina,* according to Fuentes, "the exemplary voices and virtues of medieval morality are defeated by money, passion, sex interest" (*BM,* 84).

In *Terra Nostra,* Celestina appears as the old go-between and the experienced woman who believes in love. She enters the novel in the first section, as one of two mysterious signees of a letter that Polo Febo finds on July 14, 1999. After that, she appears in Spain, initially as a *campesina* who marries the blacksmith Jerónimo and is raped by El Señor (*TN,* 110–113) while the young Felipe watches, and later she escapes with Felipe. Then she is raped by two old men in the forest. Saved by Felipe again, she engages in lengthy conversations about dreams of utopia with her newfound friends Felipe, Ludovico, and Pedro. Each speaks of dreams of ideal worlds where rebellions against repression are successful, where there is no death, and where people live in love and harmony. La Celestina bears a child and makes a pact with the devil, who promises her the wisdom she cannot attain in one lifetime. When she is in El Palacio, she frequently appears dressed as a page. After her absence from Part II in the New World, Celestina appears once again with Felipe, Ludovico, and others in Part III. As in *La Celestina,* in Part I she actively promotes sexual liberation and moves on the margins of society, often in the spaces of heterodoxy. Children claiming to have been born of Celestina appear throughout Part III. Near the end of the novel ("The Rebellion," 628–651), Celestina kisses Ludovico and promises to meet him in Paris on July 14, 1999. Her reappearance at the end of the novel, where she makes love with Polo Febo, suggests the attainment of that instant of eternal time that Fuentes and Paz have long desired in their texts.

El burlador de Sevilla (1630), by Tirso de Molina, is one of the two principal sources of the character Don Juan, a major character in *Terra Nostra.* (The other principal source is José de Zorrilla's *Don Juan Tenorio* [1844].) Multiple and transforming Don Juan figures appear in *Terra Nostra,* often with character traits from both of these classic Spanish plays. After killing Gonzalo de Ulloa, Inés's father, Don Juan is killed by some of his adversaries. A short time later, Don Juan appears in Ludovico's home, announcing that he will be reincarnated in one of Ludovico's children. After being thrown on the beaches of the Cabo de los Desastres at the age of twenty, with no awareness of his identity, he is taken into the Palacio de la Señora, where he becomes the seducer of all the women there. He then flees with Inés to the New World, where he seduces numerous women. As in the classic plays, Fuentes' Don Juan is a narcissist capable of loving only himself.

In comparison to Celestina and Don Juan, Don Quixote is a relatively minor character in *Terra Nostra.* He first appears in the narrative segment titled "The Knight of Sad Countenance" (*TN*, 530–531), which combines elements from the first and second parts of *Don Quixote*. Fuentes' Don Quixote appears to be insane because of his role as his immoral other—Don Juan. The double figure Don Quixote/Don Juan fails as Don Quixote, kills Dulcinea's father, and then acquires the identity of Don Quixote. More important than the presence of the protagonist of *Don Quixote* is Fuentes' use of Cervantes' narrative strategies, such as the story within the story, as well as what Fuentes himself has defined as Cervantine "modern" attitudes.

Erasmus' *In Praise of Folly* is more absorbed and assimilated than are *La Celestina, El burlador de Sevilla,* or other books that lend characters to *Terra Nostra*. Since his books were banned and the Spanish Crown vilified him during the Inquisition, Erasmus is the type of writer that Fuentes wishes to reclaim from Spanish cultural history. *Terra Nostra,* too, is written in praise of folly; *Terra Nostra,* too, suggests that both faith and reason had to become relative rather than absolute terms: neither Felipe's absolute faith nor Ludovico's absolute reason is acceptable. In addition, when the young boy and the old man arrive in the New World, one of the first lessons that they learn is the Erasmian idea that "appearances deceive" (*TN*, 409), a Fuentes paraphrase of *In Praise of Folly*.

The intertextual relationships with Borges are important to much of Fuentes' work, including *Terra Nostra*. One of the most important Borges pieces for the Fuentes of *Terra Nostra* and the Foucault of *Les Mots et les Choses* was the Borges story that subverted the landmarks of Foucault's thought and the West's age-old distinction between the Same and the Other. This Borges fiction refers to a Chinese encyclopedia in which it is written that animals are divided into a series of unorthodox categories, such as "belonging to the Emperor," "embalmed," "tame," "sucking pigs," "fabulous," and the like.[30] Borges' innovative subversion of traditional taxonomies and proposal of another system of thought laid the groundwork for much Latin American fiction of Fuentes' generation, much of Fuentes' own writing, and *The Order of Things*. *Terra Nostra,* as a historical project, is an invention of new historical taxonomies for the history of Spain and the Americas.

Borges' *Ficciones* is also basic to *Terra Nostra,* particularly his story "Pierre Ménard, Author of Don Quixote." Fuentes makes numerous allusions to Borges in his novel, but two of the most pervasive Borgesian ideas in *Terra Nostra* are the concept of all books as one book and the death of the author. In "Pierre Ménard," Borges suggests the former by proposing the idea of the "total book," which contains all books. And *Terra Nostra* is seemingly one of these exemplary texts, containing the canonical books of the West, as well as numerous esoteric and forgotten texts. In "Magias parciales del Quijote," Borges suggests on the one hand that fiction writing is the rewriting of other texts; on the other hand he suggests that fictitious characters can be real readers of a text and, in turn, that real readers can be fictitious.

Fuentes rewrites Borges' "Pierre Ménard," in *Terra Nostra*. This Borges story begins with a list of Ménard's works, a list of esoteric non sequiturs that recalls the bibliography of *Terra Nostra* in *Cervantes or the Critique of Reading*. Ménard's sources include "one of those parasitic books which places Christ on a Boulevard, Hamlet on the Cannebiere and Don Quijote on Wall Street." [31] This type of anachronistic spatial displacement is precisely the exercise of Fuentes in *Terra Nostra:* he has Agrippa and Celestina in the twentieth century and Polo Febo and Ulysses in the sixteenth. Ménard was also interested in "Paudet's famous plan: to unite in *one* figure, Tartarin, the Ingenious Gentleman and his square." This is also Fuentes' procedure, as he fuses Don Quijote and Don Juan into one character, and Philip II, Charles V, Charles IV, Charles II, and Francisco Franco into the character of El Señor. Several others, such as La Señora, Guzmán, and Julián, are a synthesis of several historical figures. [32] In the end, the narrator of "Pierre Ménard" views Don Quijote as a "kind of palimpsest," just as *Terra Nostra* is a kind of palimpsest with traces of writing of, above all, Cervantes and Borges—the two writers with characters least visible in *Terra Nostra,* although, in the end, Pierre Ménard does make a brief appearance.

Terra Nostra alludes to numerous other literary characters. *Les misérables* is evoked by Jean Valjean, and lines from Sor Juana Inés de la Cruz's "Primero sueño" appear in the text, as do passages from the Bible and the Kaballah. [33] The character Violetta Gautier in *Terra Nostra* is a combination of Marguerite Gautier of Alexander Dumas' *La dame aux camélias* and Violetta Valéry from Verdi's *La Traviata*.

In the narrative segment "The Chronicler" (*TN*, 233–248), Fuentes incorporates intertextually the opening lines of Kafka's *The Metamorphosis*. From Ezra Pound's poem "Cino" comes a passage in *Terra Nostra* as well as the name of Polo Febo, who originates as Pollo Phoibee in "Cino."

With respect to the intertextuality in *Terra Nostra*, it is helpful to remember that Pierre Ménard wished to "produce pages which would coincide—word for word and line for line—with those of Miguel de Cervantes." [34] *Terra Nostra* is not only a rewriting of the history of Spain but it is also an irreverent rewriting of many canonical texts of Hispanic and Western literary tradition.

Terra Nostra and El Escorial: Introduction to Structure and Architecture

The basic setting of *Terra Nostra* is sixteenth-century Spain, but in addition to this Spain of "the night of El Escorial," the novel takes place in the Roman Empire of Tiberius Caesar, the Americas of the Conquest, and Paris at the beginning of the new millennium. There are direct parallels between the structure of El Escorial and the structure of *Terra Nostra*.

Terra Nostra consists of 114 narrative segments divided formally into three parts. [35] Part I, titled "The Old World," is the longest (341 pages in Spanish; 338 pages in English). Part II, "The New World," is the shortest (139 pages in Spanish; 137 pages in English). Part III is titled "The Next World" and is of moderate length (286 pages in Spanish; 289 pages in English). In Part I, "The Old World," an anecdote with some similarity to the history of the sixteenth-century Spain of Philip II is narrated, a story of rigid Catholic orthodoxy and political repression. The character of El Señor (always capitalized) represents a synthesis of the historical figures of Charles V and Philip II. Similarly, the character of La Señora has some qualities of Juana La Loca and other Spanish queens. In Part II, a character from the first part, Pedro, travels to the New World with a young pilgrim who remains unnamed. They arrive at a land similar to the Mexico and the Tenochtitlán where Hernán Cortés arrived, where the Indians speak of Quetzalcoatl, and where there is a god named

Espejo Humeante as well as other figures that the reader associates with the Mexican Valle de Anáhuac of the sixteenth century. Part III returns to a Spain of basically the sixteenth century, but with many entirely heterodox cultural and political elements.

The structure of *Terra Nostra,* which follows the fundamental architectural scheme of El Escorial, is considerably more complex than the outline above might suggest. In the first place, the novel begins and ends with the character of Polo Febo in Paris in the year 1999. Febo helps his ninety-one-year-old concierge to give birth to a child with a cross on his back, then observes great chaos on the streets of Paris, sees masses of women giving birth to babies on these same streets, and finally meets with a woman with tattooed lips who throws a bottle into the boiling Seine River, into which Polo Febo falls. Many of the incredible characters and events of these twenty-two initial pages, whose motives seem illogical or incomprehensible on a first reading, appear and reappear in the seven hundred pages that follow. The temporal changes and the constant transformation of the identity of the characters subvert any sense of linearity that the initial description might have suggested.

Parallels between the basic structure of *Terra Nostra* and the basic architectural scheme of El Escorial are evident in the novel's three parts. El Escorial also consists of three parts, with the basilica in the center as one part, another part north of the basilica, and a third part south of the basilica. If we read the architectural plan of El Escorial from left to right, as we read books, the first and third parts of El Escorial, like the first and third parts of *Terra Nostra,* occupy the most space. Part I of El Escorial consists of the *casa real* and the *colegio.* Part II in the sequence consists of the basilica, and Part III contains the monastery. The structural complexity of El Escorial, like that of *Terra Nostra,* surpasses these initial descriptions. In addition to the multiple patios, rooms, stairways, doors, and towers, El Escorial was in a state of transformation throughout the reign of Philip II, in accordance with the plans and the adjustments to them over the three-decade period.

The constant transformations of characters in *Terra Nostra*—some of which involve three or four manifestations of the same basic character—has several equivalents in El Escorial. As mentioned above, the architecture of El Escorial underwent a process of constant transformation over the approximately three decades of its construction, including the later period when Philip II lived there at the same time that the construction of other parts continued. The biblical stories that cover the walls of El Escorial in the form of murals also underwent ongoing transformation, in both form and content. The form or style of these paintings changed in accordance with the historical period of their conception, depicting saints and other biblical figures as two-dimensional or three-dimensional, dark- or light-skinned, and the like, depending on the artistic mores and political needs of the moment. Consequently, the observer of El Escorial sees many saints called San Lorenzo and San Mauricio—all repeating different variants—just as the reader of *Terra Nostra* encounters numerous characters identified as El Señor, La Señora, and the like.

The architecture of El Escorial, as has been noted, was typical of the sixteenth century and functioned on the principle of imitation and repetition. Much architectural design, of course, operates on the basis of repetition, as does much fiction. In both El Escorial and *Terra Nostra,* nevertheless, repetition is an exceptionally notable technique and one of the predominant strategies of the two respective works. In the case of El Escorial, the major motifs of the giant exterior, such as the Greek columns and the towers, are repeated incessantly throughout the building. The structure of *Terra Nostra* is also defined by the repetition of characters and situations. For example, a green bottle appears repeatedly, as do characters with six toes and crosses tattooed on their backs. Other repetitions include the multiple appearances of the figures of Polo Febo and Don Juan.

A diachronic parallel is the space of El Escorial and *Terra Nostra.* Philip II and Fuentes conceived of their architectural models with multiple interior spaces of varying sizes, with a variety of accesses to the exterior space. The large spaces of El Escorial, such as the patio between the main entrance and the basilica, the basilica itself, and the large areas where paintings are on display, have as their equivalent the lengthy chapters of *Terra Nostra.* More precisely, the large spaces for paintings in El Escorial are the equivalent of the lengthy chapters in *Terra Nostra* on the painting from Orvieto (*TN*, 83–109). The small spaces of El Escorial, such as the Patio of the Masks and other small interior spaces, have parallels in *Terra Nostra* in the brief and spatially enclosed chapters such as "There

Is a Clock That Does Not Strike" (*TN*, 99–102) and "The Heir" (*TN*, 107–108). The self-enclosed El Escorial has, at several turns, access to outside space in the form of its numerous patios, its even more numerous windows, and its gardens. Consequently, the experience of space in El Escorial is often conveyed by abrupt change: from darkness to light, from an enclosed, hermetic interior space to a bright, open, exterior space. In *Terra Nostra,* the experience of space is parallel: the reader moves from narrative segment to narrative segment, from the small spaces of brief fragments to the larger spaces of lengthy ones, from the enclosed spaces of the tombs and small rooms to the open spaces of the forests of Spain and the jungles of the Americas.

Spaces of darkness and light in El Escorial also have their parallel in *Terra Nostra.* In El Escorial, one moves from extreme darkness to extreme light by moving from small enclosed spaces to patios, from exterior spaces to looking out windows, for example. In *Terra Nostra,* the reader is moved constantly between darkness and light, from inside to outside, from the generally inner space of Part I to the generally outer space of Part II.

The relationship between the spaces of El Escorial and the spaces (narrative segments) of *Terra Nostra,* respectively, function on the basis of metonymy rather than that of metaphor, that is, association rather than analogy. In El Escorial, the predominant images are the massive exterior walls, the four towers, the main entrance, and the basilica. Inside El Escorial, one encounters smaller walls, images of smaller reproductions of the towers, smaller entrances into rooms, and smaller images from the basilica. Each of these smaller structures and images functions as a synecdoche for the larger structure and images, thus making the experience of El Escorial, for the observer, one of continuous synecdoche. The structure of *Terra Nostra* also functions on the basis of metonymy rather than metaphor, in terms of both the relationships among the individual narrative segments and the relationships among the three parts. The individual narrative segments sometimes connect as a linear story in sequences of approximately two to ten narrative segments; other segments that do not form part of a linear narrative associate with each other metonymically. Many of these brief segments, like the small reproductions of itself within El Escorial, function as synecdoches for the larger story. The brief narration of El Señor's rape of Celestina ("Jus primae noctis," *TN*, 110–111) operates as a synecdoche for his larger rape of Spain and, in turn, for his rape of the colonies of the Americas.

El Escorial contains objects that function as synecdoches for the entire structure. The contemporary El Escorial, which Fuentes saw in 1967, contains a historical museum replete with drawings and plans of El Escorial in its different stages of development, as well as the architectural plans for associated buildings that were used as models. Numerous other objects serve as synecdoches for El Escorial itself—the already mentioned painting *San Jerónimo y San Agustín* and paintings and objects that are synecdoches for El Escorial–as–universe.

Similarly, Fuentes uses three art objects that function as synecdoches for *Terra Nostra*–as–universe: the painting *El jardín de las delicias,* a Theater of Memory, and the painting from Orvieto. (These synecdoches recall the earlier reference of Foucault to duplication and similar rhetorical strategies in Renaissance art.) The painting *El jardín de las delicias,* by Bosch, appears in Part III ("Seventh Day," *TN*, 618–628) and is the object of discussion of the young Felipe and the student Ludovico. *El jardín de las delicias,* like *Terra Nostra,* is a triptych of desire and thus functions as a synecdoche of the entire three-part novel. The garden discussed, like *Terra Nostra,* represents the opposite of El Escorial and its fictionalized version identified as El Palacio. Bosch's extraordinary painting expresses the utopian desires present throughout the novel, embodied in the characters of Felipe, Celestina, and the pilgrims to the New World. Consequently, after the exchanges between Felipe and Ludovico, El Señor closes the triptych in order to exorcise "that monstrous vision of life, passion, the Fall, the happiness and death of everything ever conceived or created" (*TN*, 628). Bosch's unorthodox painting, like Fuentes' unorthodox novel, is a triptych that celebrates desire.

The Theater of Memory (*TN*, 552–563) is the novel's second important synecdoche of itself. In this narrative segment, Ludovico visits the Venetian Valerio Camillo, who has built and operates a "theater of memory," with a historical precedent from the Middle Ages. As has been pointed out, *Terra Nostra* is structured around three worlds, just as Camillo's Theater of Memory represents three worlds: "These columns represent the seven Sephirot of the supra-celestial world, which are the seven measures of the plots of the celestial and lower worlds and which contain all the possible ideas of all three worlds" (*TN*, 558). A parallel to Fuentes' rewriting of unorthodox, heretical, and esoteric religious practices is Camillo's eclectic and unorthodox integration of diverse religious practices. Camillo places in this theater Greek divinities such as Diana, Mercury, Venus, Apollo, Mars, Jupiter, and Saturn; and he also cites the Zohar: "Three bodies and one eye; one body and three souls" (*TN*, 565). In addition, Camillo paraphrases Hermes Trismegistus: "Hermes Trismegistus has written wisely that he who knows how to join himself to this diversity of the unique will also be divine and will know all past, present, and future, and all the things that heaven and earth contain" (*TN*, 559). Camillo's explanation of Hermes' writings parallels Fuentes' writing in *Terra Nostra*, which emphasizes diversity and synthesizes the past, present, and future into one. Other allusions in the narrative section "Theater of Memory" suggest that Camillo's Theater of Memory is a synecdoche for *Terra Nostra*: Camillo refers to his theater as a "paper fortress" (*TN*, 559) and proposes memory as "total knowledge of a total past" (*TN*, 563). Obviously, *Terra Nostra* itself is not only a fortress of paper but also a manifestation of Fuentes' belief in memory as an important vehicle for understanding the past. With the inclusion of the Theater of Memory, Fuentes paraphrases Foucault's observation that, until the end of the sixteenth century, resemblance played a constructive role in the knowledge of Western culture. Painting imitated space and was posited as a form of repetition, be it the theater of life or the mirror of nature.[36] Here, a theater of life (life as mind and memory) is a mirror of both nature and *Terra Nostra* itself.

The third important object that functions as a synecdoche of *Terra Nostra* in *Terra Nostra* is the painting of Orvieto.[37] It is a magical work painted by Julián that rewrites the Jesus narrative. Orvieto's painting first appears near the beginning of the novel in the section "All My Sins" (*TN*, 89–104); the narrative of the painting is intercalated between a dialogue between El Señor and Guzmán and a narrative about the construction of El Palacio. At the beginning, the painting is described as a typical biblical narrative, telling the story of Jesus. Later in Part I, the *cuadro* appears again, but it comes to life when El Señor prays to the Jesus in the picture ("Brief Life, Eternal Glory, Unchanging World," *TN*, 148–157). Suddenly El Señor notices the movement of the nude male bodies in the pictures, with erect penises covered with blood and semen. El Señor prays more fervently, seethes with wrath, and lashes at the painting with a whip. Then Jesus begins moving his lips and delivers a speech questioning whether or not he is the Son of God. Later in Part I, in "The First Testament," El Señor has another equally devastating encounter with the painting when several characters in the painting speak, including Jesus, undermining the belief of El Señor and Guzmán in Christian doctrine as narrated in the Bible. In Part III, there are brief allusions to the painting, now rejected by El Señor (*TN*, 493), even though he prays before it (*TN*, 590). Don Juan looks at the painting ("Second Day," *TN*, 593–597) and sees himself in the figure of Jesus. Later ("Fifth Day," *TN*, 608–612), El Señor speaks to the painting and demands that the Jesus figure speak the truth, but he receives no response.

This painting from Orvieto functions as a synecdoche of *Terra Nostra* in several ways. On the one hand, the painting subverts the orthodox biblical narrative of El Señor just as *Terra Nostra* questions the institutional Catholic narrative of Hispanic political and cultural practices in the sixteenth century. It also intertwines the religious and the sexual in reproduction of the imagery of El Escorial and much of the broader narrative of *Terra Nostra* beyond the passages dealing with Orvieto's painting.

Both El Escorial and *Terra Nostra* aspire to be an "arquitectura universal." For El Escorial, the "universal" architecture is implied by the basic design based on other "universal" (i.e., European) models. The medieval, Renaissance, and neoclassical lines were the "universals" of the sixteenth century. Philip II also assured the universality of the architectural design by contracting two architects with a broad humanistic education; Bautista de Toledo and Herrera were charged with creating a "universal design." For *Terra Nostra*, Fuentes turned to canonical and equally "universal" sources: the classics of Spanish literature, as well as classic histories of the West.

El Escorial and *Terra Nostra* both employ Old World and New World architecture. The Old World architecture of El Escorial is visible in its European design and motifs. The tripartite architectural plan of *Terra Nostra,* as well as its use of some classic narrative ruses, forms part of the Old World architecture of the novel. The sources for El Escorial and *Terra Nostra,* however, are New World: the gold from the Americas serves as the financial source for the construction of El Escorial; New World pre-Columbian history and culture and New World writer Fuentes serve as the ultimate source of *Terra Nostra.*

Both El Escorial and *Terra Nostra* are architectural constructs that imagine the Americas from the space in the Guadarrama Mountains. The four towers and the imposing walls of El Escorial imagine the domination of the Americas. El Escorial's military imagery is that of a colonial power that imagines itself as a world power. *Terra Nostra,* located in the same space, imagines the Americas that appear in a dreamlike, imagined form in Part II of the novel. The locus of the narration inside the walls of this edifice, in fact, is the most logical explanation for the dreamlike quality enshrouding the conquest in this novel.

The edifice and the novel in question are, in essence, Erasmian constructs that function on the basis of the Erasmian maxim "Appearances deceive." An operating principle of El Escorial, as both a military and a religious artifact, is the creation of deceptive exterior and interior appearances: the military function is cloaked in ecclesiastic imagery; the biblical imagery, in turn, strives to re-create a medieval concept of heaven. The ceilings in many spaces of El Escorial contribute to this illusion. In *Terra Nostra,* as in much modernist fiction, the established reality of the text, once fixed, is undermined, revealing to the reader that appearances not only deceive but are appearances only. This is particularly evident in the case of character: a character named "the page" is soon revealed to be La Celestina, just as other characters ultimately assume other identities. Such ambiguity is not the exception but rather the norm for characters in *Terra Nostra.*

El Escorial and *Terra Nostra* share an architecture of desire. In El Escorial, it is the desire for utopia, which pervades its architectural design, from the basilica spires reaching toward the heavens to the internal spaces that strive to reproduce the heavens. In the structure's interior plan, the architecture expresses the desire of the voyeur for the other and the desire of the narcissist for the self in the basilica, desires that Philip II made no attempt to hide.[38] The voyeurism and narcissism of the architecture are only the most extreme examples of the utopian desires that permeate El Escorial. The ultimate utopia of El Escorial, however, is the trope of this edifice as microcosm, as universe. The original intentions of Philip II emphasized the creation of a setting isolated from the external world. The architectural object of El Escorial, like several of its predecessors, was conceived as *orbus mundi*—an architectural utopia designed to protect its inhabitants from the empirical world outside.

An architecture of desire also operates in *Terra Nostra:* the lengthy three-part novel provides for Fuentes' expression of desire. In this sense, Part III stands out; here Fuentes elaborates the heretical and esoteric texts that Philip II had repressed and that cultural and political practices following Philip II's regime had continued to repress for centuries. Fuentes seemingly accepts no spatial or temporal limits in *Terra Nostra,* for in this grand narrative he freely articulates the utopian desires that have undergirded much of his modernist writing. Fuentes' architecture of desire, unlike that of Philip II, however, is one of inclusion rather than exclusion: while the outer limits of El Escorial serve to limit and exclude, the outer limits of *Terra Nostra* expand to include. And although both employ an architecture of desire, the architectural designs of El Escorial and *Terra Nostra* reveal two entirely different concepts of utopia: the utopia of Philip II is a specific and limited place, whereas the utopia of Fuentes is, indeed, "nowhere" (the meaning of the Greek "utopia").

Finally, the tripartite structures of *Terra Nostra* and El Escorial emphasize the number three. Fuentes presents the three Sephirot in "The Sephirot" (*TN,* 523), an explanation of reality according to the Sephirot of the Kaballah. These three Sephirot were also the original letters of the Hebrew alphabet. According to the narrator, the number three represents unity: "From this trinity are born all other things, manifesting themselves progressively in love, justice, beauty, triumph, glory, generation and power" (*TN,* 523). In the New World, the Aztecs operate according to a principle of dualism. Nevertheless, the old man with memories prefers the number three, affirming the existence of three gods united in one action. In addition, *Terra Nostra* abounds in threes: there are three bottles, three primary geographical locations (Rome, Spain, Mexico), and, according to one critic, the three cosmic eras of the Kaballah are reflected in the three parts of the novel.[39]

Rereading *Terra Nostra*

Terra Nostra is Fuentes' rewriting of "the night of El Escorial," his major and culminating rereading of Indo-Afro-Ibero-American culture and history, and, in addition, his major work on identity, knowledge, and the novel itself. Fuentes has been concerned with the culture, history, and identity of the Americas since his youth. *Where the Air Is Clear, The Death of Artemio Cruz,* and *A Change of Skin* were major projects regarding these issues. Mario Vargas Llosa had asked the historical question "At what moment did Peru fuck up?" and, in an attempt to respond to this question, wrote a lengthy historical and political novel, *Conversation in the Cathedral.* Near the end of *Terra Nostra,* Fuentes poses a similar question, with a character wondering "at what moment Spanish America had fucked everything up" (*TN,* 761). In addition to the particulars of Latin American history, Fuentes is concerned with how history, culture, and identity are constructed and then understood. As an observer of El Escorial and as a reader of Ortega y Gasset and Foucault, Fuentes had concluded well before writing *Terra Nostra* that history should be understood not as the compilation of immutable truths but as a living world in transformation.

In two seminal essays on *Terra Nostra,* González Echevarría and Kerr have set forth readings of the novel that question Fuentes' proposals on Latin American culture and history; these essays deal primarily with authority and power in this novel. For González Echevarría, *Terra Nostra* is Fuentes' attempt to write what Alejo Carpentier had identified as the novel of cultural knowledge. Carpentier, in turn, had been influenced by many of the same essayists, dedicated to the study of history and culture, whose works Fuentes also read: Unamuno, Ortega y Gasset, Alfonso Reyes, José Carlos Mariátegui, Pedro Henríquez Ureña, José Lezama Lima, and Octavio Paz. More specifically, González Echevarría views Fuentes' double project of *Terra Nostra* and *Cervantes or the Critique of Reading* as a synthesis of Castro, Foucault, Cervantes, and Lukacs: "A synthesis (or reduction) of the implicit argument of Fuentes' essay would run as follows: the caste struggle (Castro) resulted in a fracture, a separation between words and things (Foucault), that produced the modern novel (Cervantes), which is the product of fragmented societies (Lukacs)."[40] According to this critic, Fuentes presents himself as the possessor of "an ultimate truth."[41] Finally, González Echevarría concludes that in *Terra Nostra,* as in a host of other Latin American novels of the 1970s, the novel of cultural knowledge is abandoned in favor of fiction in the vein of Severo Sarduy and Manuel Puig.[42] González Echevarría simplifies and reduces *Terra Nostra* with his reading, for *Terra Nostra,* as will be shown, is both modern and postmodern, both a novel of cultural knowledge and a fiction in the mode of Sarduy and Puig.

Kerr concurs with González Echevarría in his assessment of *Terra Nostra* as an archaelogy of knowledge in the Hispanic world, with its beginnings in Rome and continuation through the Middle Ages and Renaissance. In the end, however, she portrays *Terra Nostra* as an enigmatic text: "Fuentes' novel, an enigmatic text that develops around a variety of mysteries and mystery texts, aims to consider the enigmatic quality of the monarchy's enduring hegemony, which the empirical author regards as 'based on death . . . on *nada.*' "[43] Kerr's incisive reading contributes to our understanding of Fuentes' novel. Nevertheless, she misrepresents much of the work by failing to move beyond the enigma and mystery that form the basis of much fiction, including *Terra Nostra.*

With his rewriting of El Escorial, begun at the same time he was discovering Foucault, Fuentes started to explore history conceptualized beyond the terms that he, Vargas Llosa, and a host of other Latin American writers had been using in their historical inquiry into Indo-Afro-Ibero-America. The historical questions of *Terra Nostra* certainly concern issues well beyond those found in Latin American empirical experience. Foucault has pointed to a number of major functions of history in Western culture, such as: memory, myth, transmission of the word and of example, vehicle of tradition, critical awareness of the present, decipherment of humanity's destiny, anticipation of the future, or promise of return.[44] These functions provide Fuentes with material at the same time that he critiques the traditional roles of empirical history.

Fuentes' earlier understanding of history came not from Foucault but from several other scholars and historians, including R. G. Collingwood, who, in *The Idea of History* (1946), analyzes the concept of history from the Greek historian Herodotus to Descartes, Hegel, Toynbee, Dilthey, and Spengler.[45] Collingwood's historical thinking, read in the context of Fuentes' early contact with Américo Castro and Ortega y Gasset and his later contact with Foucault, has contributed to Fuentes' own thinking. Collingwood studies the steps and stages that brought the modern European idea of history into existence. Fuentes' historical vision in *Terra Nostra* is as vast and ample as Collingwood's, for he too returns to Greco-Roman history; Fuentes' central focus, however, is the history of medieval and sixteenth-century Spain and its role in the formation of the cultures of the Americas.

The conceptualization of history in classical Greco-Roman cultures, as manifested by Herodotus, Thucydides, Polybius, Livy, and Tacitus, as well as later Christian ideas of history, have direct parallels in the medieval and sixteenth-century Spain of *Terra Nostra*. The development of Greek and Roman concepts of history, respectively, as described by Collingwood, evokes the historical thinking novelized by Fuentes in *Terra Nostra*. When Herodotus converted Greek theocratic history and legend-writing into a history of events generated by human beings with reasons for acting as they did, this first "scientific" historian of the West (according to Collingwood) was laying the groundwork for Fuentes' historical project. The Greeks tended to regard society as being in perpetual change and the course of history as flexible, as opposed to the inhabitants of medieval Europe (and medieval Spain), who hoped to retain its chief features unchanged. In Greece after Herodotus, as in the Spain of Philip II, the search for unchangeable and eternal objects of knowledge stifled historical consciousness. Following the model of Herodotus, Fuentes fictionalizes a Spanish king in *Terra Nostra* who is obsessed with an unchangeable world and eternal objects.

An important change signaled by Greco-Roman historiography was the view of humans as the agents of history. In some cases, the individual was the agent; in others a collective body functioned in this role. In *Terra Nostra,* human entities similar to individuals are the agents of history, but the fragmentation of individual identity undermines any traditional conceptualization of history as generated by "great men." In *Terra Nostra,* the multiple characters of the king figure make the history of Spain and the Americas a phenomenon generated from a central space of power—El Escorial—but not controlled consistently by any one human figure. At the same time that history is motivated by these fragmented human forces, it is also moved by forces of chance and coincidence beyond human control. When Pedro and the young boy arrive, disoriented, in the New World, no human force has defined their presence there.

Medieval historiography, written under the influence of Christian doctrine, is important to *Terra Nostra* in several ways. On the one hand, Fuentes fictionalizes numerous Judeo-Christian traditions that were considered heretical during the medieval period and still censored during the sixteenth century of *Terra Nostra.* Fuentes is interested in these heretical doctrines, such as the Judaic mysticism of the Kaballah and related Judeo-Christian religious practices in general that appear in Part III, as alternatives that belong to Hispanic culture and history as well as orthodox Catholicism. On the other hand, Fuentes characterizes El Señor as a Catholic figure unsure to what extent he can control history by his own will and to what extent it is inevitable that man should accept acting in the dark—in "the night of El Escorial"—without knowing what will come of his action, in accordance with Christian doctrine.

Medieval and Christian historiography, which was of considerable interest to Fuentes when he wrote *Terra Nostra,* consisted of the task of discovering and expounding the objectives of a divine plan. Christian historiography was dedicated to a universal history, ascribing events not to the wisdom of human agents but to the workings of Providence. The parallel to this universal impulse was the insistence on a "universal design" for El Escorial. Medieval historians, according to Collingwood, "looked forward to the end of history as something foreordained by God." [46] Fuentes appropriates medieval historiography in *Terra Nostra* by creating an apocalyptic end of history in Paris in the year 1999.

The various Western conceptions of history in the different periods since the Renaissance are part of Fuentes' historical perspective. In *Terra Nostra,* the author recovers the Renaissance idea that history becomes the chronicle of human passions. The passions of El Señor, La Señora, the youths, and others break the strictures of the Spanish medieval Catholic tradition, suggesting that the events in these characters' lives, as well as the events in Spanish history, are defined by human passion more than by divine Providence. In the Americas as well, human passion occasionally decides the direction of history: the Butterfly woman in Part II affects the direction of history as much as the political events of official history do. The critical spirit of Descartes is represented in *Terra Nostra* by the questioning of authorized history, by the reinventing of the Spanish royalty, and by the evoking of the heretical texts that had been excluded and forgotten. The innovations of Giambattista Vico regarded the historical process as one whereby human beings build up systems of language, customs, law, and government. An important forerunner to Ortega y Gasset and Foucault for Fuentes, Vico laid the groundwork for Fuentes' history and critique of Hispanic culture: Fuentes understands Hispanic history not as "history" exclusively but as language, identity, and culture.

Fuentes had read Hegel, as Kadir has pointed out, and thus was aware of Hegel's new kind of history, the philosophy of history.[47] For Hegel, the new history was not merely to be ascertained as so much fact but to be understood by apprehending the reasons for things happening as they did. Collingwood points to four distinctive features of Hegel's view of history.[48] First, Hegel refused to approach history by way of nature, insisting that nature and history were entirely different. Second, all history was the history of thought, according to Hegel. Third, the force that is the mainspring of the historical process is reason. Finally, since all history of thought exhibits the self-development of reason, the historical process is a logical process. Kadir argues convincingly that Fuentes' project in *Terra Nostra* is like Hegel's, but his view of history is different.[49] Kadir characterizes *Terra Nostra* as an "ambivalent and equivocal dialogue with the Hegelian project."[50]

The concept of history that Fuentes writes against in *Terra Nostra* has its roots in nineteenth-century ideas of history that were still predominant ideological constructs in Mexico and much of Latin America in the twentieth century. The Romantic conception of history as progress, promoted by numerous Mexican institutions, including the PRI, and which Fuentes critiqued initially in *Where the*

Air Is Clear and *The Death of Artemio Cruz,* is subverted in *Terra Nostra* by the novel's structure. Kant, who had inherited from the Enlightenment the belief in a wholly irrational past and a wholly rational future, saw man as a rational being and history as a progressive advance toward rationality. In *Terra Nostra* (and essays written in the 1970s), Fuentes reverses the tradition of the Enlightenment and Kant: he fictionalizes a more rational medieval past than orthodox Christianity and an irrational future represented by a boiling Seine River, multiple births on the streets of Paris, and other equally irrational events that occur in a future beyond the year 1975, when *Terra Nostra* was published.

Kant had outlined a program for a universal history, one that emphasized the self-development of the spirit of man. Fuentes' mentor Alfonso Reyes firmly believed in this individual self-development, as did many Latin American and Spanish intellectuals of his generation. Fuentes, too, in line with his mentors Reyes and Pedroso, believes in the positive qualities of universals, at least much more than Foucault and many European post-structuralist theorists. The reading of Collingwood, who also affirmed the concept of universal history, further contributed to Fuentes' understanding of universals. Collingwood concluded his study of *The Idea of History* as follows: "Let us put together all the facts that are known to historians, look for patterns in them, and then extrapolate these patterns into a theory of universal history." Nevertheless, in *Terra Nostra,* Fuentes depicts multiple and fragmented individuals who, suffering under repressive Spanish regimes, negate the concept of the self-development of a spirit of man.

The history of *Terra Nostra* also reveals traces of a pre-Hispanic understanding of history and time. Western history, as written since the Bible, has traditionally been linear; pre-Hispanic history of indigenous cultures, as symbolized by the Aztec Sun Dial, is cyclical.[51] The ancient ritual calendar in Mesoamerica, or *tonalphohualli,* was the basis for all other calendar computations.[52] For the Maya, Aztec, and other indigenous civilizations, history was expected to repeat itself—in the case of the Maya, in cycles of 260 years. The reader's experience of history and time in *Terra Nostra* is comparable to one scholar's description of the Mayan concept of history:

The idea that given the same influences, history would repeat itself had
two interesting consequences: it tended to confound the future with
the past, and it introduced a conception of cycles of time which
partly conflicted with the imagery of time as an unending march by
its bearers into the future.[53]

One of Fuentes' predominant and most consistent ideas of history in *Terra Nostra* is history as mirror. Throughout the novel, historical characters and events resemble or are identical to other characters and events. Moreover, the history that precedes the twentieth
century mirrors that of previous centuries; the history of the New
World mirrors that of the Old World. The mirror effect begins at the
end of the novel's first narrative segment with the words of Celestina:
"Yrots ym si siht" (*TN,* 31). This phrase communicates a sense that
the entire story is, enigmatically, a mirror of another story. As Julián
explains to the Cronista in Part III, "True history is circular and eternal" (*TN,* 652).

In Part II of the novel, an explanation of the enigmatic mir-
rored story is offered. Here events and characters in the New World
of Part II frequently reflect scenes of the Escorial and the Europe of
Part I. It is suggested, for example, that the New World is a mirror
of El Palacio when the New World is described as an exact replica of
the world of El Escorial: "Endless exchanges of looks, objects, exis-
tences, memories, with the proposition of placating a predicted fury"
(*TN,* 396).

In Part III, both the old Spain of El Escorial and history appear
as mirror: Spanish society of the sixteenth century repeats Aztec society in the Americas; sixteenth-century Spanish cultural, political,
and religious history appears as a mirror of earlier periods of European history, beginning with the Romans. In Part III, for example,
the narrator states: "He asked Felipe to return to the origins of all
things, two brothers, Abel and Cain, Osiris and Set, Plumed Ser-
pent and Smoking Mirror, rival brothers" (*TN,* 594). In a manuscript written by a Stoic, read by El Señor, the Stoic states: "Rome
is the world," thus paraphrasing Philip II's belief that Spain was the
world and that, following that logic, so too was El Escorial. Similarly, toward the end of the novel, Felipe looks in a mirror near the

end of the novel and sees "the mirror of the world" (*TN*, 755). Continuing with imagery established as far back as *The Death of Artemio Cruz*, *Terra Nostra* uses the mirror as a metaphor of deceit and fragmentation.[54]

Fuentes, like Paz, has been engaged in comparisons between European and pre-Hispanic ideas of history and time since the 1950s. In *The Death of Artemio Cruz*, a considerable tension was created by the rivalry between linear and cyclical concepts of time, a conflict that essentially conveys the clash between European and pre-Hispanic notions of time.[55] In his earlier works, agreeing with Paz, Fuentes fictionalized Mexican history as it can be understood between Cortés and Doña Marina, or La Malinche. This vision of history was evident in *The Death of Artemio Cruz*.[56] In *Terra Nostra*, however, history is far more complex, with competing views of European history present and the historical roots of Latin American culture and identity predating the Spanish conquest of Mexico explored. In Paz, as in some of the earlier writing of Fuentes, humans were not makers of history but were *in history*.[57] Sommers has pointed out that in *The Death of Artemio Cruz* "history is not just a tapestry against which personal drama is enacted, it also is the field of force, restricting individual movement and freedom of choice."[58] In *Terra Nostra*, some human agents are not the makers of history, yet others are. History restricts individuals, but it also offers an ample field of choice. In this sense, in *Terra Nostra* Fuentes goes beyond Paz, thus making González Echevarría's reading of Fuentes' treatment of history in *Terra Nostra* limited and reductive.

The only hope for renovation in the work of Fuentes, according to Raymond D. Souza, lies in the future, when the weight of history has been alleviated. For this critic, "*La muerte de Artemio Cruz* es una notable expresión del ansia de libertad del pasado."[59] This desire for freedom from the past is a constant expressed in Fuentes' early fiction; it is also a desire that accompanies competing and conflictive ideas of history in *Terra Nostra*. Consequently, the ultimate place of history in *Terra Nostra* is the future: Paris in 1999. The future is implicit, however, at all historical moments in the novel, for acts in Rome, in the Middle Ages, and in the sixteenth century frequently have a future referent. Thus the Polo Febo of the late twen-

tieth century is associated with the Agrippa of Roman times, just as
Agrippa is logically associated with Febo at both the beginning and
the end of the novel.

Fuentes' history emphasizes transformation rather than the potentially static nature of things. In *Terra Nostra,* change and modernity operate in opposition to the static Palacio. The very concepts of
history, time, and space suffer constant transformation in *Terra Nostra,* in contrast to the rigidity of El Señor and the permanence of his
edifice.

The competing notions of linear versus cyclical history and
change versus permanence do find a single solution in *Terra Nostra.*
Characters can await those rare instants that stop time momentarily.
In *Terra Nostra,* these special moments are associated with love and
knowledge.[60] The Señora (mother) expresses such an idea: "Do you
know that there are moments that cannot be measured? Moments
when everything becomes one: the satisfaction of a fulfilled desire
along with its remorse, the simultaneous desire and fear of what was,
and the simultaneous terror and longing for what will be" (*TN,* 70).
Celestina lives similar moments. This special moment in time for
Fuentes has been associated with Paz.[61] In reality, however, Fuentes
and Paz express apparently similar ideas from opposite poles: Fuentes' special moment is a conjunction of all time (more similar to Borges); Paz's special moment in "Piedra de sol" is a "tiempo total donde
no pasa nada" (a total time in which nothing happens). Fuentes' own
explanation of time in *Terra Nostra,* articulated after the publication
of the novel, explains his sense of this special time:

In the end, there is a confluence of myths of the Eastern world, the Mediterranean world, the world of the Americas, that create a configuration, a time that is none of these times, that is neither the original
time, nor circular time, nor spiral time, and much less linear time,
but which constitutes a kind of Mandala that contains all these
possibilities and all the possible directions of space.[62]

A complex and significant issue in *Terra Nostra,* history surpasses the admittedly provocative interpretation of Paz concerning
the history of Mexico since the Conquest, as well as many of his
own ideas about history as formulated in *Where the Air Is Clear, The*

Death of Artemio Cruz, and *Aura*. Despite the numerous enigmas of *Terra Nostra*, it does indeed convey meaning: *Terra Nostra* suggests that history is mirror, that the future represents a liberation, and that Indo-Afro-Ibero-American history is the key to understanding, confronting, and living its culture and identity. Fuentes uses both traditional European linear ideas of time and history and cyclical concepts of time from the Mesoamerican indigenous cultures, from the Greeks, from Vico, and from Nietzsche.

History and culture undergird the concept of identity in *Terra Nostra*. The project of cultural definition, as Carlos Alonso has eloquently argued, has a lengthy history in Latin American cultural discourse, which "can be accurately depicted as a succession of statements of cultural crisis."[63] In his study of autochthonous cultural expression in Latin America, Alonso argues that "the essence of Latin American cultural production is the ever-renewed affirmation of having lost or abandoned such an essence."[64] In addition, the perennial sense of cultural crisis is characterized by "an inability to experience historical flux except in a mode of crisis."[65]

Fuentes has been well aware, of course, of the cultural discourse involved in the search for identity; it is a discourse well developed in Mexico by Samuel Ramos, Reyes, Paz, and a host of others. In his essay *La nueva novela hispanoamericana*, Fuentes was sharply critical of the *criollista* project of defining an autochthonous cultural expression in the 1920s.[66] In *Terra Nostra*, Fuentes surpasses the standard statements about Latin America's having lost or abandoned its cultural essence. Fuentes also escapes the "perennial sense of cultural crisis" fomented by his predecessors, including Paz, for *Terra Nostra* is a foundational text that turns not to any present crisis but rather to a broad historical understanding of Latin American cultural identity. Latin American cultural discourse has argued that (a) autochthonous cultural expression is to be found in the Latin American indigenous past, (b) a repressive Spanish culture dominated and destroyed much of this culture, and (c) the essence of Latin American cultural identity today stems from *mestizaje*, or the mixture of Old World and New Cultures.[67] Fuentes goes far beyond these simplistic schemes, which date from the 1920s but were still in vogue decades later, by evoking the multicultural and medieval and Renaissance cultures that he sees as the foundations of Indo-Afro-Ibero-American culture and by tracing connections between the ancient cultures of Rome and the Aztecs and contemporary Hispanic cultures too.

Fuentes subverts the very idea of cultural "essence" in *Terra Nostra*. In their search for cultural essence, literary nationalists tended to ignore or reject European literature in favor of more autochthonous forms of expression, which they considered the "essence" of their culture. With the advent of Borges and the modern Latin American novel of the 1940s, the cosmopolitan European and North American forms seemed to predominate, especially for the intellectuals of Fuentes' generation and those younger than he. In *Terra Nostra,* however, an attempt to formulate any concept of cultural essence is useless: the constant transformations of characters (from one culture to another) as well as the displacements in time and space undermine any sense of essence.

Fuentes also differs from the Latin American cultural discourse that has tended to experience cultural flux in a mode of crisis. In *Terra Nostra,* history is indeed in the same kind of flux that has characterized the empirical history of Latin America. History is not experienced, however, as being in a mode of crisis. As a series of repetitions, history in *Terra Nostra* is part of a cyclical and dialectical movement producing ever more diverse syntheses. Seen in this way, Latin American cultural identity does not suffer constant crisis but grows in a cyclical mode.

Alonso has pointed out that the problem of establishing cultural identity in Latin America has been a problem of rhetoric.[68] He suggests that the crisis in Latin American thought over the past century originated in the impossibility of reconciling the rhetoric that gave legitimacy to the emancipation movement with the historical development that ensued from that movement. Acutely aware of this gap between rhetoric and social reality, Fuentes has been a critic of political language and the attempts of authoritarian governments, such as that of Mexico, to establish monologic, dominant political discourses. *Terra Nostra* is his text of heteroglossia, of the multiple languages that challenge the static Spanish of sixteenth-century Spain as well as that of twentieth-century Mexico. Liberty in *Terra Nostra* comes not from the rhetoric of emancipation but from a consciousness of this rhetorical tradition, an awareness of its historical roots, and an understanding of its place in history. Fuentes questions cultural identity based on the specificity and singularity of autochthonous cultural characteristics and values.

History, culture, and identity are closely related concepts in *Terra Nostra*. Both traditional linear (biblical) history and cyclical (Greek, Aztec, Nietzchean) concepts of history are explored and, ultimately, negated in *Terra Nostra*. With the critique and subversion of the well-known concepts of historiography, Fuentes questions both traditional Latin American ideas about cultural essence and any possibility of history as truth.[69] By returning to El Escorial as source and foundation, he uses a historical monument that also has existed for five centuries of Western history. He employs the strategies of imitation, repetition, and duplication that characterize the architecture of El Escorial to subvert these classic rhetorical strategies of representation.

Narrating and Seeing in *Terra Nostra*

In 1916, Ortega y Gasset sat in El Escorial and wrote several volumes of essays under the title *El espectador*. In the preface to the book, he located himself in this "rigorous empire of stone and geometry": "Desde El Escorial, rigoroso imperio de la piedra y la geometría, donde he sentado mi alma, veo en primer término el curvo brazo ciclópeo que extiende hacia Madrid la sierra del Guadarrama."[70] In making this statement from El Escorial, Ortega y Gasset evokes some of the central questions of narrating and seeing that Fuentes brought to bear six decades later in *Terra Nostra*. Ortega y Gasset makes a specific point of his exact location, his act of narrating, and his act of seeing. For Fuentes, the identity and position of the narrator and the location of this narrator in time and space have always been self-consciously fundamental issues. Indeed, his allegiance to Cervantes is based on the fact that the author of *Don Quixote* "essentially imagined the world of multiple points of view."[71]

In *Terra Nostra*, who narrates and who sees and the location of these narrators and seers are all essential to the reader's experience of the novel. The narrative situation is complex and ambiguous. The work opens with a narrator outside the story, an extradiegetic-heterodiegetic narrator who tells the story of Polo Febo in Paris. At the end of this lengthy section, Celestina seems to take over the narration, making her the intradiegetic-heterodiegetic narrator of the remainder of the novel, narrative segments 2 to 143, until the final narrative segment, 144, which returns to the original situation of Polo Febo in Paris. Juan Goytisolo and other capable readers have assumed that Celestina narrates segments 2 to 143 because the narrator ends the initial narrative segment as follows: "This is my story. I want you to hear my story. Listen. Listen. Netsil. Netsil. Yrots ym raeh ot uoy tnaw I. Yrots ym si siht" (*TN*, 31). (Fuentes had already used the phrase "This is my story" in *Holy Place*.) Later in the novel, however, Fuentes subverts the reader's sense of reading Celestina's narration when it becomes evident that the narrative segments 2 to 136 are narrated by Julián. After the Cronista hears segments 2 to 136 from Julián, this Cronista relates segments 137 to 143: "Founded upon these principles, reader, I wrote both this chronicle faithful to the last years of his reign, and the life of Don Felipe, El Señor. Thus I fulfilled the fearful charge of the one who had until now narrated this story, Brother Julián" (*TN*, 669). Consequently, the Cronista writes narrative segments 2 to 143, of which 2 to 136 are related by Julián.

A series of narrators besides the Cronista intervene briefly in segments 2 to 143.[72] The Señor and Celestina narrate segments 12 to 33 together; the Señor has Guzmán write the story while, at the same time but in a different place, Celestina tells the same story to the pilgrim. Segments 84 to 126 are related alternatively by Ludovico and Celestina.[73] In the segment titled "The Duel" (*TN*, 526–528), the *monja* narrates to Celestina, Celestina narrates it to El Señor and Julián, who, in turn, tells it to the Cronista, the Cervantes figure. Similarly, the "Manuscript of a Stoic" (*TN*, 676–700) is narrated by Teodoro and written by the Cronista. Teodoro's narration alternates between first person (intradiegetic-homodiegetic) and third person (extradiegetic-heterodiegetic):

I, Theodorus, the narrator of these events, have spent the night reflecting
    upon them, setting them down upon the papers you hold, or some-
    day will hold, in your hands, reader, and in considering myself as

I would consider another person: the third person of objective narration; the second person of subjective narration; yes, Tiberius's
second person, his in the solitude that is my spare autonomy, first
person: I the narrator. (*TN*, 687)

The last narrative segment of the novel, "The Last City" (*TN*,
760–778), is related by a first-person (intradiegetic-homodiegetic)
narrator who narrates using a "you" (*tú* in Spanish) that was not
present in the opening narrative fragment of the novel. Here, Polo
Febo narrates and seemingly addresses himself in the form of *tú*.[74]

These varying points of view achieve multiple effects. Above
all, the reader is invited to conclude, as Kerr does, that all reality is
simply enigmatic. The narrative situation encourages such relativism
because it is not possible to attain definitive answers about who narrates. On the other hand, issues of history, culture, and identity, as
they have been discussed, can be clarified.

Exactly who narrates and from where is an enigmatic question
in many passages of *Terra Nostra*.[75] Equally important is the question
of who sees, for *Terra Nostra* is, to a considerable extent, a novel in
which the act of seeing is significant. As Levine has indicated, the
concept of the *mirada* has close philosophical ties to Paz, who uses
mirada imagery in his poetry to suggest a special union between male
and female in some cases and, in other situations, a union between
generic man and the universe.[76] Levine notes: "In the writings of
both authors [Paz and Fuentes] this imagery involves the physical act
of looking, meeting the eyes of another human being, seeing self as
the other, and finally feeling that self is the same as the other while
still retaining its own essence."[77] In *Terra Nostra*, looking outward
opens new possibilities for some characters. Not only is the act of
seeing important in this novel but the narrator's words often evoke
what the characters and the reader see simultaneously. The reader,
looking through the eyes of the characters, is sometimes an accom-
plice in the characters' voyeurism. At other moments in the novel, as
in Paz, the *mirada* functions as an act of unity. Similarly, the *mirada*
can signal a character seeing himself as "other" in a transformational
process.[78] An indication of the importance of the act of seeing
in *Terra Nostra* is suggested in the novel's opening scene, with the

bulging eyes of Notre Dame gargoyles peering out on the scene. Throughout this first narrative segment of the novel, the reader's framework is visual, following what Polo Febo sees.

The *mirada,* significantly enough, serves an important function at the end of each of the three sections of *Terra Nostra.* Part I ends with the narrative segment titled "Gazes" (*TN,* 340–354), in which several characters are gathered in the chapel with Felipe, awaiting the arrival of Celestina and Polo. The narrator transcribes much of what the characters observe during this scene, above all, Orvieto's painting. Much of this segment consists of the thoughts of the painter Julián as he observes the painting. He questions, for example, why the other observers do not see the "new space" he has made in the painting, "no longer the space of oneness, the invisible and invariable space of the revelation, but the many and different places of a constantly maintained and renewed creation" (*TN,* 335). It is by means of the gaze, then, that one of the novel's most consistent themes of multiplicity is communicated. Painting functions as a type of mirror that reflects back what the observer sees in the gaze: "I paint so that I may see, I see so that I may paint, I gaze at what I paint and what I paint, when painted, gazes at me and finally gazes at you who gaze at me when you gaze upon my paintings" (*TN,* 335). Throughout this lengthy series of gazes, Madre Milagros, Don Juan, El Comendador, the Dama Loca, and Felipe take turns at being the focalizer engaged in the gaze (*mirada*). Finally, at the end of Part II, the reader becomes the spectator of all these characters, and the scene ends with the reader as observer/voyeur.

In the final narrative segment in Part II, "Night of the Return" (*TN,* 478–485), the *mirada* is prominent from the beginning, when the Peregrino sees the star Venus through the clouds: "I saw shining, reborn, distant, but at the level of my gaze" (*TN,* 478). He meets young people, and their respective *miradas* signify a type of communion: "new glances for the first time new, theirs and mine" (*TN,* 479). A change in human nature is evident in the young people's new way of looking.[79] When the Peregrino embarks on his return to Spain, his boat enters a vortex, he sees Venus once again, and he falls into a chaos, losing sense of time and place. He looks into a hand mirror and sees "Venus, Hesperia, Spain, identical stars, dawn and dusk, mysterious" (*TN,* 494). With this observation, the

Peregrino sets forth, by means of the *mirada,* one of the fundamental theses of the novel: Spain is a mirror of the New World, and the New World is a mirror of Spain.

In the last narrative segment of Part III, "The Last City" (*TN,* 704–778), the *mirada* is extremely important once again. In this segment, Polo and Celestina are united by the mutual *mirada,* as well as physically. Polo becomes one with Celestina and states: "You speak, I love you, I love myself, your voice and the girl's speak at the same time, they are a single voice" (*TN,* 778).

In *Terra Nostra,* as in El Escorial, the act of seeing is fundamental. Surrounded by a visual world of architecture and painting, the characters in *Terra Nostra* are constantly reaching their understanding of the words by means of what they see. More important, these characters function as focalizers so that the reader's experience of the fictional world is predominantly that of seeing. Consequently, architecture and painting are more than just a backdrop in the setting of *Terra Nostra;* they are an integral part of the novel's texture, experience, and themes.

"L'histoire est un discours á la troisiíme personne," De Certeau has pointed out.[80] Little of *Terra Nostra* is written in the historian's third person, thus distinguishing this novel, once again, from any pretense of making historical discourse. In fact, the identity of exactly who is narrating is so problematic that the important issue is not the identity of the multiple speakers in the text but rather the place from which *Terra Nostra* is narrated: El Escorial.

Modern and Postmodern *Terra Nostra*

Fuentes has always been involved in modernizing Mexican culture and the cultures of Indo-Afro-Ibero-America; he has been closely allied with the modern and the modern novel since the beginnings of his literary career. His primary interests have always been that great object of desire for the modern writer—the grand narrative. In the 1970s and 1980s, however, he was also smitten by the bug of the postmodern. In the twelfth century, a writer named Isan i-Sabbah supposedly set forth a virtual manifesto for the postmodern, a statement oft cited by William Burroughs and the Beat Generation (the first generation of postmoderns): "Nothing is true, everything is permitted." This statement might also be seen as a manifesto for *Terra Nostra,* a modern novel considerably affected by postmodern culture.

Fuentes' search for the modern has involved both his training in the historical roots of the modern in the West and his own fictional contributions to the modern culture of the Americas. His mentors defined their idea of modernity and encouraged Fuentes and his generation of *Medio Siglo* to modernize Mexico in every possible way. For Ortega y Gasset, always influential for Fuentes, the Modern Age began with Descartes.[81] This affirmation was important for Fuentes in several ways. Fuentes had referred to Descartes throughout his career, before *Terra Nostra.* Following Ortega y Gasset's model, Fuentes has defined the pioneer modern minds in a wide range of intellectual and artistic endeavors. These early moderns, for Fuentes, were such figures as Cervantes, Fernando de Rojas, and Petrarch for literature, and Diego Velázquez and Luca Signorelli in art. Their names appear frequently in Fuentes' writings, often in reference to their respective roles, according to Fuentes, as the pioneer moderns.[82]

Fuentes was formed intellectually in the context of the modern and of being modern: the generation of intellectuals associated with the *Revista Mexicana de Literatura* desired, above all, to be the modern writers of Mexico. As a writer who grew intellectually out of a context of the modern and who held as one of his original goals as a writer to bring the modern novel to Mexico, Fuentes demonstrates many of his still fundamentally modern impulses in *Terra Nostra.* Above all, it is an ambitious grand narrative, a totalizing and utopian project that aligns itself with the modernity of *Where the Air Is Clear, The Death of Artemio Cruz,* and *A Change of Skin.* In addition, Fuentes inherited from the modernists—Joyce, Dos Passos, Faulkner, others—many of the technical devices he employed for his own modern project. In *Where the Air Is Clear,* Fuentes uses the multiple points of view and collage of *Manhattan Transfer.* And in *The Death of Artemio Cruz,* he employs the structure and narrators of Faulkner and Michel Butor. Fuentes' other debts to the European and North American modernist writers are numerous; one cannot dispute his place as one of the major contributors to the modern novel in Indo-Afro-Ibero-America, beginning with *Where the Air Is Clear* and culminating in *Terra Nostra.*

Literary modernity has its historical origins, for Fuentes, in Cervantes, Fernando de Rojas, Velázquez, Signorelli, Petrarch, and Erasmus, who represent a variety of different modern interests. Fuentes points out, as has been noted, that Cervantes "essentially imagined the world of multiple points of view" (*BM,* 177). In his essay on Cervantes, Fuentes identifies *Don Quixote* as the first modern novel. Foucault had already spoken of the modernity of *Don Quixote:*

> *Don Quixote* is the first modern work of literature, because in it we see the cruel reason of identities and differences make endless sport of signs and similitudes; because in it language breaks off its old kinship with things and enters into that lonely sovereignty from which it will reappear, in its separate state, only as literature; because it masks the point where resemblance enters an age which is, from the point of view of resemblance, one of madness and imagination.[83]

Fuentes' reading of Cervantes' modernity differs fundamentally from Foucault's: for Fuentes, the modernity of *Don Quixote* is found in its ambiguity and, above all, its self-conscious reading of itself. Fuentes' idea of self-conscious reading does find its roots in Foucault's observation about language breaking off its prior kinship with things and entering into a separate state as only literature. Nevertheless, Fuentes also speaks of the modernity in Cervantes' rupture with the medieval epic and his negation of previous forms that required order and normativity.

In reading *La Celestina,* by Fernando de Rojas, Fuentes finds another angle on modernity. This book embodies the modern, according to Fuentes, because it was the first work to offer a reflection on the interior, psychological motives behind human actions. Such ideas appear later, in different forms, in Cervantes and Shakespeare. Everything and everyone, in Fuentes' view, moves in the modern city imagined by Fernando de Rojas.

Velázquez and Erasmus are moderns because of their multiple points of view and ambiguity. With regard to Velázquez's *Las Meninas,* Fuentes points out that "we are free to see the painting . . . in multiple ways" (*BM,* 181). Speaking of Cervantes and Velázquez, Fuentes asserts: "But these two, working from within a closed society, were able to redefine reality in terms of the imagination. What we imagine is both possible and real" (*BM*, 182). For Fuentes, *In Praise of Folly* was an important forerunner to *Don Quixote*, arguing that both faith and reason had to become relative, not absolute, terms. Erasmus pleaded for the new culture of humanism that Cervantes novelizes.

Fuentes' identification of other artists as modern is also revealing. Signorelli's modernity is to be found in his rupture with the medieval order. His novelty was his negation of the need for order and normativity. For Fuentes, Petrarch was the first modern poet because what he wrote does not communicate great truths of previous ages. Rather than explaining these truths through illustration, allegory, or moralization, Petrarch returns over and over again to his own personal experience. Fuentes appreciates how this modern Italian mind resisted the temptation to be strictly abstract.

The rise of the modern novel in the late nineteenth and early twentieth centuries, with the modernists Proust, Joyce, Dos Passos, Virginia Woolf, Faulkner, and others, was a phenomenon that had considerable impact on Fuentes. Narrative strategies using fragmented structures, multiple points of view, effects of simultaneity, neologisms, and other techniques, all became part of the common literary tools of Fuentes' generation in Latin America. These European and North American modernists, as well as many of their counterparts in Latin America, tended to believe in seeking truths and rewriting history. The totalizing impulses and grand narratives of the modernists sometimes resulted in what Latin American writers and critics called the "total novel": Joyce's *Ulysses*, García Márquez's *One Hundred Years of Solitude*, Mario Vargas Llosa's *Conversation in the Cathedral*, and Cortázar's *Hopscotch*.

Terra Nostra appears to be that totalizing grand narrative, comparable in many ways to historical projects such as *One Hundred Years of Solitude* and *Conversation in the Cathedral*. Indeed, Fuentes' lengthy meditation on history, his use of multiple points of view, and an apparently fragmented structure all give *Terra Nostra* the appearance, on a first reading, of an ambitious and totalizing modernist project. Consequently, it is understandable that González Echevarría reads *Terra Nostra*, implicitly, as a modern text; this critic makes references to the novel's fragmentation and sees *Terra Nostra* as a source of "truth."[84]

Although *Terra Nostra* has some modernist, totalizing impulses, it is closer to that recent variant of modernist fiction identified by some critics as the postmodern. As a postmodern text, *Terra Nostra* articulates the twelfth-century proclamation "Nothing is true, everything is permitted." Attributed to Isan i-Sabbah in the year 1164, this quotation is particularly appropriate because Fuentes, too, frequently returns to the Middle Ages in his act of recovering history and knowledge. A polemical term and concept, postmodernism became popularized in the United States in the 1960s. Seminal articles by Leslie Fiedler, John Barth, and others laid the groundwork for future discussions by such scholars as Ihab Hassan, Brian McHale, Fredric Jameson, and Linda Hutcheon on the postmodern novel. In the 1980s, issues related to postmodernism entered prominently into the critical discourse of Latin American literature.[85]

Concepts commonly used in the context of First World postmodernism have been discontinuity, disruption, dislocation, decentering, indeterminacy, and antitotalization.[86] As Hutcheon points out, the cultural phenomenon of postmodernism is contradictory, for it installs and then subverts the very concepts it challenges. Postmodernism works to subvert dominant discourses. Hassan was instrumental in developing a critical language and concepts for postmodernism, creating parallel columns that place characteristics of modernism and postmodernism side by side.[87] As Hutcheon points out, however, such "either/or" thinking suggests a resolution of what should be seen as unresolved contradictions within postmodernism.[88]

Hutcheon has demonstrated that postmodern fiction should not be reduced to ahistorical and self-indulgent metafiction.[89] On the contrary, much postmodern fiction, such as *Terra Nostra,* can be strongly historical and political. Fuentes' awareness of historical discourse and, above all, his questioning of the very assumptions of Western historiography align *Terra Nostra* with the postmodern as described by Hutcheon. In this sense, *Terra Nostra* is more deeply historical and political than many modernist novels, including such overtly historical and political Latin American novels as *One Hundred Years of Solitude* and *Conversation in the Cathedral.*

As a postmodern text, *Terra Nostra* is Fuentes' rewriting of the medieval, Renaissance, and neoclassical architecture of El Escorial. Hutcheon, in her analysis of the postmodern, places emphasis on the unresolved contradictions of postmodern culture, a concept that Jencks also elaborates in his discussion of postmodern architecture.[90] For Jencks, one common postmodern architectural design is the skyscraper of perfectly modern lines, but with classical Greek columns in open opposition to the modern design. In this postmodern construct, no harmonic resolution of these blatantly contradictory lines is designed or desired. They remain in unresolved (postmodern) contradiction. El Palacio in *Terra Nostra* and other aspects of *Terra Nostra* function in this fashion. In his use of the *cuadro de Orvieto* (a mural by Signorelli actually located in Orvieto, Italy), Fuentes appropriates this erotic mural from Orvieto and puts it into El Señor's severe and austere Palacio. Just as the postmodern architect leaves the Greek columns on the modern building with no resolution, Fuentes leaves the Signorelli mural in the Palacio in open contradiction— with no visible resolution.[91]

In similar fashion, Fuentes appropriates the well-known novelistic ruse of the manuscript in the lost bottle and uses it anachronistically for a novel published in 1975. In the process, he juxtaposes his typically modern novelistic strategies with the anachronistically traditional. The result is comparable to the postmodern architectural image of the modern skyscraper with its Greek columns. The manuscript in the bottle is also an example of the typically postmodern procedure, according to Jameson, of pastiche rather than parody. This pastiche is repetition without the humor of parody or, as Jameson calls it, parody in blank.[92]

The double coding of the postmodern, as described by McHale, is also an important function in *Terra Nostra*. The music of "The Commitments," an imitation of Wilson Picket and Detroit soul music sung by whites in Ireland, as well as the *rancheras* of Peruvian Tania Libertad, who imitates the *rancheras* of Mexican José Alfredo Jiménez, are examples of the postmodern phenomenon of double voice. When the Commitments and Tania Libertad sing, we hear their voices at the same time that we are hearing the voices of Picket and Jiménez. Unlike parody, however, the Commitments and Tania Libertad are not by any means humorous. This double coding is parody in blank, or pastiche. The double coding in *Terra Nostra* is present in some overt cases, such as in *La Celestina* and *El burlador de Sevilla,* works with characters who are also characters in *Terra Nostra.* The double voice of Fuentes' pastiche is more subtle when the narrator intercalates the phrase *polvo enamorado* in the novel, thus evoking the simultaneous double voice of Fuentes, author of the novel we are reading, and Quevedo, author of the sonnet that ends with the words *polvo enamorado.* Similarly, the reader of *Terra Nostra* hears the double voice of Fuentes and García Márquez when the extradiegetic-heterodiegetic narrator uses the phrase "many years later" twice (near the middle and near the end of the novel). This phrase is followed by a clause in the conditional, exactly as any reader of *One Hundred Years of Solitude* immediately recognizes. González Echevarría also points out the traces of Góngora's *Soledades.*[93]

Fuentes' tendency toward double coding is evident in his characters as well. Many of them are specific historical figures while they also are not these historical figures. In most cases, such as those of the authority figures, they are and are not several historical Spanish kings and queens. Most of the novel's major figures, in addition, have double-coded identities rather than any fixed, singular identity. These multiple identities in constant transformation, which question the very concept of psychic unity and the individual subject, align *Terra Nostra* with the postmodern.

Fuentes' postmodern *Terra Nostra* follows the model of what he mentions in *Terra Nostra* as the "Arabic novel" or "Hadith-novella" (*TN,* 658). Later, a narrator who describes himself as the Chronicler mentions being in the final part of "this Hadith" precisely when the reader is in the final part of *Terra Nostra.* The hero of this Arabic novel, according to the narrator, would be the first novelistic hero to know he was being read: "This hero of mockery and hoax, born of reading, would be the first hero, furthermore, to know he was read" (*TN,* 669). This Arabic genre implies a liberated and transgressively erotic novel, too, for the Arabic is associated with liberation and the erotic. Just as *Terra Nostra* is associated with the Arabic novel, associations are also made between El Escorial and La Alhambra. This new form represents an innovative postmodern fiction in which the protagonist is aware of his status as a character being read, and it is a work of liberation and eroticism. It is also a work that has as intertexts the Arabic works *A Thousand and One Nights* and *El collar de la paloma*.

The postmodernism of *Terra Nostra* is also evidenced in the operation of what could be called the Velazquian Principle, a principle functioning in the painting *Las Meninas*. As Foucault has noted in his analysis of *Las Meninas,* a condition of pure reciprocity is manifested by the observing and the observed, with the presence of the mirror. This condition of pure reciprocity is an important characteristic of *Terra Nostra,* where mirrors observe and are observed, as in *Las Meninas.* An important corollary to this condition of pure reciprocity in *Terra Nostra* is the use of mirrors and doubles to question representation. *Terra Nostra* is laden with mirrors, doubles, and images of each. This questioning of representation, in turn, is one of the postmodern aspects of the novel. A second corollary of the Velazquian Principle, or the condition of pure reciprocity, is the presence of the gaze as a foundation, a fundamental act in a world of mirrors, as has been mentioned in the earlier discussion of *la mirada.*

A third corollary is another concept proposed by Foucault that carries the condition of reciprocity to yet another level. Foucault states that in the beginning of the nineteenth century, the laws of discourse having been detached from representation, the being of language itself became, as it were, fragmented; but these laws became inevitable when, with Nietzsche and Stéphane Mallarmé, "thought was brought back, and violently so, towards language itself, towards its unique and difficult being."[94] Foucault has noted that since Mallarmé, literature has become progressively more differentiated from the discourse of ideas. During this same period, it could be argued, literature has become progressively more postmodern, until it has nothing to do but curve back in a perpetual return upon itself. When fiction becomes markedly postmodern, as is the work of Severo Sarduy, Guillermo Cabrera Infante, and the later work of Fuentes, including *Terra Nostra,* it has nothing to do but shine in the brightness of its being, to paraphrase Foucault.[95] A key to the Velazquian Principle in *Terra Nostra* is thought brought back to language.

The fourth corollary to the Velazquian Principle concerns the reciprocity involved in critical *seeing,* a parallel to the critical writing and critical *seeing,* and a parallel to the critical writing and critical reading proposed by Fuentes himself in *Cervantes or the Critique of Reading*. Foucault states:

the previously existing law of that interplay in the painting *Las meninas*, in which representation is represented at every point: the painter, the palette, the broad dark surface of the canvas with its back to us, the paintings hanging on the wall, the spectators watching who are framed, in turn, by those who are watching them; and lastly, in the center, in the very heart of representation, nearest to what is essential, the mirror, showing us what is represented, but as a reflection so distant, so deeply buried in an unreal space, so foreign to all the gazes being directed elsewhere, that it is no more than the frailest duplication of representation.[96]

The Velazquian Principle in *Terra Nostra*, a condition of pure reciprocity, is manifested in various ways, ranging from the novel's broadest structures and issues to its imagery and minute details. The ideology of this novel should be understood as a manifestation of this condition of reciprocity, for it defines the novel's sense of history.

Terra Nostra is a transitional text that is both modern and postmodern. Just as El Escorial embodies the medieval, the Renaissance, and the neoclassical, with inherent contradictions similar to postmodern unresolved contradictions, *Terra Nostra* embodies the modern and some postmodern unresolved contradictions. In this novel Fuentes appropriates a medieval, Renaissance, and neoclassical architecture and modernizes it via the postmodern. In *Terra Nostra*, postmodern architecture is imposed on a neoclassical model of the empirical world of sixteenth-century Spain. The narrator of "Pierre Ménard, Author of the Quixote" states: "There is no intellectual exercise which is not ultimately useless. A philosophical doctrine is in the beginning a seemingly true description of the universe; as the years pass it becomes a mere chapter—if not a paragraph or noun—in the history of philosophy."[97] Such is the ultimate destiny of the apparent truths of *Terra Nostra*, a fundamentally Borgesian and postmodern text that has Pierre Ménard as a character. *Terra Nostra* is not the ultimate repository of truth that González Echevarría attempts to make it. Rather, it is a Borgesian and postmodern text that questions, undermines, and subverts Western historical truth. The ultimate destiny of *Terra Nostra* is not philosophical or historical truth but an awareness of the paragraphs or nouns that construct social systems and legitimate truths. The narrator in "Pierre Ménard" suggests this postmodern attitude toward truth: "History, *mother* of truth; the idea is astounding. Ménard, a contemporary of William James, does not define history as an investigation of reality, but as its origin. Historical truth, for him, is not what took place; it is what we think took place."[98] In this sense, *Terra Nostra* and postmodern fiction are deeply historical and political—as returns to origins of historical thinking rather than history and truth. Fuentes takes to its ultimate consequences De Certeau's proposition that "*l'écriture de histoire* est l'étude de l'écriture comme practique historique."[99] Borges, De Certeau, and Fuentes share the postmodern assumption that historical discourse is, in the end, another discourse.

Conclusion

The Spain of *Terra Nostra* was the nation that lived what Fuentes calls "the night of El Escorial," and El Escorial was the predominant architectural image of the Spanish Empire and Hispanic culture in the sixteenth century. The military exterior, the confluence of the political, the military and the religious in the interior, and the art painted and placed on the walls of El Escorial all had manifestations in Indo-Afro-Ibero-America. Fuentes uses this edifice not only to critique this imagery but also to explore the origins of Hispanic culture and identity.

With El Escorial as its point of departure, *Terra Nostra* is Fuentes' modern masterpiece and postmodern tour de force on difference and the other. He explores cultural, religious, and political difference, searching for the historical roots of the historical Spanish intolerance of difference, exploring first in sixteenth-century Spain, then in medieval Spain, then in the cultural roots of Spain and, finally, in a prediscursive logos.[100] For Fuentes, the multiple images of El Escorial are also the images of the Colonial foundations of Latin American culture. They are the images of cultural, religious, and political exclusion, and of eliminating difference.

Fuentes' understanding of culture clearly has its roots in the writings of Américo Castro, José Ortega y Gasset, and Octavio Paz. From Castro, Fuentes appropriated and reworked the idea of a potentially multicultural Spain that was suppressed by the Catholic monarchs. Ortega y Gasset's concepts of the individual, the individual in the flow of history, and the role of culture all affected Fuentes, and the Mexican writer synthesized these ideas in the simultaneous double project of *Terra Nostra* and *Cervantes or the Critique of Reading*. In *The Labyrinth of Solitude,* Paz had brought to the forefront Mexico's historically ambiguous relationship with Spain, which Fuentes dealt with first in his early works and then more elaborately in *Terra Nostra.*

One fundamental tension in both El Escorial and *Terra Nostra* is found in the issues of exclusion and inclusion. El Escorial stands with the desire to exclude and be its own hermetically autonomous world, but finds itself in a multicultural existence, thus pointing outward to the world from which it was constructed. Spain lived this contradictory existence and reproduced colonies in the Americas with identically exclusionary societies. *Terra Nostra* exploits these tensions but, above all, it exploits the opposite pole of El Escorial's exclusion—by emphasizing inclusion.

As a modern masterpiece, *Terra Nostra* is Fuentes' most lengthy expression of the grand narrative, his discourse from his days of adolescence in Chile when he and Roberto Torretti conceived of the grand narrative for a novel and the grand narrative for the international political scenario. Since then, Fuentes has clearly been concerned with the big scheme rather than with exclusively local or regional issues—always the grand narrative rather than the small narrative.[101]

Terra Nostra is Fuentes' postmodern architectural construct imposed on a medieval, Renaissance, and neoclassical architectural model. His construct rediscovers the heterogeneity of Latin American culture and the heterogeneity of postmodern culture in the Americas. Fuentes' Palacio is one of unresolved contradictions. Representation in *Terra Nostra* is not just imitation and repetition, as in El Escorial. Rather, representation in *Terra Nostra* takes El Escorial as its point of departure and then exploits the representation of *Don Quixote* and the fiction of Borges. *Terra Nostra* is neither just the modern work positing truth (as suggested by González Echevarría) nor the totally enigmatic and mysterious work with no meaning (as suggested by Kerr).

In accordance with Fuentes' reading of Foucault, and in agreement with González Echevarría's reading of *Terra Nostra,* this massive project is indeed a novel of cultural knowledge. Like the cultural thinkers who were his mentors—Reyes, Paz—Fuentes believes that culture in itself is a value that can improve society.

The problem for Fuentes' generation of Latin American intellectuals consisted not in discovering their modernity but in discovering their tradition, as Fuentes has explained; *Terra Nostra* is an exhaustive search for the origins of that tradition and an inevitable statement about its modernity. Paul De Man identifies modernity as the desire to eradicate the past by affirming the preeminence of the present moment and the desire to participate in it, an impulse evident in the writings of both Paz and Fuentes.[102] According to Paz, Spain had no Enlightenment and no Modern Age, and Latin America's experience of modernity essentially paralleled that of Spain.[103] Alonso tends to see Latin American modernity as rhetorical—an appropriation of modern discourses and gestures.[104] He also argues that Latin American modernity must be understood as a cultural activity possessing meaning unto itself.[105] Fuentes' dual project of *Terra Nostra* and *Cervantes or the Critique of Reading* tacitly agrees with Paz's assertion about Spain's lack of an Enlightenment and modernity. Fuentes, however, recognizes a pre-Enlightenment culture in Spain that offered cultural alternatives as potentially liberating as those of the Enlightenment. In addition, Fuentes self-consciously appropriates discourses of a later modernity, questioning the very Western dichotomy of the modern versus the traditional or the modern versus the Rennaissance.

Fuentes had been concerned about identity since the 1940s, when he and Sergio Pitol sat in the study of their mentor Alfonso Reyes, and when the writings of Paz's predecessor, Samuel Ramos, were in fashion. Then there was the canonical book on Mexican identity—Paz's *Labyrinth of Solitude.* Fuentes' *Where the Air Is Clear* was an initial narrative response to Paz's essay. With his discovery of El Escorial and Foucault in 1967, and with his rereading of Américo Castro and Ortega y Gasset, Fuentes initiated a search for Mexican and Latin American identity, turning directly to the roots of Hispanic culture in medieval and Renaissance Spain. With *Terra Nostra,* Fuentes discovered both his tradition and his identity as a Mexican and as a man of the Americas.

"Faire l'histoire, c'est un practique," De Certeau has asserted.[106] This statement echoes Foucault and synthesizes Fuentes' operations in *Terra Nostra* as he makes history both linear and cyclical. He also makes static history as well as transformative history, and he makes history as a series of mirrors reflecting forward and back in time and space. Fuentes' making of history makes everything from an architectural object to historiography, in the end, the same—discourse. De Certeau also points out that historiography began in the sixteenth century with "l'écriture conquérante": "Aprés un moment de stupeur sur ce seuil marqué d'une colonnade d'arbres, le conquérant va écrire le corps de l'autre et y tracer sa propre *histoire.* Il va en faire le corps historié—le blason—de ses travaux et de ses fantasmes. Ce sera l'Amérique 'latine.' "[107] Four centuries later, *Terra Nostra* is one response—another mirror image—to this sixteenth-century historiography.

El Escorial and *Terra Nostra* function internally on the basis of metonymic associations, while both works function as metaphors for Hispanic culture. El Escorial is a metaphor for Spain as a Colonial power and "a dwelling place for God." *Terra Nostra* is a metaphor for the monumental grand narrative of the Boom—indeed, one of the most lengthy, complex, and elaborate novels ever to be published in Latin America. As such, it is one more text of the curse of heterodoxy, taking its place after the Kaballah, the Zohar, the Sephirot, and the like. Thus, *Terra Nostra* finds its place among the most important Latin American novels—as an Arabic novel.

After the image of El Escorial, the central image of *Terra Nostra* is that of the mirror. The mirror provides much of the unity to this diffuse novel; the mirror ties together one understanding of history (history as mirror), the Velazquian Principle operating in the book, and its postmodern effects. The mirror also highlights the constant examination of the self and the other in Hispanic culture: the Spanish kings versus the other, El Escorial versus the other, the self and the other as reflected in the gaze (*mirada*), language itself and its multiple others throughout the ages.

Rereading Fuentes

Spanish American literature . . . is both a return and a search for tradition. In searching for it, it invents it. But invention and discovery are not terms that best describe its purest creations. A desire for incarnation, a literature of foundations.

— OCTAVIO PAZ

T*erra Nostra* and El Escorial are central to an understanding of Fuentes. Nevertheless, the importance of Fuentes as a major writer of the century rests not in this one work only but in the entirety of his oeuvre. *Terra Nostra* contributes to the significance of his total work, and vice versa. *Terra Nostra* elucidates much of his other fiction, while an awareness of his other works affects the reading of *Terra Nostra*. Fuentes' other fiction and this mutual interaction are the subject of Part III. *Terra Nostra* is a major foundational work in the history of Latin American literature; Fuentes' total work should be seen, to cite Paz, as a "literature of foundations."

In rereading Fuentes in light of El Escorial and *Terra Nostra*, it is evident that many of the concerns, issues, and themes of *Terra Nostra* can be found early in his work. The beginnings of *Terra Nostra* can be located in the story "Tlactocatzine, del Jardín de Flandes" (from *Los días enmascarados*), *Aura*, and *Holy Place*. Works written after *Terra Nostra*, such as *Distant Relations, Christopher Unborn*, and *The Orange Tree*, further elaborate many of the topics of *Terra Nostra*.

"La Edad del Tiempo"

Since the mid-1980s, Fuentes himself has conceptualized his total fiction in fourteen cycles titled "La Edad del Tiempo," which consists of twenty-eight volumes of fiction, eighteen of which he had published by the end of 1993.[1] Few other modern writers have constructed such a broad master scheme of their work, although Jean Paul Sartre, an extremely influential figure for Fuentes' generation of Latin American writers, had conceived *Les chemins de la Liberté,* and Fuentes has mentioned others.[2] "La Edad del Tiempo" has a circular structure, with the foundational text, *Terra Nostra,* near the beginning of the cycle and *The Orange Tree* at the end; this last book in the cycle also probes into the historical origins of Hispanic culture and politics, as does *The Campaign.* Fuentes presents himself as Fuentes-historian, for the fourteen cycles appear, generally speaking, in historical chronological order. (The work also negates history, however, opening and closing with a set of books that seek atemporality in a variety of ways.) This is the history about which one of the sons of Hernán Cortés, Martín, says in *The Orange Tree:* "The true history, not the dusty archives, will tell it all one day. The living history of memory and desire . . . which always takes place right now, not yesterday, not tomorrow" (62). According to Fuentes' own explanation, "La Edad del Tiempo" is a lengthy reflection on time.[3] He views his total work as an ongoing consideration of a series of temporal issues, such as how we situate ourselves in time, why some time seems so short, why some time seems so long, and numerous others matters related to time.[4]

(1) El Mal del Tiempo

The four works that Fuentes has described as "El Mal del Tiempo," which open the cycle, deal with the problem of time itself. They play with the past, the present, and the future in such a way that, in the end, any sense of Western linear time is blurred. In different ways, they undermine and destroy time. According to Fuentes, in El Mal del Tiempo "I want to announce that my concept of time is linear. It is at times circular, at times of eternal returns, at times spirals like those in Joyce."[5] If it were not for the obvious importance of this announcement, this first cycle of four books could have been called "Distant Relations" just as well.

This first cycle precedes and negates Western historiography. The protagonist in *Aura*, Felipe Montero, is a historian who responds to a newspaper advertisement for a young historian to complete the papers of a deceased general. In these four books of fiction—*Aura, Birthday, Distant Relations,* and *Constancia and Other Stories for Virgins*—linear time is negated by patently enigmatic human relations that are privileged over time. They are all books of "distant relations" that blur many of the traditional human relations created by space and time. Consequently, they are not only enigmatic, they are also self-consciously ambiguous works that desire to create, above all, even more enigmas. Fuentes uses a variety of settings in these four works, but the old Mexico City of the palaces appears frequently—evoking the central architectural image of his work, El Escorial.

After the story "Tlactocatzine, del Jardín de Flandes," roots of *Terra Nostra* are to be found in *Aura* and *Birthday; Aura* contains some of the most clearly delineated beginnings. The transformation of one character into another from another century is one of the most direct links between the two novels; the rewriting of history is another. With *Aura*, Fuentes begins his attack on time, initiated with the use of a second-person *tú* combined with an enigmatic future tense that both negates and destroys time.[6]

The basic framework of *Aura* has numerous parallels with *Terra Nostra*. The protagonist enters the enclosed space of a building (an old Colonial home in the *centro* of Mexico City) to engage in this historical project, an act that prefigures the entrance into El Escorial in *Terra Nostra* to carry out a different type of historical project. When the nineteenth-century general Llorente is fused with the twentieth-century Felipe Montero, it is the beginning of a much more elaborate parallel process of doubling, and later multiple doubling, in *Terra Nostra*.

Other minor details appear in *Aura* that lay groundwork for *Terra Nostra*. Montero walks up exactly twenty-two stairs into the home, just as El Señor carefully counts the thirty-three steps in El Palacio. Montero notices paintings of Jesus, Mary, and other religious figures on the walls of the home, and they almost—but not quite—come to life, as in *Terra Nostra.* For example, in one exotic scene in which Montero and Aura dance, she directs a *mirada* at the figure of Christ, again, as if he were a live character: "dirige miradas furtivas al Cristo de madera" (*Aura,* 48).

The young historian of *Aura* reveals the desires of Fuentes-the-historian in *Terra Nostra,* mentioning his wish to write an *opus magnus* similar, perhaps, to *Terra Nostra:* "A work that synthesizes all the different chronicles, makes them intelligible, finds correspondences between all the enterprises and adventures of the Golden Age, among the human prototypes and the fact of the Rennaissance" (*Aura,* 33). Taking into account all these elements to be more fully developed in *Terra Nostra,* the sixty-two page *Aura* functions as a small-scale synecdoche for *Terra Nostra.*

In *Birthday,* Fuentes develops some of the experiments of *Aura* in a more radical way. Some of the concepts suggested as themes and possibilities in Fuentes' other fiction are put in practice in this book, his most hermetic and experimental novel. Set in London, the story deals with a multiple set of identities: George, his son Georgie, his wife, characters named Nuncia and Nino, and the thirteenth-century Averroist philosopher Siger of Brabant. Their constantly transforming identities and distant relations associate and overlap in the most enigmatic fashion of any of Fuentes' novels until *Terra Nostra.* As one informed critic explained about *Birthday:* "The book is a complex meditation on the nature of time and the continuity of mind through time, and probably other things as well."[7]

The most important of these "other things" is space, a factor that is signaled initially by George's profession of architect. The point of departure is a room that George and his wife occupy with their son, Georgie, but this novel lacks a space to be identified as a center, and space is experienced as an element of the novel in continual transformation. In *Birthday,* Fuentes effects with space what Juan Rulfo had done with time in *Pedro Páramo* and Julio Cortázar had done with character in *62: A Model Kit:* radical innovation. *Birthday* is a lengthy meditation on space; experience is not separated into the worlds of inside and outside.

Birthday was written during the initial stages of the conception and writing of *Terra Nostra,* and the two novels share a common conception of space and other elements. The descriptions of hermetically closed spaces occasionally evoke the equally hermetic space of El Escorial, and the Diocletian Palace of Spalato and other palaces that served as precedents of El Escorial are described in the text (in the context of Siger of Brabant). The architectural constructs in *Birthday,* like those of El Palacio in *Terra Nostra,* are severe. George's house is even compared to such palaces: "I have compared this house to a Yugoslav city and a Mediterranean palace" (*B,* 29).

The conceptualization of architecture and space are the most important connections with *Terra Nostra.* The synthesis of the thirteenth-century Siger of Brabant and the twentieth-century George is also a notable precedent to the maneuvers of *Terra Nostra. Birthday* is even more experimental with space than *Terra Nostra* is; only in the former are there concepts such as "la casa está siendo" (*B,* 65). In the second half of the novel the figure of Siger of Brabant raises theological questions that are precedents for some of the anguishing of Felipe II (El Señor) in *Terra Nostra.* Siger of Brabant's affirmations, however, are the opposite of El Señor's: "The world is eternal, since there was no creation; the truth is double, since it can be multiple; the soul is not immortal, but the common intellect of the human species is unique" (*B,* 98). He insists on multiplicity, the same multiplicity that undergirds *Terra Nostra.* (The *náufrago* of *Terra Nostra* also appears in *Birthday.*)

Distant Relations expands and develops several of the problems found in *Aura.* The complex plot tells of a Heredia family in Mexico attempting to find its connections with Heredias in France. One of Fuentes' most accomplished novels, *Distant Relations* deals with the Latin American cultural heritage from France, as *Terra Nostra* had done with Spain. Nevertheless, *Distant Relations* suggests much about Fuentes as writer and his interests in literature, for this is the book that promotes the idea that living, in the end, is predicated on the act of telling a story. It suggests that in a work of art "the solution of its enigma creates a new enigma" (*DR,* 200). This book also fictionalizes a concept of culture in which nothing exists in an isolated way. Consequently, culture is recognized not only in a multicultural world but also in a culturally interdependent one, even though relations may be, at a first glance, distant ones.

Written after *Terra Nostra, Distant Relations* can be read as an extension of the former in the sense that it continues Fuentes' lengthy meditation on European-Mexican relations. Near the end, it is revealed that the person listening to the Compte de Branly is a man named Fuentes who, instead of returning to his native Mexico from Buenos Aires in 1945, remained in the Río del Plata until 1955, when he went to France. This is an option for another Fuentes, one more of numerous alternatives in a fictional world of continual and multiple alternatives. As in *Terra Nostra,* the New World is conceived as a lost opportunity to create a universal culture, as Branly explains to Fuentes: "You, who come from there, should understand when I tell you that the New World was the last opportunity for European universalism" (*DR,* 124). Above all, *Distant Relations* is a complex elaboration of two concepts from *Terra Nostra:* that the self and the other are inextricably bound in distant relations and that human existence depends on the act of storytelling.

Constancia and Other Stories for Virgins also deals with distant relations, now elaborated in five stories located in a variety of settings ranging from the heart of the old historical center of Mexico City—the center of the formerly grandiose palaces—to Savannah, Georgia. Like El Señor in El Escorial, some of the characters in this volume have a very particular and personal sense of their *morada* (abode) as an architecture of their respective desires. Not since *Terra Nostra,* in fact, had architecture been so important. In the last story, "Reasonable People," architecture is a central element, and it plays a role in all of these stories. Like *Terra Nostra,* these are also stories that return inevitably to enigmatic origins, enigmatic deaths.

In the first story, "Constancia," the protagonist Whitby Hull refers to his *hogar* (home) as a *morada* (abode), thus recalling the description of El Escorial, according to Felipe II, as a *morada de Dios* (home of God). Hull is a physician from the South who meets a beautiful young woman from Seville, Constancia, in Spain, marries her, and brings her back to Savannah. His neighbor, an eccentric Russian actor exile named Polotnikov, had known the young woman in Spain, and had fathered a child by her, a fact that Hull realizes after forty years of marriage—when he is sixty-nine years old and she is sixty-one.

Hull fancies himself a very logical and rational man, and he searches desperately for a full understanding of the increasingly incredible situation, which reaches its emotional zenith when he discovers the corpse of his wife's son in the coffin of Polotnikov. Near the end, Hull makes the same discovery that the reader makes with all four books of El Mal del Tiempo: "The enigma reveals another enigma" (*Constancia*, 47).

In "Constancia," human relations and time assume a meaning different from that in the other fiction in this first cycle. "Distant relations," in this case, has multiple meanings. The relationship between Hull and Constancia seems to have been always psychologically distant. The intimate relationship between Polotnikov and Constancia, on the other hand, is distant in time.

In "Reasonable People," distant relations are also an important factor in the story's development. On the one hand, a group of students and their mentor, an architecture professor named Santiago Ferguson, form one set of special relations. On the other, the relationship between these youths and Ferguson's daughter, Catarina, is characterized by its paradoxically distant intimacy. Here, Fuentes' subversion of time is similar to the procedure in *Aura*. The narrator (one of the youths) explains time as follows: "We are formed not merely by our ancestors but by our contemporaries, especially our teachers" (*Constancia*, 263).

A significant constant in these stories is the desire to return to origins, and this is a motivating force in the life of Ferguson. Ferguson wishes to be buried within the architectural construct of an English church: "I like the religious secret of my old islands. I would like to be buried in an English cathedral. I would go back there in rebellion, in affirmation of the sacred, the incomprehensible" (*Constancia*, 264). He had once gone back to find his family origins, traveling to Scotland, where he had "encountered the past" (*Constancia*, 282). When he dies, the two characters do indeed accompany him to his *última morada* (last abode) in England, thus repeating language of El Escorial as a *morada de Dios* (God's abode). The narrator describes the monasteries of Canterbury and Chichester as "hulls of stone" (*Constancia*, 330), a description that could have been used for El Escorial. According to this narrator, "Ferguson had *become* architecture" (*Constancia*, 333).

Like the story "Constancia," "Reasonable People" deals with numerous conflicts between rational and irrational understandings of the world. The two brothers who follow Santiago Ferguson's life are caught between their experience of the miraculous or the sacred, and the rational. As modern-day students of architecture, they project an external image as *gente de razón* (reasonable people), but their most profound experiences deal with the miraculous.

"La Desdichada" is a nostalgic piece set in the old part of Mexico City and, once again, its palaces, but now in the 1930s. The two main characters, Toño and Bernardo, are students who came from the provinces to Mexico City, where they share an apartment among the palaces. Their relationship is superb until Toño buys a mannequin from a store, which they call "La Desdichada." In the lively imaginations of these future writers, "La Desdichada," like the figures of saints and dolls that they see, takes on a real life. Her presence is so real in the apartment, in fact, that it creates distance in their relationship, eventually causing them to part ways.

The two remaining stories, "Viva mi fama" and "The Prisoner of Las Lomas," present the engimas and several of the issues already observed in *Constancia and Other Stories for Virgins*. The architecture of the characters' homes is particularly important in "The Prisoner of Las Lomas"; painting surfaces once again in "Viva mi fama," a story in which Goya appears as a twentieth-century character, after his physical death centuries before. "Viva mi fama" deals with a humble Spaniard, his relationship with his wife, his career as a *torero* and, ultimately, his death. "The Prisoner of Las Lomas" is an enigmatic story about an enigmatic death. All five of these stories, in fact, have death as a constant backdrop, an unexpected presence among all these distant relations.

This first cycle of Fuentes' fiction indeed could well have been called "Distant Relations," and it contains some of his most accomplished work. He cultivates a variety of enigmas and includes in this cycle his most enigmatic fictional experiment of all, *Birthday*.

(2) *Terra Nostra* (Tiempo de Fundaciones)

Terra Nostra is the foundational novel for the total cycle of "La Edad del Tiempo," which also closes with another foundational text, *The Orange Tree*. With *Terra Nostra,* time is set in motion in Fuentes' cycle, beginning with the Western and Native American roots of the Americas. Fuentes himself has spoken of his intention to surpass all conventional understandings of time.[8] As discussed in Part II, *Terra Nostra* both incorporates and negates Western linear time as well as Aztec circular time. It is Fuentes' most elaborate and complex version of the distant relations theme.

With his rewriting of El Escorial, Fuentes fictionalizes the foundations of Indo-Afro-Ibero-American culture, using as its central metaphor the architecture of El Escorial. This architecture serves as a mirror image of the numerous palaces that Fuentes fictionalizes in his work set in Mexico City: the palaces in *Aura, Hydra Head, Burnt Water,* and *Constancia and Other Stories for Virgins.*

(3) El Tiempo Romántico

El Tiempo Romántico consists of three novels, one of which Fuentes has written and two more that he has conceived. With *The Campaign,* Fuentes continues from the foundation in *Terra Nostra* to the independence period of the early nineteenth century. It relates the story of Balthasar Bustos, a Latin American child of the Enlightenment who is obsessed with a woman and who joins the revolutionary forces that forged independence in the early nineteenth century. The novel follows this independence movement in the Río del Plata, in the region of today's Bolivia, in Chile, in Peru, up the west coast of South America to Colombia and Venezuela, and ends in Veracruz, Mexico. It is Fuentes' only novel set in Latin American nations other than Mexico, but it is one of several works with characters in search of origins and truth. In the case of *The Campaign,* truth is to be found in the ideas of the Enlightenment, for the young revolutionaries are guided by the ideas of Rousseau, Voltaire, and Diderot. The central conflict of the novel is posited between the culture of the Enlightenment and the culture of the Catholic Church.

In *The Campaign* history is moved not by the forces of economics or by individual psychology but by ideas. More than in any of Fuentes' novels since *Where the Air Is Clear,* characters in *The Campaign* tend to represent ideas. The character Dorrego is associated with the ideas of Voltaire, Bustos with those of Rousseau, and Varela (the narrator) with those of Diderot. Similarly, a wise old figure named Simón Rodríguez states: "I am the idea of light before light was ever seen" (*Campaign,* 86). Balthasar tends to conceive of history as a set of ideas and other factors, too: "He accepted the fact that history, the conglomeration of ideas, facts, and desires which he fought for or against, came to be only in the company of others, in something shared with others" (*Campaign,* 43). Near the end of the novel, the characters themselves come to recognize that they are products of the written word: "The written is the real and we are its authors" (*Campaign,* 215).

Like *Terra Nostra* and *The Orange Tree, The Campaign* is a foundational text. Unlike these two, which review the foundations in Spain and from Spain before, during, and after the Conquest, *The Campaign* looks at the ideological roots of the new republics in the Americas at the moment of the independence movements. These are the foundations of European reason and rationality that produced the liberal constitutions of the Latin American states in the early nineteenth century. They are also the roots of the nation-state that appear, in *The Campaign,* more as self-contradictory and question-able ideological constructs than as nations in the European sense. They appear in this novel as nations in search of a discourse. As in *Terra Nostra,* the Americas are conceived as the mirror image of Spain: "Spain was reiterated in its colonies" (*Campaign,* 71).

This cycle contains, in addition, two novels yet to be writ-ten, *La novia muerta* and *El baile del Centenario.* According to Fuentes, *La novia muerta* takes place in Paris in the nineteenth cen-tury, the main characters being from Latin America's oligarchy: "The characters from *The Campaign,* from Chile, Mexico, and Argentina, now have aged and are living in Paris, as the nineteenth-century Latin American oligarchy wished to live. This is a family that asks the painter Courbet to paint their portrait, and it is his resistance to painting a bourgeois work for a rich Mexican family when he was accustomed to painting cows."[9] *El baile del Centenario* is a novel of the *porfiriato,* the late-nineteenth-century dictatorship of Porfirio Díaz in Mexico: "It occurs during the centennial indepen-dence celebrations of Mexico, with Porfirio Díaz, with military pa-rades, an army that looks Prussian, with German helmets and uni-forms. Worldwide delegations praising the labor of Díaz and the peace and prosperity that he brought to Mexico, a letter from Tolstoy praising Díaz the peace maker, and two months later the country was in flames."[10]

(4) El Tiempo Revolucionario

Fuentes fictionalizes the time of the Mexican Revolution with two novels. *Old Gringo* continues the historical chronology, entering into the period of the Mexican Revolution of the early twentieth century. It is the story of two Americans in Mexico, Ambrose Bierce and Harriet Winslow, and it is classic Fuentes with his best storytelling. Here Fuentes uses language and the gaze (*mirada*) as well as he ever has. Much of the novel consists of the actions and adventures already associated with the Mexican Revolution, those of the sort Mariano Azuela had related in his classic novel of the revolution, *The Underdogs* (1915). One of the early scenes of the novel, in fact, evokes an early scene in *The Underdogs,* when the old gringo crosses the Rio Grande and looks back at a burning bridge: "As soon as he crossed the Río Grande, he heard the explosion and turned to see the bridge in flames" (*OG,* 10). (In *The Underdogs,* the protagonist Demetrio Macías looks back at his burning home in a key early passage.) Fuentes also follows Azuela's model in characterizing the men of the revolution using animal imagery.

In the fiction of Fuentes, individuals always live in relationship to others, and their actions affect others. In *Old Gringo,* the destinies of the three main characters are fully dependent upon others. As is especially evident in *Hydra Head,* they do not act as individuals with a particular identity, but they play roles that are the fulfillment of an identity: Harriet Winslow always takes the role of the American woman who is the daughter of an American; the old gringo assumes the role of the American dreamer and writer; Tomás Arroyo plays the role of the proto-Mexican in the Mexican Revolution. They can play other roles, too, in the movement of constant substitutions. The most intense of these games of substitutions is a scene in which Harriet dances with Arroyo thinking of her father, while Arroyo dances with her imagining his mother.

Like *Terra Nostra, Old Gringo* is really a novel about language and writing. The old gringo carries *Don Quixote* along with him to Mexico, claiming that he wants to read it before dying. But all the characters are obsessed with texts, with dreaming, and with stories. Throughout this novel, reality is portrayed not as it is observed in the empirical world around the characters but as it is conceived within the bounds of their language, their imaginations, and their stories. As in *Distant Relations,* in *Old Gringo* the power of storytelling predominates over empirical reality.

Old Gringo, like *Terra Nostra,* is a novel about frontiers, difference, and the other. Once the two Americans cross the Rio Grande, these issues are evoked, generated as much by the history of the relations between the two nations as by the actions of the characters. Harriet and Arroyo are fully aware of the baggage they carry as an American woman and a Mexican man in the discourse each represents on the other side of the border. Harriet also understands that the psychological frontiers are as real as the physical border: "And the frontier in here?" (*OG,* 5). Arroyo responds: "The frontier of our differences with others" (*OG,* 5).

Written after *Terra Nostra, Old Gringo* is a work that continues the interest in frontiers that Fuentes evidenced in *Terra Nostra.* In the latter work, it was the cultural frontier between Spain and the Americas; in *Old Gringo,* it is the frontier between Mexico and the United States. In this novel, the border is a source of language, a discourse of clichés and misunderstanding.

Fuentes' fourth cycle contains one more novel yet to be written, *Emiliano en Chinameca,* which will also be set in the period of the Mexican Revolution and will describe the final days in the life of agrarian leader Emiliano Zapata.

(5) *Where the Air Is Clear*

Fuentes began his first novel by establishing a distinction between "novel" and "history" that he never again delineated so clearly and definitively in a book of fiction: a page appears at the beginning with a chronological outline of the *novela* and another with the events of Mexican *historia.* (After *Where the Air Is Clear,* "novel" and "history" become self-consciously problematized, and the author does not again establish such clear dichotomies.) After this six-page chronological overview, Fuentes offers a four-page guide to all of the eighty-three characters, with brief, one-line descriptions of the role of each. They are classified, to a large extent, by social class. After *Where the Air Is Clear,* many of Fuentes' characters have unfixed identities in a process of transformation; the fixed characterizations delineated at the beginning of *Where the Air Is Clear* are not feasible.

Where the Air Is Clear deals with the modern Mexico of the 1940s and 1950s and the issue of identity. The modernity of Mexico is, in itself, fictionalized within a context of rapid capitalization and promotion of industrial and technological "progress." This progress is fictionalized in a context of the successes and failures of individuals, with their respective ascents and descents in Mexican society. Identity, in fact, is frequently conceptualized in this novel in opposition to progress: the modern Mexican is portrayed as an uprooted individual who has lost any sense of past and identity. The modern Mexican is also the citizen of the novel's setting in Mexico City: a culturally complex and historically bound urban area.

Where the Air Is Clear appeared at a time when identity was a major issue for Mexican intellectuals, especially since the publication of the essays of Samuel Ramos and Alfonso Reyes in the 1930s and Paz's *Labyrinth of Solitude* in 1950. *Where the Air Is Clear* is closely associated with the ideas of Ramos and Paz, who had described the Mexican as a hermetic being, hidden behind masks, with an identity difficult to discover. Along these same lines, the character Rodrigo Pola writes: "I, carried along by my personality dialectic, no longer know my true face" (*Where*, 190). Near the end of the novel, Pola's final meditations on Mexico emphasize the mask of the modern Mexican's identity:

. . . names dripping like drops of your unique mascara, that of your anonymity, face flesh hiding fleshed faces, the thousand faces, one mask Acamapichtli, Cortés, Sor Juana, Itzcóatl, Juárez, Tezo-zómoc, Gante, Ilhuicamina, Madero, Felipe Angeles, Morones, Cárdenas, Calles . . . (*Where*, 363)

Where the Air Is Clear conceives of the Mexican and Mexican concerns primarily in the context of the present and past of Mexico City, with little allusion to Spain and the issues of *Terra Nostra*. Writer Manuel Zamacona, however, does make a reference to Spain that asks one of the questions implied by *Terra Nostra:* "What closed the door to European participation on a nation that today lives shut off from all expressions of intelligence?" (*Where*, 44). And *Where the Air Is Clear*, like much of Fuentes' early writing, presents characters and a nation in the situation of choosing between options of historical import. Consequently, the Mexico of the 1950s is seen at the same crucial juncture as the Spain of the late sixteenth century: "We stand at the crossroad. Which, of all the roads, shall we choose?" (*Where*, 49). In addition, continual questioning of origins is, in effect, an important precedent, leading to the writing of *Terra Nostra* a decade later.

(6) *The Death of Artemio Cruz*

The Death of Artemio Cruz, one of Fuentes' major novels, as well as his first contribution to the Boom, is his critique of the modern state developed in Mexico. He continues his project of simultaneously constructing historical times and destroying the subjective time of the individual. An omniscient (extradiegetic-heterodiegetic) narrator constructs historical time in the twelve narrative segments that take place in years identified from 1889 to 1955. This partially historical novel of twentieth-century Mexico loses any sense of chronological *histoire* through the use of various strategies. On the one hand, these historical sections do not appear in chronological order; on the other, the sections narrated by "*yo*" (I) and "*tú*" (you) create a variety of atemporal effects. When the "*tú*" narrator states, "lo que pasará ayer" (that which will happen yesterday), the temporal oxymoron has the effect of destroying Western concepts of linear time; the important changes in this novel are temporal by nature.

In *The Death of Artemio Cruz,* Fuentes once again fictionalizes several of the ideas about Mexican identity—ideas with roots in Reyes and Ramos of the 1940s—that he and Paz had been popularizing since the publication of Paz's *Labyrinth of Solitude* in 1950. Consequently, several passages of *The Death of Artemio Cruz* portray the Mexican as the heir of Malinche, the *hijo de la chingada,* the *gran chingón.* Such ideas, clearly paraphrased from *The Labyrinth of Solitude,* are a relatively minor sidelight to the totality of the novel. The most significant identity for protagonist Cruz is that of survivor: his only consistent and certain affirmation on his deathbed is "yo sobreviví" (I survived).

Some of the issues and themes of *Terra Nostra* are more fully developed in *The Death of Artemio Cruz* than they had been in *Where the Air Is Clear* or *The Good Conscience*. As in *The Good Conscience,* the matter of individual choice is extremely important in *The Death of Artemio Cruz*. The protagonist's failure as a human being is portrayed as the culmination of a series of poor moral decisions, just as one of Spain's historical problems lies, according to Fuentes, in her decision to isolate herself from the Europe of the Renaissance and the Enlightenment. Seeds of *Terra Nostra* are to be found in certain passages of *The Death of Artemio Cruz,* in which the circumstance of Mexico is linked to its past with Spain:

> You will walk toward the facade, early Baroque, Spanish but rich in vine columns and aquiline-nosed keystones: the facade of the Conquest, severe yet jocund, with one foot in the dead Old World and the other in the New, which did not begin here but on the other side of the ocean: the New World arrived when they arrived; facade of austere walls to protect their avaricious, sensual, happy hearts. (*AC,* 31)

This particular passage is a key referent to *Terra Nostra,* for it represents an early stage of the development of ideas for the latter novel. Other aspects of *The Death of Artemio Cruz* point more indirectly to the future creation of *Terra Nostra*. The fragmentation of the character of Cruz into three is Fuentes' most elaborate subversion of individual identity in his fiction to date, thus laying groundwork for a much more elaborate and complex fragmentation of the individual subject in *Terra Nostra*. In *The Death of Artemio Cruz,* Fuentes also begins to question the Western Manichaean bipolar systems of thought.

(7) Los Años con Laura Díaz

Fuentes' plan for this novel, according to the novelist himself, is "in a certain way it is a companion novel to *The Death of Artemio Cruz*. The characters are from the same period, but the story is told about a woman, a point of view very different from that of Artemio Cruz as a man. It has a little of my own family story, the story of a family in Veracruz." [11]

(8) Dos Educaciones

Fuentes identifies *The Good Conscience* and *Holy Place* as "two edu-
cations" and, indeed, they are Bildungsromans, albeit very different
types. In both works the protagonist passes through a *rite de passage*.
In *The Good Conscience,* it is the young Jaime Ceballos who suffers
the experience of growing up in the traditional and provincial society
of Guanajuato. This novel is dedicated to Luis Buñuel, the person
who had insisted that Fuentes visit El Escorial. *The Good Conscience*
and El Escorial share with *Terra Nostra* a concentration upon a
closed, hermetic space within a closed and hermetic society. The narrator states: "There was faith in the city of noble stone that Saturday"
(*GC*, 41), thus evoking images of the palace of El Escorial.

   The Good Conscience focuses on the Ceballos family, which is
depicted by Fuentes-the-historian as the history of Guanajuato, with
a strong sense of the development of a new oligarchy after the Mexican Revolution. The young protagonist faces the same decisions concerning religious faith and a life of rigidity under the restrictions of
the Catholic Church that El Señor faces in *Terra Nostra*. A character
named Jaime Ceballos suffers the "upset spirit" of El Señor in *Terra
Nostra:* "On the one hand the complex theorems of love and sin,
man's fall and salvation; on the other life's vulgar plain reality: to
fornicate, to conform to class and breeding, to die" (*GC,* 142).

   The protagonist of *Holy Place,* Guillermo Nervo, is older than
most fictional characters of the Bildungsroman: he is the twenty-
nine-year-old son of a celebrity actress who frequently overshadows
him, causing an identity crisis. The only significant action of *Holy
Place,* however, is the act of transformation. As Guillermo observes
at one point, "Nothing unfolds, all is transfigured" (*HP,* 55). Consequently, this protagonist's identity is never fully established, as he is
reduced to little more than a series of meaningless gestures.

   Published in 1967, *Holy Place* is closer to *Terra Nostra,* containing numerous direct connections to it. Like *Terra Nostra,* it has a
three-part structure. The chapters within these three parts move
from Mexico to Europe and back, as portions of material do in *Terra
Nostra*. Near the beginning of the novel, Guillermo ends a chapter
with the words "This is my story," thus prefiguring Celestina's opening in *Terra Nostra,* "Este es mi cuento," followed by the same words
as reflected in a mirror. Fuentes continues the practice, already begun

in *Aura*, of creating characters who are in a state of ongoing transformation. As a modern-day Ulysses, Guillermo prefigures Polo Febo as well as all the Polo Febo figures in *Terra Nostra*. From *Aura* to *Holy Place*, the concept of character in the fiction of Fuentes questions any idea of fixed identity or psychological unity, a concept fully exploited in *Terra Nostra*.

Painting figures prominently in *Holy Place*, as do references to a triptych (of Leonora Carrington) that is comparable to the triptych (of *El jardín de las delicias*) in *Terra Nostra*. In *Holy Place*, Fuentes begins to experiment with the mutual interaction between characters in a novel and the paintings around them. The protagonist of *Holy Place* goes to Orvieto, Italy, the site of the painting from Orvieto in *Terra Nostra*, and the Italian painter of the murals in the Chapel of Orvieto, Signorelli, is also mentioned (as he is subsequently in *A Change of Skin*).

(9) Los Días Enmascarados

According to Octavio Paz, the "masked days," or what Fuentes calls "Days in which it's better to stay home," were special in Aztec civilization.[12] For Paz, the title of Fuentes' first volume of short stories "alludes to the final days of the Aztec calendar, the *nemontatani*. In the spirit of Fuentes, without doubt, the term also has a meaning of questioning . . . what is behind the masks?"[13] The idea of "the masked days" appears throughout Fuentes' fiction, from his first book of short stories, through *Terra Nostra*, and in his later novel *The Orange Tree*. The cycle that Fuentes identifies as Los Días Enmascarados contains four volumes of short fiction—some of his very best writing: *Los días enmascarados, Cantar de ciego, Burnt Water*, and one more volume to be written, *La frontera de cristal*.

The book titled *Los días enmascarados* consists of six stories written with the aesthetic agenda of Borges and Arreola: now, everything is seemingly possible in fiction. In "Chac Mool," the statue of an Aztec god comes to life to dominate a human being; in "Tlactocatzine, del Jardín de Flandes" a historian finds himself transformed into Maximilian (in the method of *Aura*); in "Por boca de los dioses," another Aztec god takes control of a human being. In these stories, Fuentes does indeed stop time for the sacred days, undermining the rationale behind many traditional understandings of time and space, as well as human interaction within the traditional human boundaries of time and space. History begins to live in the present and future, as it will on a much larger scale in his later fiction.

Cantar de ciegos contains seven stories that are more explicitly cosmopolitan than *Los días enmascarados,* more subtle in their human relationships, and equally effective in subverting any established sense of order. *Los días enmascarados* engages in the fantastic with a strong sense of the Aztec past; *Cantar de ciegos* does not involve a definition of Mexican identity by means of the past. Rather, each story of *Cantar de ciegos* takes place in contemporary Mexico. The characters of "Las dos Elenas," for example, are self-consciously modern, and the distant historical past is not an issue. The issue is the relationship among the three individuals—a young married couple and their mother/mother-in-law. The surprise ending reveals a relationship between the husband and his mother-in-law.

Burnt Water represents Fuentes' return to Mexico after having published a series of books situated outside of Mexico. It also represents a return to his historical thinking about Mexico. The stories of *Cantar de ciegos* could have taken place anywhere (and were not historical). *A Change of Skin* enters into European history, *Birthday* is set in London (and totally devoid of Mexican referents), and *Terra Nostra,* of course, is set primarily in Spain. Fuentes' next work, *Hydra Head,* is set in contemporary Mexico, thus making the "narrative quartet" titled *Burnt Water* his first historically driven book set in Mexico since *The Death of Artemio Cruz.* And like *The Death of Artemio Cruz,* it deals with that generation of Mexicans who came to power during the Mexican Revolution. *Burnt Water* consists of four narratives that can be read separately but that fit together tightly as characters and situations overlap in each of the stories. The colloquial and personal tone of the language makes it a very Mexican book.

The central figure of *Burnt Water* is Vicente Vergara, a patriarch who was a captain during the revolution and who lives out his old age in the fancy Pedregal neighborhood of modern Mexico City. He is present as a key figure or important implicit referent in each of the stories. In the first, "Mother's Day," Vergara is the grandfather of the narrator, Plutarco, who adores this last family hero. A dominant and violent figure representing the best and the worst of the old order of the *porfiriato,* Vergara engages in the same irrational and inhumane violence in modern Mexico as he had during the revolution. Like many characters in *Burnt Water,* he lives intensely in the past, negating the present and thus differentiating himself from many of Fuentes' major characters, who often live the past and the future in the present. In this book, the past refers to the glory days of the revolution and the 1920s.

The physical space of *Burnt Water* is also from the past, the same space as *Aura:* the old Colonial and nineteenth-century buildings of the central downtown area of Mexico City. Vergara lives there until he moves to the Pedregal, as does Manuelita, Vergara's maid and the protagonist of the second narrative, "These Were Palaces." The decrepit and poverty-stricken Manuelita lives in an imaginary world of modern Mexico, the imagined past grandeur of the aristocracy who inhabited the "palaces" of old Mexico City.

The success of the stories in *Burnt Water* lies not in their nostalgic references to the past but in their multiple enigmas. Vergara and Manuelita are enigmatic characters, as are Federico Silva and Bernabé of the last two stories. Silva is a property owner in the old part of the city (of Vergara and Manuelita) and Bernabé is a modern-day product of the Mexican Revolution—first a window washer, then a thug. When Bernabé becomes involved in organized violence at the end, his boss observes (citing the protagonist of *The Underdogs*), "Look at that rock, how it keeps rolling" (*BW,* 230).

La frontera de cristal, the last volume of the Los Días Enmascarados cycle, will consist of seven stories, all dealing with border themes, such as Mexicans in the United States and individuals of other nationalities who have crossed other national boundaries.

These stories of the cycle Los Días Enmascarados have numerous connections with *Terra Nostra,* which mentions "los días enmascarados" near the beginning of Part II (*TN,* 403). Of the stories in *Los días enmascarados,* "Tlactocatzine, del Jardín de Flandes" contains the earliest identifiable roots of *Terra Nostra* in Fuentes' fiction. It represents an early effort to transform characters, to be "transhistorical"—blending characters from different time periods into one, and to create a sense of atemporality.

Cantar de ciegos and *Burnt Water* have less in common with *Terra Nostra.* The former, however, was a step toward the more universal interests in *Terra Nostra*. Most of the stories in *Cantar de ciegos* could take place anywhere, and in this sense move beyond the question "What is Mexico?" As one critic has pointed out, now Fuentes turns to the question "Who are the Mexicans?"[14] *Burnt Water* appeared after *Terra Nostra*, reaffirming the fact that Fuentes' narrative always returns to its central referent: Mexico and its past.

(10) El Tiempo Político

This tenth cycle consists of one published novel, *Hydra Head*, and two forthcoming works, *El sillón del águila* and *El camino a Texas*. They represent yet another concept of time—"political time." In the first volume of this cycle, *Hydra Head*, political time is fundamentally the linear time of the spy thriller. In reality, the numerous elements of the spy thriller or detective fiction—including the fast-moving plot—are the trappings of this pastiche of mystery novels and spy films. The protagonist, Félix Maldonado, an overly punctual bureaucrat, becomes unwillingly involved in a plot to assassinate the president of Mexico as well as a plot of international intrigue concerning Mexico's oil reserves. A double of him is killed, and he has plastic surgery and assumes a new identity, now calling himself Diego Velázquez. He owns a reproduction of *Las Meninas* because he and his wife had noticed physical similarities between him and Velázquez.

As one critic has aptly pointed out, *Hydra Head* is actually a novel of pseudo-detection.[15] The protagonist plays the role of detective and does eventually discover that the murderers of the woman of his amorous obsessions—Sara Klein—had been killed by his own wife, Ruth. In the process of this discovery, as well as the process of his transformation into his new identity as Diego Velázquez, however, Felix seems to be living out the lives of a series of film characters, from Humphrey Bogart to James Bond. Consequently, the reader experiences a humorous distance from the events at hand and observes with intellectual aloofness the fact that the characters are caught in enigmatic relationships of power.[16]

As in *Terra Nostra*, Fuentes is interested in the multiple and transforming aspects of character that result, in much of his fiction, in doubles and multiples of characters. *Hydra Head* is entirely predicated on the double Felix Maldonado/Diego Velázquez. In the end,

Felix fully assumes his new identity. But Felix has other doubles, including Theseus, Trevor, Hamlet, the March Hare from *Alice in Wonderland,* Humphrey Bogart, even Woody Allen. In a novel of numerous and ongoing substitutions, it is notable that Felix is a substitute for Velázquez just as his painting is a substitute for *Las Meninas.*

The most significant affinity with *Terra Nostra,* however, is found in the function of painting.[17] As in *Terra Nostra,* the paintings that occupy the space on the walls in the novel play an active role in the plot rather than the traditional passive role of scenery or setting. Paintings of Ricardo Martínez and John Everett Millais, consequently, have as active a function in this novel as the paintings of Signorelli and Bosch do in *Terra Nostra.* The most important painting is *Las Meninas,* by Velázquez, the same painting that is so important for Foucault, and for Fuentes in *Terra Nostra.* Felix and his wife, during a visit to El Prado, find similarities between the self-portrait of Velázquez and Felix, purchase a reproduction, and place it prominently in their home, where Felix sees it regularly. After Felix assumes his new identity, he feels increasingly at home in his new role, and eventually he *becomes* Diego Velázquez.

Among his observations on *Las Meninas* in *Les Mots et les Choses,* Foucault notes that "representation, freed finally from the relation that was impeding it, can offer itself as representation in its pure form."[18] Fully aware of certain limits of the novel as compared to the visual arts, Fuentes incorporates painting and film to suggest the nature of literature.[19] By incorporating *Las Meninas* into the novel, Fuentes creates a *mise en abyme* that emphasizes the fictional nature of the characters. Just as in *Don Quixote* and *Terra Nostra,* the characters never strive for "reality"; rather, they constantly reveal their fictionality, repeating lines from Shakespeare and from films, as well as acting in situations that recall Shakespeare and films.

As in *Terra Nostra,* in *Hydra Head* Fuentes fictionalizes a world in constant transformation. Relationships and alliances transform as quickly as identities. As the narrator states, "Any day, the alliances can change radically" (*HH,* 284).

As a postmodern work published in post–*Terra Nostra* Mexico, *Hydra Head* assumes a comic attitude toward some of the topics discussed intensely in Mexico with the rise of Paz and Fuentes in the

1950s. Since the publication of Paz's *Labyrinth of Solitude* in 1950, identity has been a central theme of Mexican literary discourse. In *Hydra Head*, Fuentes finally assumes a playful distance from this topic, using it for satirical ends. He satirizes the president of Mexico by portraying him as a character similar to the hapless Felix: "The President suffered the same malady as Felix Maldonado. He had no face. He was nothing but a name, a title" (*HH*, 57). The narrator also makes a reference that can be read as a satire of the numerous writings of Paz on Mexican identity, referring to the National Palace as "the fixed center of a country fascinated with its own navel" (*HH*, 190).

(11) *A Change of Skin*

Fuentes had suggested the idea for the title of *A Change of Skin* near the middle of *Where the Air Is Clear*. The character Rodrigo Pola thinks "they needed changes of seasons and skin to know themselves, and also others" (*Where*, 260). *A Change of Skin,* like the works of the first cycle, negates linear time and, in addition, looks to the future. Following the model of Borges in "The Garden of Forking Paths," Fuentes creates a labyrinth of time comparable to the infinite novel left by Ts'ui Pen in the Borges story. The basic referents in *A Change of Skin* are Palm Sunday, April 11, 1965, and the town of Cholula in Mexico. The four main characters—Javier, Elizabeth, Franz, and Isabel—make a car trip to Cholula, the site of one of Mexico's most renowned pyramids. But the novel moves back into different historical times, including the Spain of the Inquisition, German concentration camps, Hiroshima, and Vietnam. Fuentes' own experience in the United States in the 1930s and in Argentina in the 1940s results in characters acting in New York in the 1930s and in Buenos Aires in the 1940s. An opening section of the novel moves back and forth, from one paragraph to the next, between the twentieth-century travel of the four main characters and the sixteenth-century conquest of Mexico by Hernán Cortés. The past, the present, and the future exist here and now. As Fuentes himself has suggested in an interview about this book, "There is no historical progress . . . only a repetition of a series of ceremonial acts." [20] In this lengthy and complex novel, Fuentes pursues another time and another world. [21]

Published in 1967 with *Holy Place, A Change of Skin* is a transitional work read in the context of *Terra Nostra*. It is the Fuentes novel before *Terra Nostra* that most clearly incorporates an Aztec view of cyclical time. The Aztecs had accepted the inevitability of change, but they believed that every fifty-two years a cycle was closed and the past had to be "cancelled, denied, destroyed or covered like the seven successive pyramids at the ceremonial center of Cholula." [22] *A Change of Skin* is clearly centered on this cyclical view of time (represented by the seven pyramids): Mexico has kept the original conception of sacrifice as necessary to maintain the order of the cosmos. [23] Continuing his search for the eternal moment suggested in some of his previous work (and later elaborated in *Terra Nostra*), Fuentes strives for the experience of creative re-creation, as represented in the poems *Death without End,* by José Gorostiza, and *Sunstone,* by Octavio Paz, where, as one critic has observed, "Western linear discourse struggles with the spirit of Indian cyclical time in order to reestablish reality on a new foundation." [24] *Terra Nostra* ends in apocalypse; *A Change of Skin* ends with Javier in a state of (postmodern) exhaustion.

There are numerous other allusions of lesser importance in *A Change of Skin* that connect it to *Terra Nostra*. Like *Terra Nostra*, it has a framing story: in *Terra Nostra* it is the frame of Polo Febo in Paris; in *A Change of Skin* it is the frame of an external narrator who is named. In *Terra Nostra,* numerous characters perceive reality and themselves through mirrors; in *A Change of Skin* the four main characters are in the constant presence of a mirror in the car in which they travel. In *Terra Nostra* characters move in and out of the light and shadows of the Palacio; in *A Change of Skin* they move in and out of the same light and shadows when they explore the pyramid of Cholula. *Terra Nostra* has Polo Febo and other transfigurations of Polo Febo (such as the *peregrino*) functioning as Ulysses figures; in *A Change of Skin* Javier becomes, in one part of the novel, a Ulysses (and Polo Febo) figure.

(12) *Christopher Unborn*

Fuentes conceived the entire idea of his "La Edad del Tiempo" when he was writing *Christopher Unborn*. He was a visiting professor on the faculty of Dartmouth College, the same campus on which Diego Rivera had resided while painting his celebrated mural. During that time, while writing this novel about the present and future of Mexico, Fuentes began thinking about the temporal implications of his total work, thus arriving at the global plan of "La Edad del Tiempo."

One of Fuentes' most innovative fictions, *Christopher Unborn* is also one of his lengthy, ambitious, and totalizing books, with most obvious parentage in *A Change of Skin* and *Terra Nostra*. Here, a return to origins takes on a different meaning, for the narrator, Cristóbal, narrates on January 6, 1992, from the womb of his mother, Angeles, who has conceived him in 1992 in Acapulco (also identified as Kafkapulco). As in the story "Apollo and the Whores," in *The Orange Tree,* Fuentes imagines a Mexico of the future, a postpostmodern Mexico that has trivialized not only its national myths and its institutions but also its very identity.

Christopher Unborn is Fuentes' most irreverent fictional critique of the modern state of Mexico; the questioning of the nation's modernization to be found in *Where the Air Is Clear* and *The Death of Artemio Cruz* culminates, in *Christopher Unborn*, in images of a nation lost in the garbage and defecation that are the products of its own development. The *suave patria* of the (nationalistic) early-twentieth-century poet Ramón López Velarde is now a mutilated land where the "external debt" has become an "eternal debt," where the jungle has been destroyed and the nation is covered with cement highways and excrement. Mexico has reached a state of total exhaustion. The Mexico of *Where the Air Is Clear* in which Federico Robles was a businessman on the move is now the Mexico of his son, Robles Chacón, a minister in this fragile and tired state, "cursing right and left about the language of economists" (*CU,* 27). In this postpostmodern world of no truths, "The only truth . . . is that that the vast majority of the people . . . are *screwed*" (*CU,* 28). It is the nation where "nothing works but everything survives" (*CU,* 52). Perhaps the most devastating critique, however, is the fact that Cristóbal, narrating from the womb, has no past at all, a postmodern condition unlike the Mexican characters of Fuentes' early fiction.

Christopher Unborn is a 563-page dialogue with López Velarde, written in a language as provisional and disposed to substitutions as the post-postmodern Mexico of an imagined future with an "Avenida Warehz," a "Colonia Whatamock," and "Jardines Flotantes de Suchamilkshake." The *suave patria* of 1992 is where "shit meets shit" (*CU*, 204).

As in *A Change of Skin, Holy Place*, and *Terra Nostra*, in *Christopher Unborn* Fuentes plays, above all, with language. This is a novel of postmodern play, a world of seemingly infinite substitutions. Humorous associations, such as the following, are common: "Your cherry jubilee in my hungry mouth, your scherezada from tampique with its chilis and little beans which I'm digging up with my longer finger, your cunt, your raccunto, your ass chérie, your cherry ass, Chere Sade, flagellated by my furious whip . . . " (*CU*, 7). It is one of Fuentes' most self-conscious metafictions, which plays off his own words and other institutionalized languages in Mexico, both literary and political. In this sense, *Christopher Unborn* is the Bakhtinian text par excellence: a text of heteroglossia with competing languages at play. The narrator's father articulates this Bakhtinian situation in a statement to his wife: "Adored Angeles: please realize that we live in an arena where all languages fight it out" (*CU*, 17).

The characters in *Christopher Unborn* seem to be lost in time and space, possessing no past. This ahistoricism, however, does not represent the situation of Fuentes in *Christopher Unborn*. To the contrary, he is well aware of the past, parodying and subverting Mexican writers, such as the traditionalists Ramón López Velarde and Mariano Azuela, as well as some of the writers present in much of his work—Cervantes, Erasmus, and Gogol.

The naming of Cervantes and Erasmus also evokes *Terra Nostra*, and *Christopher Unborn* has numerous connections with Fuentes' fictional centerpiece. Like *Terra Nostra*, with the pilgrim who travels across the oceans, it plays off Homer's *Odyssey*. The narrator mentions Homer, for example, in the following context: "Homer, oh mere, oh mer, oh madre, oh merde origin of the Gods: Thalassa, Thalassa" (*CU*, 12).

(13) El Tiempo Actual

This thirteenth cycle consists of three works, two of which have yet to be published. They were originally titled *Crónica del guerrillero y el asesino, Crónica de una actriz renuente,* and *Crónica de una víctima de nuestro tiempo,* but their titles in 1994 became *Diana, o la cazadora solitaria; Aquiles, o el guerrillero y el asesino;* and *Prometeo, o el precio de la libertad.* They are contemporary fictitious chronicles. *Diana, o la cazadora solitaria* is considerably autobiographical, dealing with an affair Fuentes had with an American actress in the 1960s.

(14) *The Orange Tree*

In *The Orange Tree* Fuentes, like García Márquez, uses an image as his point of departure.[25] In this novel, the central image is the *naranjo,* or orange tree, which provides the unity to the volume. Although not a common image in Fuentes' fiction, the orange had appeared in *Hydra Head* as a Spanish image when the narrator describes Felix in the context of a Velázquez painting: "But Felix's face did not have the smile of Velázquez, the satisfaction of those lips that had just tasted plums and oranges" (*Orange,* 35). The orange also appears prominently in *Constancia and Other Stories for Virgins.*[26] The final work in the cycle of "La Edad del Tiempo," this book can be read as a five-chapter novel or a volume of five short stories. The image of the orange tree and the consistency of themes, however, invite the reader to consider it a novel.

The first of these stories (or Chapter 1 of the novel) is narrated by the historical character Jerónimo de Aguilar, a historical character: he was a Spaniard who was shipwrecked on the Yucatán Peninsula and then began living with the Maya inhabitants there.[27] Like the narrator in *Pedro Páramo,* Aguilar narrates from the tomb. The story is divided into ten sections, beginning with the tenth and ending with the first; each highlights, above all, what Aguilar *sees* as a witness of the encounter between two worlds. In the story, he describes himself as the translator between Cortés and Chief Guatemuz, but he says that he purposely distorted and invented in his act of translation. He describes such historical events as the arrival of the Spaniards in the splendid Aztec city of Tenochtitlán on November 3, 1520, and the encounter with Moctezuma, as well as the encounter in Cholula. This narrator presents himself, indirectly, as a writer figure, always emphasizing that as translator, he is a man of language or "the master of language" (*Orange,* 32). In his role as translator, he learns of the power of language. After the misunderstandings and the destruction involved with the encounter, in fact, the only thing that remains is language: "the words remained." As a foundational text, then, *The Orange Tree* emphasizes the origins of the cultures of the Americas in language. At the end of this first chapter (or story), only language remains in Spain, too, for the Aztecs go to Spain and conquer it.

The second story, "The Sons of the Conquistador," continues the foundational narration with the story of two sons of Cortés with identical names—Martín. Identified in the text as Martín 1 and Martín 2, they alternate as the narrators of the story. Once adults and "the real owners of New Spain," they play the role of their father, just as the different kings of Spain in *Terra Nostra* played their roles as the rulers of Spain. In the struggle for establishing authority in Mexico, these sons seem to claim their authority as the heirs of Cortés: "That there is no higher authority in New Spain than I myself?" (*Orange*, 77). In reality, Martín 1 is the recognized heir (the white or criollo son) and Martín 2 is the mestizo son of Malinche. "The Sons of the Conquistador" is fundamentally the *mestizaje* part of the foundational story, for their identity is understood as mestizos, as sons of Cortés and Malinche. Martín 2 clearly has a sense of his identity when he states to his brother: "You're a son of a bitch. You're my brother. You're the fucking son of *La Chingada*" (*Orange*, 89). Despite their realization of their own identity as criollo and mestizo, they cannot even imagine the concept of a new nation. The story ends with Martín 2 observing, "I don't understand how a nation is born" (*Orange*, 100).

In the third story, "The Two Numantias," the roots of Spanish history and culture are observed from the opposite side of the mirror—not from Mexico but from the Roman Empire during the conquest of Spain. Seen by the Romans, the other in Spain represents the savage and the uncivilized that, centuries later, the Spaniards used to define the Native Americans they discovered in Mexico. A Roman narrator opens the story by stating: "They, the Spaniards, are a coarse, savage, and barbarous people whom we Romans lead, whether they like it or not, toward civilization" (*Orange*, 101). "The Two Numantias" relates the story of Roman armies conquering the walled city of Numancia, which becomes Spain and which mirrors Roman civilization back upon itself. A Roman narrator realizes at

one point that he came to Numancia not to conquer it but to duplicate it (*Orange,* 129).

The entertaining fourth story, "Apollo and the Whores," initially seems to be an anomaly to the volume, for it is a narrative set
in contemporary Mexico and relates the last hours in the life of
Vince Valera, a fifty-five-year-old American B-movie actor who goes
on vacation to Acapulco. He rents a boat and takes a group of young
Mexican prostitutes for an afternoon of sexual play at sea but suffers
a heart attack while engaged in sex with the first of these eighteen-
year-olds. The only connection to the other stories, until the last one
in the volume, is the sprouting of an orange tree, at the end of the
story, next to Valera's tomb. The boat he rents is called *The Two
Américas,* the title of the next story.

In the fifth and last story of the volume, "The Two Américas,"
Christopher Columbus narrates his diary, in which he explains the
original importance of the orange. Columbus has loved oranges since
his childhood because they remind him of sucking at his mother's
breast. They also seem as perfect as the sun to him and, as an adult,
he receives great sensual pleasure from oranges, the pleasures of "wet
nurses, breasts, the sphere, the world, the egg" (*Orange,* 219). This
Columbus is also a Sephardic Jew who lives long enough into the
twentieth century to witness the selling of the Americas to Japanese
and other multinational companies, becoming "Paradise Inc." In the
end, the only survivors of the paradisiacal multinational company are
the orange tree, the wolf, and Columbus himself. The ultimate mirror effect appears in the story's last lines, in which he promises to
return to Europe to plant the seeds of an orange tree.

The image of the orange tree, which recurs throughout the
book, is the image of Spain. As Jerónimo de Aguilar explains, "Could
any image verify a Spaniard's identity better than the sight of a
man eating an orange?" (*Orange,* 37). The orange and the orange
tree appear throughout the volume and provide a thread of continuity among the five stories. In "The Numantias," the seeds of this
strange, oriental fruit—*naranja*—are brought to Rome by a Greek
and planted in the Roman's patio. The orange tree grows in the center of the image of the circle, the circle of the patio and the circle of
time that is the conceptual framework of this volume of stories.
Aguilar planted the seeds of the first inherently Spanish image in the

Americas. When Martín, the son of Cortés, goes to Spain to be with his decrepit and dying father, Cortés smells of defecation and oranges: "The stench of my father's shit could not, however, wipe out the fresh scent of an orange tree that grew to the height of his window and which, during those months, bloomed splendidly" (*Orange,* 52–53). The son also relates that Cortés, when he arrived at Yucatán, was amazed to find the orange trees that Jerónimo de Aguilar and Gonzalo Guerrero had planted: "He remembered that when he reached Yucatán, he was astonished to see an orange tree whose seeds had been brought there by the two disloyal castaways, Aguilar and Guerrero" (*Orange,* 63–64). Cortés was so impressed with the seeds from Yucatán that he planted them in Acapulco, thus expanding the mirror image of Spain throughout Mexico.

In July 1992, Fuentes returned to El Escorial and wrote a portion of *The Orange Tree.* It was a return to his origins—for Fuentes and for his lifetime writing project. The circles of time in *Terra Nostra* also reappear in *The Orange Tree.* Like the pilgrim in *Terra Nostra,* Jerónimo de Aguilar can claim "I knew both shores" (*Orange,* 22). And like generations of Latin Americans, particularly the early generations that came most recently from Spain, Aguilar found himself "divided between Spain and the New World" (*Orange,* 22). This first story can be read as a continuation of *Terra Nostra:* in this novel the Americas are portrayed as a mirror image of Spain and vice versa; in this story, Mexico conquers Spain in a mirror image of the Conquest. All that remains on both shores—Spain and the Americas—is language, in both *Terra Nostra* and *The Orange Tree.* The second story continues the foundational history, relating the dilemmas of being the sons of Cortés, the first generation of children of Spaniards born in Mexico as the first mestizos. "The Two Numantias" functions as a mirror image of Part II of *Terra Nostra,* which tells a story of Spaniards conquering the other in the Americas; "The Two Numantias" mirrors the conquest story by writing of the conquest of Spain as the other by the Romans. The inhabitants of Numancia become the other dreamed of by the dominant power, just as the other of Spain dreamed in Part II of *Terra Nostra.* The Columbus of *The Orange Tree* has parents who originate from the same Jewish neighborhood as "The Toledo Jewry" of Part III of *Terra Nostra.* *Terra Nostra* had conceptualized Latin America as a mirror image of

Spain and vice versa; this mirror imagery continues in *The Orange Tree,* when Columbus returns to Europe to plant the seeds of an orange tree.

Narrating and Seeing

Cervantes had imagined a world of multiple points of view, and that is one of the main reasons for Fuentes' lifetime fascination with *Don Quixote.* Similarly, exactly who narrates and who sees and the location of these narrators and seers are important to the reader's experience in *Terra Nostra.* The complex narrative situation in *Terra Nostra* had precedents, of course, in Fuentes' fiction. Reality tends to be enigmatic in all his fiction, and the presence of multiple narrators and seers contributes to the enigmas.

From *Where the Air Is Clear* through *Birthday,* Fuentes had explored in numerous experiments the possibilities and potentialities of multiple narrators and seers. In *Where the Air Is Clear,* he was already using first-, second-, and third-person narrations to fictionalize modern Mexico City and the problems of identity for the modern Mexican. The use of these three points of view was more systematically and fully developed in *The Death of Artemio Cruz,* with a regular rotation of the first, second, and third persons that provides varying insights into the psychic and spiritual makeup of the protagonist, as well as his past. The multiple points of view in *The Death of Artemio Cruz* are also one of the vehicles for destroying linear time. Similarly, the "*tú*" ("you") of *Aura,* used in the future, subverts the rationality of Western linear time.

A Change of Skin and *Birthday* were radical experiments with point of view quite close to the effects in *Terra Nostra,* for beyond the modernist interests in "multiple points of view," Fuentes questions the very being of the narrator. In *A Change of Skin* and *Birthday* the identity and location of narrators and seers move beyond the sphere of epistemology to ontology: the issues are not knowing but being. *Distant Relations* continues the questioning of identity by means of the act of narration, for in this novel, affirmation of self is found by the very act of telling a story.

The gaze (*mirada*) in Fuentes' fiction, as has been noted, had close ties to the work of Paz, who uses *mirada* imagery to suggest a special union between male and female in some situations and a union between generic man and the universe in other cases.[28] The *mirada* appears with this and a variety of other functions from the early stories of *Los días enmascarados* to those of *The Orange Tree*. In "Tlactocatzine, del Jardín de Flandes," the narrator/protagonist's turning point occurs when he realizes that the mysterious old woman in the house has no eyes. In *Aura*, the protagonist is fascinated with Aura's green eyes, and there is always a special level of communication effected through the *miradas* exchanged between the protagonist and *Aura*. The point of departure and circumstance of Artemio Cruz revolve around his looking, associating, and remembering on his deathbed. In *Holy Place*, the protagonist's identity and relationship with his mother are defined, to a large extent, by how she sees him, by the circumstances in which they see or don't see each other, and by Claudia's ability to be seen and not be seen. The four main characters in *A Change of Skin* engage in an ongoing communication on the basis of *miradas*, and the *miradas* have several specific functions in the text. On the one hand, the *mirada* is often used to communicate the distant relations that the characters suffer, despite their physical proximity. Their observing through a mirror, as they often do while riding in the car, underlines this distance, with the physical object of the car's mirror intervening between the characters. On the other hand, as in *Aura*, the enigmatic qualities of the characters seem to be hidden behind their equally enigmatic *miradas*. Isabel's green eyes, like those of Aura, are particularly visible and enigmatic in *A Change of Skin*. In accordance with Paz's idea of the Mexican who hides behind his mask, several characters in this novel hide behind their masks, revealing only an ever-changing *mirada*. Consequently, the *mirada* of the other, as well as a mirror, can be momentarily revealing or momentarily trivial, depending on the situation, in *A Change of Skin*.

The *mirada* is a powerful, defining element in *Birthday* and *Terra Nostra*, and a factor in *Hydra Head* and *Distant Relations*. In *Birthday*, the subtle human relationships are such that to see without being seen is an exercise of power, and *miradas* can deny identity. As has been discussed already, the *mirada* opens new possibilities for some characters in *Terra Nostra*, and it has important functions at the end of each of the novel's three parts. The *mirada* is less significant in *Hydra Head* and *Distant Relations* than in most of Fuentes' fiction. Nevertheless, the relationship between the protagonist and his wife in *Hydra Head* is characterized by communication via the *mirada*. In *Distant Relations,* the act of narrating is more important than the act of seeing or observing, although conversations are sometimes accompanied by a suggestive *mirada*.

Old Gringo is one of Fuentes' most visually rich books and one of his novels that most elaborately and self-consciously uses the *mirada*. From the beginning of the work, the old gringo, repeating the first significant act of his predecessor Demetrio Macías of *The Underdogs,* looks back over the Rio Grande to observe a burning bridge. In both novels, the symbolic value of the burning is evoked by the very act of observing it with such intensity and care. In the mind of the old gringo, the *mirada* is an act of imagination and memory. He understands and interprets the world around him, to a large extent, on the basis of what he literally sees visually. As used by the other characters, the ubiquitous *mirada* fulfills many of the functions of Fuentes' previous fiction. After one verbal exchange between characters, for example, the narrator states: "His look [*mirada*] was more eloquent than his words" (*OG,* 14). Indeed, the characters strive to understand the other as much by visual as by verbal means. As in *Distant Relations,* reality is ultimately defined as story, but in *Old Gringo* the process of communication in a world of stories is effected largely by the *mirada*.

Fuentes also uses the device of the *mirada* in *The Campaign* and *The Orange Tree*. *The Campaign* is a novel more of history and ideas than of human relationships and *miradas,* and the latter are only minimally present in his work. The protagonist does become aware, nevertheless, of the presence of the *mirada* as a "zone of heat in the bodies around him" (*Campaign,* 85). In a key passage in the novel, Balthasar reflects upon his new identity among *gauchos,* and he uses the *mirada* to judge himself. He asks himself: "How could his eyes change?" (*Campaign,* 111). *The Orange Tree* is a much more visual novel than *The Campaign,* and the *mirada* serves different functions throughout the work. As in previous works, the *mirada* is used for moments of illumination on the part of individual characters, to suggest nonverbal communication among characters, and as an expression of desire.

The *mirada* of Fuentes' fiction is an intermediary mode of communication, unlike direct statements by characters and narrators. It functions as an image or action that frequently carries a special meaning determined by the particular context of each *mirada*.

Fuentes: The Modern and the Postmodern

Fuentes was smitten by the modernity of Cervantes, Dos Passos, Borges, Kafka, and Faulkner at a young age, and soon by the postmodernity of Joyce, Borges, and Cortázar as well. The transitional work in his oeuvre, embodying the modern and the postmodern, was *Terra Nostra*. Following the impulses of the moderns, Fuentes has published such powerfully modernist works as *Where the Air Is Clear* and *The Death of Artemio Cruz, Holy Place, Terra Nostra, Hydra Head, The Campaign,* and *The Orange Tree.* His predominantly postmodern fiction is *A Change of Skin, Birthday, Terra Nostra, Distant Relations, Old Gringo,* and *Christopher Unborn.*

The most powerful of Fuentes' modernist works are *Where the Air Is Clear, The Death of Artemio Cruz,* and *Holy Place.* In these three novels, Fuentes fully exploits the technical devices pioneered by First World modernists to explore the past and present of modern Mexico. In *Where the Air Is Clear,* he uses the multiple points of view and collage of this work's most important predecessor, *Manhattan Transfer.* The structure and narrators of the fiction of Faulkner and Butor are evident in *The Death of Artemio Cruz.* In both novels, Fuentes-the-modernist moves from a fictional world of an apparent fragmented chaos to one of order and harmony. *Holy Place,* a work written under the influence of film, uses many of the same narrative strategies. For McHale, *The Death of Artemio Cruz* and *Holy Place* represent variants of the modernist interior-monologue novel that focuses on a grid that each mind imposes on the outside world, or through which it assimilates the outside world.[29] This early Fuentes, like his modernist predecessors, was still searching for truths and still producing the totalizing grand narrative.[30]

Terra Nostra, The Campaign, Hydra Head, and *The Orange Tree* represent a continuation, to different degrees, of Fuentes' modernist project. Now that he is writing in a Western culture increasingly aware of the end of modernity, he has tempered the modernist and totalizing impulses in these four novels by the postmodern. Nevertheless, *Terra Nostra, The Campaign,* and *The Orange Tree* are historical and truth-seeking works still written under the influence of his earlier modernist interior-monologue novels. *The Campaign, Hydra Head,* and *The Orange Tree* all reach denouements more typical of modern ambiguity than of postmodern indeterminacy.

As a product of modernism rather than an opposition to it, postmodern fiction shares some modernist impulses; this is the case in Fuentes' predominantly postmodern novels *A Change of Skin, Birthday, Terra Nostra, Distant Relations, Old Gringo,* and *Christopher Unborn. A Change of Skin* was one of his early experiments with characters of multiple (rather than just double) identity, as well as with characters and space in constant transformation. When it is revealed at the end that the text of *A Change of Skin* has been produced by the mad inmate of an insane asylum, it is apparent that Fuentes' fiction has moved from concerns over the epistemological to the ontological, a sign of the postmodern.[31] *Birthday* is his most radical experiment with space, an experiment continued with *Terra Nostra* and later novels. If innovation with time was predominant in Fuentes' modern texts (*Where the Air Is Clear, The Death of Artemio Cruz*), in his postmodern works, particularly *Birthday* and *Terra Nostra,* the predominant innovation is with space.[32] The postmodern elements of *Terra Nostra* are so evident that McHale has identified it, along with Pynchon's *Gravity's Rainbow,* as one of the "paradigmatic texts of postmodernist writing, literally an anthology of postmodernist themes and devices."[33]

Distant Relations, Old Gringo, and *Christopher Unborn* continue the postmodern themes and strategies of *A Change of Skin, Birthday,* and *Terra Nostra.* Characters of multiple and transforming identities are evident in these three texts, and Fuentes flaunts the unresolved contradictions that are a sign of the postmodern. As frequently happens in postmodern texts, the reality of texts, of fiction, or of storytelling predominates over empirical reality and often subverts it. These are fictional worlds that inevitably revert to language as their principal subject.

Fuentes' postmodern fiction, despite its unresolved contradictions and metafictional qualities, is deeply historical and political. His postmodern work is a "transhistorical carnaval" (as McHale calls it) in which characters in their projected worlds and empirical reality interact.[34] Simultaneously, Fuentes engages in multiple intertextual boundary violation, including fictional characters from other novels in his texts. Consequently, the reader of Fuentes' postmodern fiction experiences an even more complex confrontation with history than in his overtly historical and political modern texts, *Where the Air Is Clear* and *The Death of Artemio Cruz*.

History, Culture, Identity

History and culture undergird the concept of identity in most of Fuentes' fiction. For Fuentes, writing implies an engagement with history, culture, and identity. The foundations of Latin American history and culture are found primarily in *Terra Nostra*, but then they are elaborated in the foundational texts *The Campaign* and *The Orange Tree*.

Fuentes' early fiction—*Los días enmasacarados, Where the Air Is Clear, Aura, The Death of Artemio Cruz*—coincides with Paz's formulations on Mexican identity. Paz traces Mexican identity back to the key moment when Cortés, by fathering the first Mexican with La Malinche, created the first Mexican of Spanish and Indian identity. Since that moment, according to Paz, the Mexican woman is *la chingada*, the proto-male is *el chingón*, and Mexicans have lived behind the mask of an identity difficult to penetrate or define. Such questioning of Mexican identity had been discussed among Mexican intellectuals since the 1940s, in the writings of Samuel Ramos, Alfonso Reyes, and José Vasconcelos. Fuentes returned to the Aztec past and La Malinche in his early fiction.

In the late 1960s, Fuentes' understanding of identity began to evolve beyond the predominant ideas of Paz in the 1950s. In *Holy Place, A Change of Skin, Birthday*, and *Terra Nostra*, his transhistorical vision is more universal and less focused on the Aztec past as the primary means of understanding the present. Now Fuentes begins including Europe as part of a historical vision beyond the Mexican Colonial past; he also begins questioning the very concept of fictional space. The multiple identities of his characters undermine any concept of the unified subject, thus rejecting Paz's formula for Mexican identity. History, culture, and identity in *Terra Nostra* are concepts that also reject the 1950s versions of both Paz and Fuentes. Now Fuentes fictionalizes history and culture as the foundations for not just Mexican identity but Latin American identity as well. In these works of the late 1960s and 1970s, his vision is, in effect, as universal as he and his generation of intellectuals had desired back in the 1950s when they published the *Revista Mexicana de Literatura*.

With *Hydra Head* and *Old Gringo,* Fuentes looks back at the Paz vision of Mexican identity as a cliché. The very idea of the mask and identity are material for satire in several passages of *Hydra Head,* thus mocking the ideas of Paz at the distance of more than three decades. In *Old Gringo,* the actions of both the Mexican and the American characters are more the manifestations of national clichés than the expression of individual identities. In this post–*Terra Nostra* work, as in *Terra Nostra* itself, Fuentes questions cultural essence and history as truth.

Conclusion

The fourteen cycles of "La Edad del Tiempo" represent one of the most significant bodies of literature to have been created and projected by a Latin American writer since the beginnings of Indo-Afro-Ibero-American culture. A vast body of work in time and space, it is set in all of the Hispanic world, from Spain to the Americas, from Argentina to the borders between Mexico and the United States, and it represents a rewriting of history from Roman times to the present. In his total work, of course, Fuentes explores many of the issues synthesized in *Terra Nostra*.

Fuentes' fiction in general, like *Terra Nostra,* exhibits a constant belief in the power of imagination as a value in itself. Liberation always returns, sooner or later, to imagination. After imagination,

Fuentes privileges the power of ideas over other forces, such as the economic or the sexual.

Much of Fuentes' fiction explores the spaces and the times of change. He is interested in those forces that transform individuals, cultures, and societies. Many of his novels are located precisely in the space of change; for example, *The Campaign* is located temporally at that key moment of transformation from colony to republic, *Terra Nostra* during the conquest and colonization, *Christopher Unborn* during the post-modernization of NAFTA.

El Escorial is the central architectural image of the Hispanic culture transferred to the Americas in the sixteenth century. But palaces have been a central body of space in Fuentes' fiction throughout his writing career. The mirror image of El Escorial in much of Fuentes' fiction is, in fact, the image of the multiple palaces of the Colonial period that have still survived in the ancient downtown area called the *centro histórico*.

A constant pattern in Fuentes' fiction is that of a character trapped within the confines of an architectural construct, desiring or needing to escape. Such is the basic circumstance, in different ways, of the protagonists of "Chac Mool," "Tlactocatzine, del Jardín de Flandes," *The Death of Artemio Cruz, Aura, Birthday, Terra Nostra,* and *Christopher Unborn.* In some of Fuentes' fiction, characters find the enclosed space sacred, as is the case of the protagonists of *Holy Place* and *Terra Nostra.* The exact definition of this enclosed space— as a punishing hell or as a sacred utopian enclosure—returns the reader to the conflict between the rational and the irrational or between the scientific and the sacred in the fiction of Fuentes.

La Edad del Tiempo:
An Interview with Carlos Fuentes, Los Angeles, California, April 1994

WILLIAMS: The first notice I saw of "La Edad del Tiempo" was the plan in the Spanish edition of *Christopher Unborn*, which is when you announced twelve of the fourteen cycles that are presented in the Spanish edition of *The Orange Tree*. Was this the first announcement, in *Christopher Unborn*?

FUENTES: I believe so, because I believe that I wrote the project for the first time at Dartmouth College in 1981. I was writing *Christopher Unborn*, and then I conceived of all the novels in a more or less organic and articulated fashion.

WILLIAMS: Do you remember the date, by chance, that you conceived of the idea for "La Edad del Tiempo"?

FUENTES: In January of 1981.

WILLIAMS: So you began to think of your cycle a while ago.

FUENTES: Fourteen years, right? And perhaps the books go through a metamorphosis many times, changing their positions like a constellation of mobile stars, changing places.

WILLIAMS: Like the characters of your novels, who are in a constant process of transformation. It is not very common that a novelist has such an overall vision of his complete work.

FUENTES: Very Balzacian, right? I've been reading Balzac since I was young. He has always been a teacher of mine, a teacher of good habits, and, at times, of bad habits. I also read other authors with complete novelistic cycles: Roger Martin Du Gard, Jean-Paul Sartre, Anthony Powell, even Faulkner. There's a tradition. The circumstances at Dartmouth, I believe, were that I was writing in a cubicle in Baker Library, and I spent a desolate winter there, which Orozco called a "white hell." Nevertheless, I found it a very stimulating setting with good friends, of course, but a place which is so isolated, Raymond, that it had to generate a cultural life of its own. In contrast, Princeton did not have its own cultural life because New York and Philadelphia are nearby. Hanover is so far away that they had to construct a cultural center, the Hopkins Center, with good films, theater, and fine chamber music. I was writing *Christopher Unborn* in a very exciting world, and the novel itself stimulated me tremendously. Perhaps because it is a novel based in the future, a prophetic novel, it permitted me, paradoxically, to look back and to try to understand my work in its entirety. Moreover, I was teaching a course on time in the novel and the novel of time. This also has something to do with my impression that there is certainly no novel without time, while there certainly have been times without novels. Many times conspire in the novel: the time in which it was written, the time of the writer, the time in which it could be written, the time it takes the reader to read it and the times that are created within the novel, the writing time, the time to which the novel refers and the historical time of the novel, the fact that while the novel occurs in the present it will transform into an historical time, as in Orwell's *1984* that has already gone by. So, all of these permutations of time are essential to the novel. There can be time without novels, as in ancient Greece and Rome, right? But there can be no novel without time. It is impossible to write a novel without the time factor at the core of the work.

   WILLIAMS: Before talking about five or six of these cycles, and the idea of "La Edad del Tiempo," why did you choose this title?

   FUENTES: Look, it is a paradoxical title because, on the one hand, I am thinking about time as an element which is essential to our era. The reflection on time as a constant, fundamental fact of modern fiction. Among the stages of history: What is modernity? When does modernity start? Are we modern? How are we modern? How do we need history? Is history beginning anew? Are we not coming to the end of a century? The end of a millennium? The beginning of a new century? A new millennium? How do we situate ourselves within this flow of history? When did the twentieth century begin? When did it end? Why are there centuries as short as ours which began in Sarajevo in 1914 and ended in Sarajevo in 1994? Why are there centuries as long as the nineteenth century, that began perhaps with the French Revolution and ended with World War I? Why are there these long cultural stages like the one which began with Goethe and the romantics but did not end until Picasso? Why are there cultural stages as short as ours, which began with Picasso and ended with Picasso? Ours is a century of crime, of homicide, of the rupture of the illusion of progress. What will we do starting with this conception of our position in history? Has history ended, like Fukuyana says, or are we incapable of identifying a new history that has grown within the parameters of the calendar that we are accustomed to? The novel is a great captor of these changes, of these historical transformations. Look, I would like to go into a little bit of depth to explain what I am talking about and add that the novel, as the novel of time, began for me with *Don Quixote*, the clearest statement that an age has ended—the Middle Ages. It turns out that in *Don Quixote* all that appears to be certain in literature is not certain in reality. For him the windmills are giants because that is what his reading taught him. The great heritage of *Don Quixote* is the idea that literature is literature and that literary time is a total fabrication of the novelist. Don Quixote knows that he is read, Tristam Shandy knows that he exists on pages. But from Napoleon Bonaparte, and the French Revolution forward, the history of the novel becomes linear. It is the history of a hero, it is the history of a psychology, but with Kafka psychology dies. Just as Don Quixote went out to the Castilian countryside to find out that the world had changed, Gregor Samsa believes that he is an insect. His era announces the end of human dignity, the concentration camps, the abolition of justice, of reason, and of progress. This is what Kafka announced in a marvelous and horrifying nightmare. And that is what Beckett finally says: "I do not exist. The fact is evident." And my question is, Do we give up in the presence of this evidence presented by Beckett? Don't we exist? Do we recognize a human being only to see his monstrosity and cut off the head of the insect? Or are we beginning to create a new conception of the person, a person who is more complex, less psychological, less secure, but more connected to the world, to the reality of time, to the reality of the world, to the reality of others? Finally, are they characters or are they figures? Cortázar wrote a page recalling another from Novalis in which he speaks of the contrast between a figure and a character. And in *Terra Nostra*, above all, I tried to create myths of the figure through the three shipwrecked boys who constantly return to a Cantabrian beach and have no more by way of an identity than a cross on their backs. That is, they are human beings in gestation, surprised at existing, mutants. We are in a time without a name and every novel is an exploration backwards, forwards, in the present; but they are explorations in time. I believe that something that the poetry of our century and some great prose writers like Jorge Luis Borges have taught us, above all, is that the past invites us to discover its novelty constantly. The past is not a permanent given. We have to discover not only the novelty of the future but also of the past.

WILLIAMS: The beginning of "La Edad del Tiempo" surprised me a little because I would have thought that perhaps *Terra Nostra* would be the beginning of the whole thing. But "El Mal del Tiempo" begins with *Aura, Birthday,* and *Distant Relations.*

FUENTES: And *Constancia.*

WILLIAMS: Oh, you have *Constancia* there now?

FUENTES: The volume that is coming out in May or June of 1994 now has *Constancia* in "El Mal del Tiempo." Your question is very pertinent because, although the cycle follows certain chronological periods after *Terra Nostra,* I want to announce with *Aura, Birthday, Distant Relations,* and *Constancia* that my conception of time is not linear. Sometimes it is a circular conception, sometimes of eternal returns, sometimes of Vican spirals like the ones we have seen in Joyce, inspired by the historical philosophy of Giambattista Vico, what Joyce calls his "Vicocyclometer." My time is a constant recuperation of the past in the present and of the future in the present. It is a constant reminder that the past is novelty and that the future is present. It is a declaration that past time is memory in the present, and that which we call the future is also desire in the present.

WILLIAMS: Then the second cycle is *Terra Nostra.* Could we say that here there is at least a certain beginning, in principle, of a chronological order?

FUENTES: Yes, although *Terra Nostra* is also based on a simultaneity of historical time, right? Many times occur at the same time. It is a way of recovering a past, but always remembering that this past is present, that this past has a present and it has a future.

WILLIAMS: Is this the reason that it is the second novel in the cycle?

FUENTES: Yes, it is called "Tiempo de Fundaciones" because it contains much of the cultural reality on which this series of novels from "La Edad del Tiempo" is based. In *Terra Nostra,* reality is presented like a star with three points. There is undoubtedly a personal, subjective reality. There is an objective material reality. But there is also a collective individuality, in which I shake hands with my culture, with others, and this is the reality that interests me the most. Collective individuality is the reality in which I identify with my culture.

WILLIAMS: The cycle called "El Tiempo Romántico" is apparently the nineteenth century.

FUENTES: Of course, this is already the chronological scheme, the "exceptions" that confirm the rule, right?

WILLIAMS: Could you say something about your general plan for *La novia muerta* and *El baile del Centenario*?

FUENTES: Sure. *La novia muerta* takes place in Paris in the middle of the nineteenth century. The characters from *the Campaign,* from Chile, Mexico, and Argentina, now have aged and are living in Paris, as the nineteenth-century Latin American oligarchy wished to live. This is a family that asks the painter Courbet to paint their portrait, and it is his resistance to painting a bourgeois work for a rich Mexican family when he was accustomed to painting cows. It is a family of oligarchs. We have the Latin American oligarchy in nineteenth-century Paris, when Europe became the Latin American utopia. Guatemala proclaimed that Guatemala was the Paris of Central America, hoping that Paris would one day proclaim itself the Guatemala of Europe.

WILLIAMS: And what is *El baile del Centenario* about?

FUENTES: *El baile del Centenario* appears to be a novel written today. It occurs during the centennial independence celebrations of Mexico, with Porfirio Díaz, with military parades, an army that looks Prussian, with German helmets and uniforms. Worldwide delegations praising the labor of Díaz and the peace and prosperity that he brought to Mexico, a letter from Tolstoy praising Díaz the peacemaker, and two months later the country was in flames. And instead of Porfirio Díaz, we have Madero, Zapata, and Pancho Villa.

WILLIAMS: Are Zapata and Pancho Villa characters in the work?

FUENTES: Well, it is about that period.

WILLIAMS: The idea of "Los días enmascarados" is the Aztec concept in which times stops, right?

FUENTES: Yes, it serves to synchronize the events that happen on the sad days of the year, the days of waiting, on the days in which it is better to stay home and not go out.

WILLIAMS: Will *La frontera de cristal* be a book of short stories?

FUENTES: It is a book of short fiction that constitutes a novel in seven stories. It represents the border theme as a common topic. At times it is basically more about Mexico or Mexicans than the United States, or North Americans in Mexico, or Mexicans in Spain, and even Mexicans discussing our border with Central America. Many borders are crossed in this book, but there is always a family, the Barroso family, which appears on all of the borders of the world.

WILLIAMS: The Barroso family, then, is like the orange in *The Orange Tree,* that is, the unifying element.

FUENTES: It is the Orange family.

WILLIAMS: What will *Los años con Laura Díaz* be about?

FUENTES: In a certain way it is a companion novel to *The Death of Artemio Cruz.* The characters are from the same period, but the story is told by a woman, a point of view very different from that of Artemio Cruz as a man. It has a little of my own family story, the story of a family in Veracruz. It is the fate of a provincial woman in Mexico City, exiled from her province after the Revolution.

WILLIAMS: The side of your family from Veracruz, however, is not your mother's side, but your father's, right?

FUENTES: Yes.

WILLIAMS: But is Laura Díaz from the same generation as Artemio Cruz?

FUENTES: Yes.

WILLIAMS: What indeed worries me a little is the order in which *A Change of Skin* appears in your "La Edad del Tiempo," because one would suppose that it might have appeared at the end of the fourteen cycles.

FUENTES: It is really a novel about Mexico's encounter with the world. In *A Change of Skin* there is a parallel between our life and contemporary life, and the life of today's world. It is the inseparable character of these two stories, of these two experiences, above all, through the element of violence. When I was a child in the schools of Washington, they told me that violence was a special trait of the poor, of the underdeveloped peoples, of dark-skinned people. On the other hand, the United States and Europe were free of this fated violence. This, despite the butchery of World War I, of racism, of everything we know but was never mentioned. I believe that Hitler and Stalin showed that European history is also violent and that the United States is also gradually discovering that it, too, is violent. But today it is clear that we are all implicated in violence. Thus, in *A Change of Skin* these connections interest me, the connections that go beyond the chronological order that is found, let's say, between "El Tiempo Romántico" and *Los años con Laura Díaz* with the linear chronological element, if you wish. Consequently, if I go back to the beginning, I return to "La Edad del Tiempo," as a circular theme. In *Christopher Unborn* there is the connection between present-day Mexico with its possible future as in the science fiction novel. In *The Orange Tree,* I finally permit myself all of the liberties of intrahistorical connections. It is a problem of the chronicles of our time.

WILLIAMS: And what does "El Tiempo Actual" consist of?

FUENTES: "El Tiempo Actual" consists of contemporary chronicles.

WILLIAMS: So after these novels of "La Edad del Tiempo" could you work on yet another plan for a cycle of novels?

FUENTES: I don't think that I will have enough time to write more novels.

WILLIAMS: Finally, are you still in agreement with the plan that you conceived of that January in Hanover?

FUENTES: Yes, even as I insist that I am writing a mutant project, a challenge to my own mortality. Imagine me in Buenos Aires last December, connecting my old readings of Borges, Bioy, Arlt, and Macedonio Fernández both with my life as a very young man in Buenos Aires and with my new friends Héctor Libertella, Luisa Valenzuela, and Martín Caparrós. Suddenly, I imagined a new novel of hopes and pratfalls, outrageous commonplaces, topias and dystopias. I might simply call it, like Scarron's work *Le Roman Comique.* Argentina and Poland are the last two cultures that believe in the universality of the French language. Is Gombrowicz the bridge between the two?

Milan Kundera and I, perhaps because we belong to the same generation, believe that he does in Europe what I cannot do in Latin America and I do in Latin America what he cannot do in Europe. Literature is made of communication, finding out what relates all things. It complements our absences, our needs. It is founded on the world, but it adds something new to the world.

"La Edad del Tiempo"

A. "La Edad del Tiempo," Version I, 1987

    I. EL MAL DEL TIEMPO
        1. *Aura*
        2. *Cumpleaños*
        3. *Una familia lejana*

    II. *TERRA NOSTRA* (Tiempo de fundaciones)

    III. EL TIEMPO ROMANTICO
        1. *La campaña*
        2. *La novia muerta*
        3. *El baile del Centenario*

    IV. EL TIEMPO REVOLUCIONARIO
        1. *Gringo viejo*
        2. *Emiliano en Chinameca*

    V. *LA REGION MAS TRANSPARENTE*

    VI. *LA MUERTE DE ARTEMIO CRUZ*

    VII. *LOS ANOS CON LAURA DIAZ*

    VIII. DOS EDUCACIONES
        1. *Las buenas conciencias*
        2. *Zona sagrada*

IX. LOS DIAS ENMASCARADOS
  1. *Los días enmascarados*
  2. *Cantar de ciegos*
  3. *Agua quemada*
  4. *Constancia*

X. EL TIEMPO POLITICO
  1. *La cabeza de la hidra*
  2. *El rey de México, o El que se mueva no
     sale en la foto*

XI. *CAMBIO DE PIEL*

XII. *CRISTOBAL NONATO*

B. "La Edad del Tiempo," Version II, 1993

I. EL MAL DEL TIEMPO
  1. *Aura*
  2. *Cumpleaños*
  3. *Una familia lejana*

II. *TERRA NOSTRA* (Tiempo de fundaciones)

III. EL TIEMPO ROMANTICO
  1. *La campaña*
  2. *La novia muerta*
  3. *El baile del Centenario*

IV. EL TIEMPO REVOLUCIONARIO
  1. *Gringo viejo*
  2. *Emiliano en Chinameca*

V. *LA REGION MAS TRANSPARENTE*

VI. *LA MUERTE DE ARTEMIO CRUZ*

VII. *LOS AÑOS CON LAURA DIAZ*

VIII. DOS EDUCACIONES
  1. *Las buenas conciencias*
  2. *Zona sagrada*

IX. LOS DIAS ENMASCARADOS
  1. *Los días enmascarados*
  2. *Cantar de ciegos*
  3. *Agua quemada*
  4. *Constancia*
  5. *La frontera de cristal*

X. EL TIEMPO POLITICO
  1. *La cabeza de la hidra*
  2. *El sillón del águila*
  3. *El camino de Texas*

XI. *CAMBIO DE PIEL*

XII. *CRISTOBAL NONATO*

XIII. EL TIEMPO ACTUAL
  1. *Crónica del guerrillero y el asesino*
  2. *Crónica de una actriz renuente*
  3. *Crónica de una víctima de nuestro tiempo*

XIV. *EL NARANJO, O LOS CIRCULOS DEL TIEMPO*

C. "La Edad del Tiempo," Version III, 1994

  I. EL MAL DEL TIEMPO
  Tomo I
    1. *Aura*
    2. *Cumpleaños*
    3. *Una familia lejana*

Tomo II
   1. *Constancia*

II. *TERRA NOSTRA* (Tiempo de fundaciones)

III. EL TIEMPO ROMANTICO
   1. *La campaña*
   2. *La novia muerta*
   3. *El baile del Centenario*

IV. EL TIEMPO REVOLUCIONARIO
   1. *Gringo viejo*
   2. *Emiliano en Chinameca*

V. *LA REGION MAS TRANSPARENTE*

VI. *LA MUERTE DE ARTEMIO CRUZ*

VII. *LOS ANOS CON LAURA DIAZ*

VIII. DOS EDUCACIONES
   1. *Las buenas conciencias*
   2. *Zona sagrada*

IX. LOS DIAS ENMASCARADOS
   1. *Los días enmascarados*
   2. *Cantar de ciegos*
   3. *Agua quemada*
   4. *La frontera de cristal*

X. EL TIEMPO POLITICO
   1. *La cabeza de la hidra*
   2. *El sillón del águila*
   3. *El camino de Texas*

XI. *CAMBIO DE PIEL*

XII. *CRISTOBAL NONATO*

PART I

1. Carlos Fuentes, "How I Started to Write," in Carlos Fuentes, *Myself and Others,* p. 83. Further quotations are from this same edition.

2. Personal interview with Berta Fuentes (Carlos Fuentes' mother), Mexico City, December 1989.

3. Personal interview with Carlos Fuentes, Mexico City, August 1989.

4. Ibid.

5. Personal interview with Roberto Torretti, San Juan, Puerto Rico, July 27, 1991.

6. Ibid.

7. Roberto Torretti's books include *Manuel Kant: Estudio sobre los fundamentos de la filosofía crítica* (Santiago: Ediciones de la Universidad de Chile, 1967); *Philosophy of Geometry from Riemann to Poincaré* (Dordreth: D. Reidel Publishing, 1978); *Relativity and Geometry* (Oxford: Pergamon Press, 1983); *Creative Understanding: Philosophical Reflections on Physics* (Chicago: University of Chicago Press, 1990).

8. John Reese Stevenson, *The Chilean Popular Front,* p. 72.

9. Personal interview with Berta Fuentes (Carlos Fuentes' sister), Mexico City, July 10, 1991.

10. John S. Brushwood, *Narrative Innovation and Political Change in Mexico,* pp. 31–46.

11. Personal interview with Berta Fuentes (sister), Mexico City, July 10, 1991.

12. Personal interview with José Campillo Sainz, Mexico City, July 12, 1991.

13. Carlos Fuentes, lecture, Coloquio de Invierno, Mexico City, February 10, 1992.

14. Personal interview with Porfirio Muñoz Ledo, Mexico City, September 22, 1991.

15. Personal interview with Sergio Pitol, Mexico City, July 14, 1991.

16. Personal interview with José Campillo Sainz, Mexico City, July 12, 1991.

17. Ibid.

18. Personal interview with Víctor Flores Olea, Mexico City, July 15, 1991.

19. Personal interview with Berta Fuentes (sister), July 10, 1991.

20. Ibid. Berta Fuentes showed me a family album with Carlos Fuentes' picture during this period.

21. Personal interview with Carlos Fuentes, London, July 15, 1992.

22. Ibid.

23. David G. La France, "Mexico Since Cárdenas," p. 213.

24. *Novedades,* December 5, 1954, no. 298, p. 2.

25. Fuentes purposely did not receive his law degree, even though he completed his coursework, in order to avoid holding the title of *Licenciado.*

26. Brushwood, *Narrative Innovation and Political Change,* p. 49.

27. *Revista Mexicana de Literatura,* no. 6 (July–August 1956): 581–589.

28. Personal interview with Sergio Pitol, Mexico City, July 14, 1991.

29. Ibid.

30. La France, "Mexico Since Cárdenas," p. 213.

31. José Donoso, *Historia personal del "boom."*

32. Roderic A. Camp, *Intellectuals and the State in Twentieth-Century Mexico,* p. 141.

33. Personal interview with Pierre Schori, Boulder, Colorado, December 6, 1993. The Swedish political scholar and politician, who has followed Fuentes' politics since the late 1960s, describes Fuentes' current political stances as those of a "radical democrat."

34. Ibid.

35. Personal interview with Gabriel García Márquez, Mexico City, February 11, 1992.

36. Ibid.

37. In *Aura,* at least two beginnings of *Terra Nostra* are evident: (1) the transformation of characters and (2) the particular use of history in which historical characters are duplicated in later generations.

38. John S. Brushwood coined the term "small-screen fiction" in *The Spanish American Novel: A Twentieth-Century Survey,* pp. 267–286.

39. In a letter from John S. Brushwood to me dated November 8, 1993, Brushwood states: "You didn't necessarily have to be a celebrity to be invited to Fuentes' Sunday gatherings. My student Frobén Lozada called Fuentes and was invited to one of them."

40. Personal interview with Gabriel García Márquez, Mexico City, February 11, 1992.

41. Personal interview with William Styron, Mexico City, February 11, 1992.

42. Ibid.

43. Wendy Farris, *Carlos Fuentes,* p. 138.

44. Juan Goytisolo, *Realms of Strife,* p. 64.

45. Despite Fuentes' criticism of some aspects of the Cuban regime, he maintained his friendship with Julio Cortázar until the Argentine's death in 1984, and he is still a very close personal friend of Gabriel García Márquez, as both Fuentes and García Márquez have confirmed with me in personal interviews.

46. Farris, *Carlos Fuentes,* p. 79.

47. Personal interview with Carlos Fuentes, London, July 15, 1992.

48. Personal interview with William Styron, Mexico City, February 11, 1992.

49. Jonathan Tittler, "Interview: Carlos Fuentes," p. 54.

50. For a list of the books in each of the three versions of "La Edad del Tiempo," see Appendix II.

51. Enrique Krauze's critique of Fuentes appeared as "The Guerrilla Dandy," in *The New Republic,* June 27, 1988, pp. 28–38.

52. The conflicts between Paz and Fuentes took the form of polemics between intellectuals affiliated with Paz's magazine *Vuelta* and Héctor Aguilar Camín's magazine *Nexos.* In February 1992, articles supporting or attacking these groups appeared in the daily press. In the months of March, April, and May, *Vuelta* published a series of articles criticizing the "Coloquio de Invierno" in general and Carlos Fuentes personally.

53. Personal interview with Carlos Fuentes, Santa Monica, California, April 23, 1994.

PART II

1. Both *Los días enmascarados* and *Where the Air Is Clear* deal with issues to be developed later in *Terra Nostra.* Fuentes' early considerations of time and history appear in the story "Tlactocatzine, del jardín de Flandes." I discuss the relationship of both these books to *Terra Nostra* in Part III.

2. George Kubler discusses the relationship between the architecture of El Escorial and the monasteries in Tarragona, Yuste, and Granada in *Building the Escorial.*

3. The Diocletian Palace in Spalato is mentioned in *Terra Nostra,* pp. 552–553.

4. Geoffrey Woodward provides background to this Erasmianism in Spain in *Philip II,* pp. 2, 5, 48, 53, 117.

5. Ibid., p. 51.

6. Ibid., p. 72.

7. Ibid.

8. M. López Serrano, *El Escorial,* p. 12.

9. See Kubler, *Building the Escorial,* for background on Herrera.

10. Michel Foucault, *The Order of Things: An Archeology of the Human Sciences,* p. 17.

11. Ibid., p. 25.

12. Miguel de Unamuno refers to El Escorial as "la gran piedra lírica," in *Andanzas y visiones españolas,* p. 83.

13. Eduardo Lemaitre, *Cartagena Colonial,* p. 12.

14. Ibid.

15. Fredric Jameson sets forth the concept of the "political unconscious" in Chapter 1 of *The Political Unconscious: Narrative As a Socially Symbolic Act.*

16. Miguel de Unamuno, *Andanzas y visiones españolas,* p. 83.

17. Woodward, *Philip II,* p. 5.

18. See Charles Jencks, *What Is Post-Modernism?*

19. Foucault, *The Order of Things,* p. 30.

20. Carlos Fuentes, *Cervantes o la crítica de la lectura,* first page.

21. José Ortega y Gasset, *Historia como sistema,* p. 39.

22. Ibid., p. 50.

23. Ibid., p. 4.

24. Ibid., p. 5.

25. Foucault, *The Order of Things,* pp. 126–127.

26. Roberto González Echevarría's basic argument concerning *Terra Nostra* is as follows: Fuentes simplifies and plagiarizes Castro, Foucault, Cervantes, and Lukacs in his attempt to portray Latin American culture. González Echevarría also reads *Terra Nostra* as a repetition of the themes set forth by Octavio Paz in *El laberinto de la soledad.* With respect to Hispanic culture, González Echevarría reads *Terra Nostra* as an effort to reach back to the original words found in a prediscursive logos that retains the keys to a homogeneous Hispanic culture. In Part II and Part III, I attempt to demonstrate the intertextuality of *Terra Nostra,* as well as the differences between the ideas of Paz in *El laberinto de la soledad* and those of Fuentes in his double project of *Terra Nostra* and *Cervantes o la crítica de la lectura.* See Roberto González Echevarría, "*Terra Nostra:* Theory and Practice."

27. González Echevarría, "*Terra Nostra,*" p. 135.

28. I use the term "intertextuality" here and throughout the remainder of Part II not in the interest of discussing any writers' possible influence upon Fuentes, nor in tracing literary "sources," but as a sign system.

29. I use the term "intertextuality" as originally proposed by Julia Kristeva and later developed by Jonathan Culler, as a sign system. In this usage, as explained by Gerald Prince, the term designates the relations between any text and the sum of knowledge, the potentially infinite network of codes and signifying practices that allows it to have meaning. See Julia Kristeva, *Desire in Language: A Semiotic Approach to Literature;* Jonathan Culler, "Presuppositions and Intertextuality," in Jonathan Culler, *The Pursuit of Signs: Semiotics, Literature, Deconstruction;* Gerald Prince, *Dictionary of Narratology,* p. 46. In addition, see Gérard Genette, *Palimpsests: La Littérature au second degré;* Laurent Jenny, "The Strategy of Form"; Gustavo Pérez Firmat, "Apuntes para un modelo de la intertextualidad en literatura"; Jean Ricardou, *Pour une theorie du nouveau roman;* Michael Riffaterre, *Semiotics of Poetry;* Michael Riffaterre, *Text Production;* and Meir Sternberg, "Proteus in Quotation Land."

30. Foucault, *The Order of Things,* p. xv.

31. Jorge Luis Borges, "Pierre Ménard, Author of *Don Quixote,*" in Jorge Luis Borges, *Ficciones,* p. 48.

32. Ingrid Simson, *Terra Nostra de Carlos Fuentes,* pp. 226–231.

33. Ibid., pp. 138–184.

34. Jorge Luis Borges, "Pierre Ménard, Author of *Don Quixote,*" in Borges, *Ficciones.*

35. *Zona sagrada,* published in 1967, had the three-part division of *Terra Nostra.*

36. Foucault, *The Order of Things,* p. 17.

37. The original painting described in *Terra Nostra* as the *cuadro traído de Orvieto* is located in a chapel in Orvieto, Italy.

38. For a psychoanalytic study of *Terra Nostra,* see Marc Nacht, "Coeur blanc de l'inacces."

39. Catherine Swietlicki discusses the Kaballa's three cosmic eras and the three parts of *Terra Nostra* in "*Terra Nostra:* Carlos Fuentes' Kaballistic World."

40. See González Echevarría, "*Terra Nostra,*" p. 137.

41. In his critique of Fuentes' historical vision, Roberto González Echevarría reads Fuentes as a modern writer, seemingly ignoring that *Terra Nostra* is, in the end, a fiction and not a text usually considered part of the discipline of history.

42. González Echevarría, "*Terra Nostra,*" p. 143.

43. Lucille Kerr, "On Shifting Ground: Authoring Mystery and Mastery in Carlos Fuentes' *Terra Nostra,*" in Lucille Kerr, *Reclaiming the Author: Figures and Fictions from Spanish America,* p. 67.

44. Foucault, *The Order of Things,* p. 367.

45. The English edition of R. G. Collingwood's *The Idea of History* appeared in 1946. The Mexican edition appeared in 1952, published by the Fondo de Cultura Económica.

46. Collingwood, *The Idea of History,* p. 46.

47. See Djelal Kadir, "Quest's Impossible Self-Seeking," in Djelal Kadir, *Questing Fictions: Latin America's Family Romance.*

48. Collingwood, *The Idea of History,* pp. 114–117.

49. Kadir, "Quest's Impossible Self-Seeking."

50. Kadir, *Questing Fictions,* p. 123.

51. Fuentes, Paz, and numerous others have written on the Aztec concept of time. See, in particular, Fuentes' *Tiempo mexicano* and Paz's "La máscara y la transparencia."

52. Alfonso Caso, *The Aztecs: People of the Sun,* p. 66.

53. J. Eric S. Thompson, *The Rise and Fall of Maya Civilization,* p. 166.

54. Raymond D. Souza, *La historia en la novela hispanoamericana,* p. 115.

55. Ibid., p. 116.

56. Ibid., p. 120.

57. Joseph Sommers, *After the Storm: Landmarks of the Modern Mexican Novel,* p. 160.

58. Ibid.

59. Souza, *La historia,* p. 128.

60. Simson, *Terra Nostra de Carlos Fuentes,* p. 199.

61. Ibid. Simson quotes Paz's "piedra de sol" as "tiempo total donde no pasa nada" [total time where nothing happens].

62. Marcelo Coddou, "*Terra Nostra* o la crítica de los cielos," p. 9.

63. Carlos Alonso, *The Spanish American Regional Novel: Modernity and Autochthony,* p. 13.

64. Ibid., p. 15.

65. Ibid., p. 17.

66. Carlos Fuentes had called these "autochthonous" writers "*primitivos.*" See *La nueva narrativa hispanoamericana,* pp. 9–14.

67. Alonso, *The Spanish American Regional Novel,* p. 17.

68. Ibid., p. 19.

69. Since Fuentes questions these concepts of time and truth, Roberto González Echevarría misreads Fuentes when he states that Fuentes claims to be "the ultimate source of truth." See González Echevarría, "*Terra Nostra.*"

70. José Ortega y Gasset, *Obras completas,* p. 19.

71. Carlos Fuentes, *The Buried Mirror,* p. 177.

72. Simson offers explanations for the Cronista's interventions. See Simson, *Terra Nostra de Carlos Fuentes,* pp. 44–53.

73. Narrative segments 84, 86–89, 91, 93, 95, 100, and 102–125 are narrated by Ludovico; narrative segments 90, 94, 96, 98, 99, 101, and 126 are narrated by Celestina; 85 and 92 seem to be narrated by both.

74. Fuentes uses the "*tú*" for the *náufrago.* See *Terra Nostra,* pp. 63–69 (Mexican edition in Spanish).

75. Lucille Kerr has discussed the enigma of the manuscript in the bottle as follows: "The manuscript sealed in a bottle is a familiar device of mystery fiction and has a double function. It is both a mystery and a solution; it both suggests and solves a problem." See Kerr, *Reclaiming the Author,* p. 79.

76. See Susan F. Levine, "Heresy and Hope in the Works of Carlos Fuentes," Chapter 3.

77. Ibid., p. 99.

78. Ibid., p. 101.

79. Ibid., p. 111.

80. Michel De Certeau, *L'écriture de l'histoire,* p. 60.

81. Ortega y Gasset, *Historia como sistema,* p. 8.

82. Fuentes also mentions Signorelli on several occasions in *Zona sagrada.*

83. Foucault, *The Order of Things,* p. 48–49.

84. González Echevarría, "*Terra Nostra.*"

85. The issue of postmodernism in Latin America has been most widely discussed in Argentina, Chile, and Mexico. The enormous volume of articles and books published in Latin America precludes any complete bibliography in the context of this study on Fuentes, but representative publications include Nicolás Casullo, ed., *El debate modernidad postmodernidad; Nuevo Texto Crítico. Modernidad y posmodernidad en América Latina (1);* Josep Pico, ed., *Modernidad y postmodernidad;* George Yúdice, "¿Puede hablarse de postmodernidad en América Latina?"

86. Linda Hutcheon, *A Poetics of Postmodernism,* p. 3.

87. See Ihab Hassan's parallel columns in *The Postmodern Turn: Essays in Postmodern Theory and Culture,* pp. 91–92.

88. Hutcheon, *Poetics of Postmodernism,* p. 49.

89. Linda Hutcheon has argued convincingly in favor of the political content in postmodern cultural production in *The Politics of Postmodernism.*

90. See Hutcheon, *Politics of Postmodernism,* and Jencks, *What Is Post-Modernism?*

91. In reality, Signorelli is never named per se in *Terra Nostra.* In an essay that appeared soon after the publication of *Terra Nostra* (later republished in his book

Disidencias), Juan Goytisolo identified the painting from Orvieto as Signorelli's. In my own personal interview with Fuentes in March 1993 in Denver, he confirmed that the painter for him is, indeed, Signorelli.

92. Fredric Jameson, *Postmodernism, or the Cultural Logic of Late Capitalism,* Chapter 1, pp. 1–54.

93. González Echevarría, "*Terra Nostra,*" p. 139.

94. Foucault, *The Order of Things,* p. 306.

95. Ibid., p. 300.

96. Ibid., p. 307.

97. Jorge Luis Borges, "Pierre Menard, Author of *Don Quixote,*" in Jorge Luis Borges, *Ficciones,* p. 53.

98. Ibid.

99. De Certeau, *L'écriture de l'histoire,* p. 4.

100. Roberto González Echevarría has suggested that Fuentes returns to a prediscursive logos in *Terra Nostra.* See "*Terra Nostra.*"

101. Jean-François Lyotard has coined the terms "grand narrative" and "small narrative" in *The Postmodern Condition: A Report on Knowledge.*

102. Paul De Man, *Blindness and Insight,* p. 148.

103. Octavio Paz, *Children of Mire: Modern Poetry from Romanticism to the Avant-Garde.*

104. Alonso, *The Spanish American Regional Novel.* See especially Chapter 1.

105. Ibid., p. 32.

106. De Certeau, *L'écriture de l'histoire,* chap. 1.

107. Ibid., p. 3.

PART III

1. The books that Fuentes proposes to write for "La Edad del Tiempo" but that he had not yet published by early 1994 are *La novia muerta; El baile del Centenario; Emiliano en Chinameca; La frontera de cristal; El sillón del águila; El camino a Texas; Aquiles, o el guerrillero y el asesino; Prometeo, o el precio de la libertad. Diana, o la cazadora solitaria* appeared in 1994 after the completion of this manuscript.

2. In addition to Sartre, other writers with cycles whom Fuentes has mentioned in our interviews are Balzac, Roger Martin Du Gard, and Anthony Powell.

3. Personal interview with Carlos Fuentes, Appendix I.

4. Ibid.

5. Ibid.

6. Richard Reeve has discussed the development of the *tú* in Fuentes' early fiction. See Richard Reeve, "Carlos Fuentes y el desarrollo del narrador en segunda persona: un ensayo exploratorio."

7. Frank Dauster, "The Wounded Vision: *Aura, Zona sagrada,* and *Cumpleaños.*"

8. For Fuentes' discussion of time, see Marcelo Coddou's interview, "*Terra Nostra,* o la crítica de los cielos," and my interview in Appendix I.

9. Personal interview with Carlos Fuentes, Appendix I.

10. Ibid.

11. Ibid.

12. Ibid.

13. Paz, "La máscara y la transparencia," p. 7.

14. Richard Reeve, "El mundo mosaico del mexicano moderno: *Cantar de ciegos,* de Carlos Fuentes."

15. Mary E. Davis, "On Becoming Velázquez: Carlos Fuentes' *The Hydra Head,*" p. 149.

16. Ibid., p. 154.

17. Emma Kafalenos has discussed the paintings in *Hydra Head* in "The Grace and Disgrace of Literature: Carlos Fuentes' *Hydra Head.*"

18. Foucault, *The Order of Things,* p. 16.

19. See Kafalenos, "The Grace and Disgrace of Literature."

20. Emir Rodríguez Monegal, "Carlos Fuentes," p. 23.

21. Julio Ortega, *La contemplación y la fiesta,* pp. 80–81.

22. Fuentes, *Tiempo mexicano,* p. 27.

23. Malva E. Filer, "*A Change of Skin* and the Shaping of a Mexican Time," pp. 122–123.

24. Ibid., p. 125.

25. Gabriel García Márquez has discussed the fact that his fiction always uses an image as the point of departure. See "The Visual Arts, the Poetization of Space, and Writing: An Interview with Gabriel García Márquez."

26. The orange and orange tree are not common in Fuentes' fiction. He mentions an orange in *Zona sagrada* as an insignificant object that Guillermo notices. See *Zona sagrada,* p. 4.

27. Jerónimo de Aguilar was mentioned fifty-eight times in *Verdadera historia de la conquista de la Nueva España,* by Bernal Díaz del Castillo.

28. See Levine, "Heresy and Hope in the Works of Carlos Fuentes," Chapter 3.

29. Brian McHale, *Postmodernist Fiction,* p. 15.

30. I have discussed the issue of truth in modern and postmodern fiction in Latin America in "The Discourse of Truth and Latin American Postmodernism." An expanded version of this piece appeared as "Western Truth Claims in the Context of the Modern and Postmodern Latin American Novel," in *Readerly/Writerly Texts.*

31. For a discussion of the ontological and the epistemological as part of contemporary fiction, see McHale, *Postmodernist Fiction,* Chapter 1, pp. 3–40.

32. David Harvey discusses the space of postmodern fiction in *The Condition of Postmodernity,* Chapter 3, pp. 39–65.

33. McHale, *Postmodernist Fiction,* p. 16.

34. Ibid., p. 17.

WORKS BY CARLOS FUENTES

Agua quemada. Mexico City: Fondo de Cultura Económica, 1981. [English edition, *Burnt Water.* New York: Farrar, Straus, and Giroux, 1980.]

Aura. Mexico City: Era, 1962. [English edition, New York: Farrar, Straus, and Giroux, 1968.]

Las buenas conciencias. Mexico City: Fondo de Cultura Económica, 1959. [English edition, *The Good Conscience.* New York: Obolensky, 1961.]

La cabeza de la hidra. Barcelona: Argos, 1978. [English edition, *The Hydra Head.* New York: Farrar, Straus, and Giroux, 1978.]

Cambio de piel. Mexico City: Joaquín Mortiz, 1967. [English edition, *A Change of Skin.* New York: Farrar, Straus, and Giroux, 1968.]

La campaña. Madrid: Mondadori, 1990. [English edition, *The Campaign.* New York: Farrar, Straus, and Giroux, 1991.]

Cantar de ciegos. Mexico City: Joaquín Mortiz, 1964. [Some stories appeared in *Burnt Water.*]

Casa con dos puertas. Mexico City: Joaquín Mortiz, 1970.

Cervantes o la crítica de la lectura. Mexico City: Joaquín Mortiz, 1976. [English edition, *Don Quixote or the Critique of Reading.* Austin: Institute of Latin American Studies, 1976.]

Constancia y otras novelas para vírgenes. Mexico City: Fondo de Cultura Económica, 1990. [English edition, *Constancia and Other Stories for Virgins.* New York: Farrar, Straus, and Giroux, 1990.]

Cristóbal nonato. Mexico City: Fondo de Cultura Económica, 1987. [English edition, *Christopher Unborn.* New York: Farrar, Straus, and Giroux, 1989.]

Cuerpos y ofrendas. Madrid: Alianza Editorial, 1972.

Cumpleaños. Mexico City: Joaquín Mortiz, 1969.

Los días enmascarados. Mexico City: Los Presentes, 1954. [English edition, partial. Some stories from this volume appeared in *Burnt Water,* 1980.]

El espejo enterrado. Mexico City: Fondo de Cultura Económica, 1992. [English edition, *The Buried Mirror.* London: André Deutsch, 1992.]

Geografía de la novela. Mexico City: Fondo de Cultura Económica, 1993.

Gringo viejo. Mexico City: Fondo de Cultura Económica, 1985. [English edition, *The Old Gringo.* New York: Farrar, Straus, and Giroux, 1985.]

"Latin America and the Universality of the Novel." In *The Novel in the Americas,* edited by Raymond Leslie Williams, pp. 1–12. Boulder: University of Colorado Press, 1992.

La muerte de Artemio Cruz. Mexico City: Fondo de Cultura Económica, 1962. [English edition, *The Death of Artemio Cruz.* New York: Obolensky, 1964.]

El mundo de José Luis Cuevas. Bilingual ed. Mexico City: Galería de Arte Misrachi, 1969.

Myself and Others. New York: Farrar, Straus, and Giroux, 1988.

La nueva narrativa hispanoamericana. Mexico City: Joaquín Mortiz, 1969.

Orquídeas a la luz de la luna. Barcelona: Seix Barral, 1982.

París: O la revolución de mayo. Mexico City: Era, 1968.

La región más transparente. Mexico City: Fondo de Cultura Económica, 1958. [English edition, *Where the Air Is Clear.* New York: Farrar, Straus, and Giroux, 1960.]

Los reinos originarios: Teatro hispanoamericano. Barcelona: Seix Barral, 1971.

Righe per Adami. Venice: Alpieri, 1968.

"Situación del escritor en América Latina." *Mundo Nuevo* 1 (July 1966): 5–21.

Terra Nostra. Mexico City: Joaquín Mortiz, 1975. [English edition, *Terra Nostra.* New York: Farrar, Straus, and Giroux, 1975.]

Tiempo mexicano. Mexico City: Joaquín Mortiz, 1971.

Todos los gatos son pardos. Mexico City: Siglo XXI, 1970.

El tuerto es rey. Mexico City: Joaquín Mortiz, 1970.

Una familia lejana. Mexico City: Era, 1980. [English edition, *Distant Relations.* New York: Farrar, Straus, and Giroux, 1982.]

Valiente mundo nuevo. Madrid: Mondadori, 1990.

Zona sagrada. Mexico City: Siglo XXI, 1967. [English edition, *Holy Place,* in *Triple Cross.* New York: Dutton, 1972.]

OTHER SOURCES

Alonso, Carlos. *The Spanish American Regional Novel: Modernity and Autochthony.* Cambridge: Cambridge University Press, 1990.

Andrada, R., et al. *El Escorial: Octava maravilla del mundo.* Barcelona: Editorial Escudo de Oro, 1987.

Báez, Antonio Martínez, et al. *Testimonios sobre Mario de la Cueva.* México: Editorial Porrúa, 1982.

Bakhtin, M. M. *The Dialogic Imagination: Four Essays.* Austin: University of Texas Press, 1981.

Bernal, Ignacio. *The Olmec World.* Berkeley: University of California Press, 1969.

Bettenson, Henry. *Documents of the Christian Church.* London: Oxford University Press, 1963.

Borges, Jorge Luis. *Ficciones.* New York: Grove Press, 1962.

———. *Obras completas.* Buenos Aires: Emecé Editores, 1974.

Boschi, Liliana Befumo, and Elsa Calabrese. *Nostalgia del futuro en la obra de Carlos Fuentes.* Buenos Aires: Fernando García Cambeiro, 1974.

Botero, Juan Carlos. "Confesiones a Botero." *Semana* (Bogota), December 21, 1993, pp. 116–121.

Brody, Robert, and Charles Rossman, eds. *Carlos Fuentes: A Critical View.* Austin: University of Texas Press, 1982.

Brushwood, John S. "A Comparative View of Mexican Fiction of the Seventies." In *The Novel in the Americas,* edited by Raymond Leslie Williams, pp. 77–90. Boulder: University of Colorado Press, 1992.

———. *Mexico in Its Novel: A Nation's Search for Identity.* Austin: University of Texas Press, 1966.

———. *Narrative Innovation and Political Change in Mexico.* University of Texas Studies in Contemporary Spanish-American Fiction, vol. 4. New York: Peter Lang Publishing, 1989.

———. "Sobre el referente y la transformación narrativa en las novelas de Carlos Fuentes y Gustavo Sainz." *Revista Iberoamericana* 47, nos. 116–117 (1981): 49–54.

———. *The Spanish American Novel: A Twentieth-Century Survey.* Austin: University of Texas Press, 1975.

Calderón, Emilio. *Amores y desamores de Felipe II.* Madrid: Editorial Cerene, 1991.

Callan, Richard. "The Jungian Basis of Carlos Fuentes' *Aura.*" *Kentucky Romance Quarterly* 18 (1971): 65–75.

Camp, Roderic A. *Intellectuals and the State in Twentieth-Century Mexico.* Austin: University of Texas Press, 1985.

Carballo, Emmanuel. "Carlos Fuentes." In *Diecinueve protagonistas de la literatura mexicana del siglo XX,* pp. 427–448. Mexico City: Empresas, 1965.

Carrasco, David. "Desire and Frontier: Apparitions from the Unconscious in *The Old Gringo.*" In *The Novel in the Americas,* edited by Raymond Leslie Williams, pp. 101–119. Boulder: University of Colorado Press, 1992.

Caso, Alfonso. *The Aztecs: People of the Sun.* Norman: University of Oklahoma Press, 1958.

Castro, Américo. *España en su historia.* Buenos Aires: Editorial Losada, 1948.

———. *La realidad histórica de España.* Mexico City: Editorial Porrúa, 1954.

Casullo, Nicolás, ed. *El debate modernidad postmodernidad.* Buenos Aires: Puntosur, 1989.

Coddou, Marcelo. "*Terra Nostra* o la crítica de los cielos." *American Hispanist* 3, no. 24 (1978): 9.

Collingwood, R. G. *The Idea of History.* Oxford: Oxford University Press, 1946.

Conde Ortega, José Francisco, et al. *Carlos Fuentes: Cuarenta años de escritor.* México: Universidad Autónoma Metropolitana, 1993.

Culler, Jonathan. *The Pursuit of Signs: Semiotics, Literature, Deconstruction.* Ithaca: Cornell University Press, 1981.

Dauster, Frank. "The Wounded Vision: *Aura, Zona sagrada,* and *Cumpleaños.*"

In *Carlos Fuentes,* edited by Robert Brody and Charles Rossman, pp. 106–120. Austin: University of Texas Press, 1982.

Davis, Mary E. "On Becoming Velázquez: Carlos Fuentes' *The Hydra Head.*" In *Carlos Fuentes,* edited by Robert Brody and Charles Rossman, pp. 146–155. Austin: University of Texas Press, 1982.

De Certeau, Michel. *L'écriture de l'histoire.* Paris: Editions Gallimard, 1975.

De Guzman, Daniel. *Carlos Fuentes.* New York: Twayne Publishers, 1972.

De Man, Paul. *Blindness and Insight.* New York: Oxford University Press, 1971.

Díaz del Castillo, Bernal. *Historia verdadera de la Conquista de la Nueva España.* Mexico City: Editorial Porrúa, 1955.

Doezma, Herman P. "An Interview with Carlos Fuentes." *Modern Fiction Studies* 18 (Winter 1972–1973): 491–503.

Donoso, José. *Historia personal del "boom."* Barcelona: Seix Barral, 1972.

Dostoievsky, F. M. *The Diary of a Writer.* Translated and annotated by Boris Brasol. New York: Charles Scribner's Sons, 1949.

Durán, Gloria. *The Archetypes of Carlos Fuentes: From Witch to Androgine.* Hamden, Conn.: Shoestring Press, Archon, 1980.

Dwyer, John. "Una Conversación con Carlos Fuentes." In *Autorretratos y espejos,* edited by Gloria and Manuel Durán, p. 63. Boston: Heinle and Heinle, 1988.

Eco, Umberto. *The Open Work.* Translated by Anna Cancogni. Cambridge: Harvard University Press, 1989.

Elliot, J. H. *Imperial Spain, 1469–1716.* New York: Penguin Books, 1990.

Farris, Wendy. *Carlos Fuentes.* New York: Ungar, 1983.

Fell, Claude. "Mito y realidad en Carlos Fuentes." In *Homenaje a Carlos Fuentes,* edited by Helmy F. Giacoman, pp. 367–376. New York: Las Américas, 1971.

Filer, Malva E. "*A Change of Skin* and the Shaping of a Mexican Time," in *Carlos Fuentes,* edited by Robert Brody and Charles Rossman. Austin: University of Texas Press, 1982.

Fortson, James R. *Perspectivas mexicanas desde París: Un diálogo con Carlos Fuentes.* Mexico City: Corporación Editorial, 1973.

Foucault, Michel. *The Order of Things: An Archeology of the Human Sciences.* Translation of *Les mots et les choses.* New York: Vintage Books, 1973.

García de Aldridge, Adriana. "Herejía y portento en 'Carne, esferas, ojos grises junto al Sena,' de Carlos Fuentes." *Cuadernos americanos* 32, no. 3 (Mexico City, 1973): 231–246.

Garibay, K. Angel María. *Historia de la literatura nahuatl.* Mexico City: Editorial Porrúa, 1954.

Gertel, Zunilda. "Semiótica, historia y ficción en *Terra Nostra.*" *Revista Iberoamericana* 47, nos. 116–117 (1981): 63–72.

Genette, Gérard. *Figures III.* Paris: Editions du Seuil, 1972. [English edition, *Narrative Discourse: An Essay in Method.* Ithaca: Cornell University Press, 1980.]

———. *Palimpsests: La Littérature au second degré.* Paris: Editions du Seuil, 1982.

Giacoman, Helmy F., ed. *Homenaje a Carlos Fuentes.* New York: Las Américas, 1971.

Gibbon, Edward. *The Decline and Fall of the Roman Empire.* New York: Washington Square Press, 1962.

Gilman, Stephen. *The Spain of Fernando de Rojas: The Intellectual and Social Landscape of La Celestina.* Princeton: Princeton University Press, 1972.

Gilman, Stephen, and Edmund L. King. *An Idea of History: Selected Essays of Américo Castro.* Columbus: Ohio State University Press, 1977.

González Echevarría, Roberto. "Carlos Fuentes: *Terra Nostra.*" *World Literature Today* 52, no. 1 (1978): 84.

———. "*Terra Nostra:* Teoría y práctica." *Revista Iberoamericana* 47, nos. 116–117 (1981): 298–321.

———. "*Terra Nostra:* Theory and Practice." In *Carlos Fuentes,* edited by Robert Brody and Charles Rossman, pp. 132–145. Austin: University of Texas Press, 1982.

———. *The Voice of the Masters: Writing and Authority in Modern Latin American Literature.* Austin: University of Texas Press, 1985.

Goytisolo, Juan. *Disidencias.* Barcelona: Seix Barral, 1977.

———. *Realms of Strife.* London: Northpoint Press/Quartet Books, 1990.

Gyurko, Lanin. "Freedom and Fate in Carlos Fuentes' *Cambio de piel.*" *Revista/Review Interamericana* 7, no. 4 (1977–1978): 703–739.

———. "Identity and the Mask in Fuentes' *La región más transparente.*" *Hispanófila* 65 (January 1979): 75–103.

———. "The Myths of Ulysses in Fuentes' *Zona sagrada.*" *Modern Language Review* 69 (April 1974): 316–324.

———. "Novel into Essay: Fuentes' *Terra Nostra* As Generator of *Cervantes o la crítica de la lectura.*" *Mester* 11, no. 2 (1982): 16–35.

———. "The Pseudo-Liberated Woman in Fuentes' *Zona sagrada.*" *Journal of Spanish Studies: Twentieth Century* 3 (1975): 17–43.

———. "The Self and the Demonic in Fuentes' *Una familia lejana.*" *Revista/Review Interamericana* 12 (Winter 1982–1983): 572–620.

Harss, Luis, and Barbara Dohmann. *Into the Mainstream: Conversations with Latin American Writers.* New York: Harper and Row, 1967.

Harvey, David. *The Condition of Postmodernity.* Cambridge: Blackwell Publishers, 1990.

Hassan, Ihab. *The Postmodern Turn: Essays in Postmodern Theory and Culture.* Columbus: Ohio State University Press, 1987.

Hazm de Córdoba, Ibn. *El collar de la paloma.* Translated by Emilio García Gómez. Madrid: Alianza Editorial, 1952.

Hernández de López, Ana María, ed. *La obra de Carlos Fuentes: Una visión múltiple.* Madrid: Editorial Pliegos, 1988.

Hutcheon, Linda. *A Poetics of Postmodernism: History, Theory, Fiction.* London: Routledge, 1988.

———. *The Politics of Postmodernism.* London: Routledge, 1989.

Jameson, Fredric. *The Political Unconscious: Narrative As a Socially Symbolic Act.* Ithaca: Cornell University Press, 1981.

———. *Postmodernism, or the Cultural Logic of Late Capitalism.* Durham: Duke University Press, 1991.

Jencks, Charles. *What Is Post-Modernism?* New York: Academy Editions/St. Martin's Press, 1986.

Jenny, Laurent. "The Strategy of Form." In *French Literary Theory Today,* edited by Tzvetan Todorov, pp. 34–63. Cambridge: Cambridge University Press, 1982.

Kadir, Djelal. "Fuentes and the Profane Sublime." In *The Other Writing: Postcolonial Essays in Latin America's Writing Culture,* pp. 73–110. West Lafayette, Ind.: Purdue University Press, 1993.

———. *Questing Fictions: Latin America's Family Romance.* Theory and History of Literature, vol. 32. Minneapolis: University of Minnesota Press, 1986.

Kafalenos, Emma. "The Grace and Disgrace of Literature: Carlos Fuentes' *Hydra Head.*" *Latin American Literary Review* 15, no. 29 (January–June 1987): 141–158.

Kamen, Henry. *The Spanish Inquisition.* New York: New American Library, 1965.

Kerr, Lucille. "The Paradox of Power and Mystery: Carlos Fuentes' *Terra Nostra,*" *PMLA* 95, no. 1 (1980): 91–102.

———. *Reclaiming the Author: Figures and Fictions from Spanish America.* Durham: Duke University Press, 1992.

Kestner, Joseph A. *The Spatiality of the Novel.* Detroit: Wayne State University Press, 1978.

Kristeva, Julia. *Desire in Language: A Semiotic Approach to Literature.* New York: Columbia University Press, 1980.

Kubler, George. *Building the Escorial.* Princeton: Princeton University Press, 1982.

La France, David G. "Mexico Since Cárdenas." In *Twentieth-Century Mexico,* edited by W. Dirk Raat and William H. Beezley, pp. 206–222. Lincoln: University of Nebraska Press, 1986.

Lemaitre, Eduardo. *Cartagena Colonial.* Bogota: Canal Ramírez Antares, 1973.

Levin, Harry. *Contexts of Criticism.* Cambridge: Harvard University Press, 1958.

Levine, Susan F. "'Cuerpo' y 'No-Cuerpo'—Una Conjunción entre Juan Goytisolo y Octavio Paz." *Journal of Spanish Studies: Twentieth Century* 5, no. 2 (Fall 1977): 123–135.

———. "Heresy and Hope in the Works of Carlos Fuentes." Ph.D. diss., University of Kansas, 1980.

———. "The Lesson of the *Quijote* in the Works of Carlos Fuentes and Juan Goytisolo." *Journal of Spanish Studies: Twentieth Century* 7, no. 2 (1979): 173–185.

———. "Poe and Fuentes: The Reader's Prerogatives." *Comparative Literature* 36, no. 1 (Winter 1984): 34–53.

———. "The Pyramid and the Volcano: Carlos Fuentes' *Cambio de piel* and Malcolm Lowry's *Under the Volcano.*" *Mester* 11, no. 1 (1982): 25–40.

Lyotard, Jean-François. *The Postmodern Condition: A Report on Knowledge.* Translated from the French by Geoff Bennington and Brian Massumi. Foreword by Fredric Jameson. Theory and History of Literature, vol. 10. Minneapolis: University of Minnesota Press, 1984.

McHale, Brian. *Postmodernist Fiction.* New York: Methuen, 1987.

Mead, Robert. "Carlos Fuentes, Mexico's Angry Novelist." *Books Abroad* 38 (1964): 380–382.

Menton, Seymour. *Latin America's New Historical Novel.* Austin: University of Texas Press, 1993.

———. *Narrativa mexicana.* Mexico City: Universidad Autónoma de Tlaxcala/Universidad Autónoma de Puebla, 1991.

Nacht, Marc. "Coeur blanc de l'inacces." *Confrontation* 6 (Autumn 1981): 57–67.

Nuevo Texto Crítico. Modernidad y postmodernidad en América Latina 1, no. 6 (1990). Stanford: Department of Spanish and Portuguese, Stanford University.

Nuevo Texto Crítico. Modernidad y postmodernidad en América Latina 2, no. 7 (1991). Stanford: Department of Spanish and Portuguese, Stanford University.

Ordiz, Francisco Javier. *El mito en la obra narrativa de Carlos Fuentes.* México: Universidad de León, 1987.

Ortega, Julio. *La contemplación y la fiesta.* Lima: Editorial Universitaria, 1968.

———. *The Poetics of Change: The New Spanish-American Narrative.* Translated by Galen D. Greaser. Austin: University of Texas Press, 1984.

Ortega y Gasset, José. *The Dehumanization of Art.* Princeton: Princeton University Press, 1968.

———. *El espectador.* Book 2 of *Obras completas* (1916–1934). 5th ed. Madrid: Revista de Occidente, 1961.

———. *Historia como sistema.* Madrid: Revista de Occidente, 1962.

———. *La rebelión de las masas.* Barcelona: Editorial Planeta, 1985.

Ortiz Vásquez, Javier, et al. *Carlos Fuentes.* Barcelona: Editorial Anthropos, 1988.

Oviedo, José Miguel. "Fuentes: Sinfonía del Nuevo Mundo." *Hispamérica* 6, no. 16 (1977): 19–32.

Patán, Federico. "Recent Mexican Fiction." In *The Novel in the Americas,* edited by Raymond Leslie Williams, pp. 91–100. Boulder: University of Colorado Press, 1992.

Paz, Octavio. *Children of Mire: Modern Poetry from Romanticism to the Avant-Garde.* Cambridge: Harvard University Press, 1974.

———. *The Labyrinth of Solitude.* New York: Grove Press, 1961.

———. "La máscara y la transparencia." Introduction to Carlos Fuentes, *Cuerpos y ofrendas,* pp. 7–15. Madrid: Alianza Editorial, 1972.

Peden, Margaret Sayers. "*Terra Nostra:* Fact and Fiction." *American Hispanist* 1, no. 1 (1975): 4–6.

Pérez Firmat, Gustavo. "Apuntes para un modelo de la intertextualidad en literatura." *Romanic Review* 69 (1978): 1–14.

Pico, Josep, ed. *Modernidad y postmodernidad.* Madrid: Alianza Editorial, 1988.

Poniatowska, Elena. *¡Ay, vida, no me mereces!* Mexico City: Joaquín Mortiz, 1985.

Prince, Gerald. *Dictionary of Narratology.* Lincoln: University of Nebraska Press, 1987.

Raat, W. Dirk, and William H. Beezley, eds. *Twentieth-Century Mexico.* Lincoln: University of Nebraska Press, 1986.

Ramírez Mattei, Aida Elsa. *La narrativa de Carlos Fuentes.* San Juan: Editorial de la Universidad de Puerto Rico, 1983.

Reeve, Richard. "Carlos Fuentes y el desarrollo del narrador en segunda persona:

un ensayo exploratorio." In Helmy F. Giacoman, ed., *Homenaje a Carlos Fuentes,* pp. 75–87. New York: Las Américas, 1971.

————. "El mundo mosaico del mexicano moderno: *Cantar de ciegos,* de Carlos Fuentes." *Nueva narrativa Hispanoamericana* 1, no. 2 (September 1971): 79–86.

Reyes, Alfonso. "Ultima Tule." In *Obras completas.* Vol. 11, pp. 10–155. Mexico City: Fondo de Cultura Económica, 1960.

Ricardou, Jean. *Pour une theorie du nouveau roman.* Paris: Seuil, 1971.

Riffaterre, Michael. *Semiotics of Poetry.* Bloomington: Indiana University Press, 1978.

————. *Text Production.* Translated by Teres Lyons. New York: Columbia University Press, 1983.

Rodríguez Monegal, Emir. "Carlos Fuentes." In *Homenaje a Carlos Fuentes,* edited by Helmy F. Giacoman, pp. 25–65. New York: Las Américas, 1971.

Runes, Dagobert D. Foreword to *The Wisdom of the Kabbalah.* New York: Citadel Press, 1967.

Sánchez-Albornoz, Claudio. *La España Musulmana.* Buenos Aires: Librería El Ateneo, 1946.

Schmidt, Donald. "Changing Techniques in the Mexican *Indigenista* Novel." Ph.D. diss., University of Kansas, 1972.

Séjourné, Laurette. *Pensamiento y religión en el México antiguo.* Mexico City: Fondo de Cultura Económica, 1957.

Serrano, M. López. *El Escorial.* Madrid: Editorial Patrimonio Nacional, 1976.

Simson, Ingrid. *Realidad y ficción en Terra Nostra de Carlos Fuentes.* Frankfurt: Vervuert, 1989.

Smitten, Jeffrey R., and Ann Daghistany. *Spatial Form in Narrative.* Ithaca: Cornell University Press, 1981.

Sommers, Joseph. *After the Storm: Landmarks of the Modern Mexican Novel.* Albuquerque: University of New Mexico Press, 1968.

Souza, Raymond D. *La historia en la novela hispanoamericana moderna.* Bogota: Tercer Mundo Editores, 1988.

Sternberg, Meir. "Proteus in Quotation Land." *Poetics Today* 3, no. 2 (Spring 1982): 107–156.

Stevenson, John Reese. *The Chilean Popular Front.* Philadelphia: University of Pennsylvania Press, 1942.

Strauss, Leo. *Persecution and the Art of Writing.* Glencoe, Ill.: Free Press, 1952.

Swietlicki, Catherine. "Doubling, Reincarnation, and the Cosmic Order in *Terra Nostra.*" *Hispanófila* 79, no. 1 (1983): 93–104.

————. "*Terra Nostra:* Carlos Fuentes' Kabbalistic World." *Symposium* 35, no. 2 (1981): 155–167.

Thompson, J. Eric S. *The Rise and Fall of Maya Civilization.* Norman: University of Oklahoma Press, 1954.

Tittler, Jonathan. "Interview: Carlos Fuentes." *Diacritics* 10, no. III (September 1980): 46–56.

————. *Narrative Irony in the Contemporary Spanish-American Novel.* Ithaca: Cornell University Press, 1984.

Unamuno, Miguel de. *Andanzas y visiones españolas.* Madrid: Alianza, 1988.

Valbuena y Prat, Angel. *La novela picaresca española.* Madrid: Aguilar, 1956.

Valdés, M. L. "Myth and History in *Cien años de soledad* and *La muerte de Artemio Cruz.*" *Reflexión* 2, nos. 3–4 (1974– 1975): 243–255.

Weinstein, Leo. *The Metamorphoses of Don Juan.* New York: AMS Press, 1967.

Williams, Raymond Leslie. "The Discourse of Truth and Latin American Postmodernism." *Profession* (November 1992): 6–9.

———. "Observaciones sobre el doble en *Terra Nostra.*" In *Actas: Simposio Carlos Fuentes,* edited by Isaac Jack Levy, pp. 175–183. Columbia: University of South Carolina Press, 1979.

———. "The Octavio Paz Industry." *American Book Review* 14, no. 3 (August– September 1992): 3–10.

———. "The Visual Arts, the Poetization of Space, and Writing: An Interview with Gabriel García Márquez." *PMLA* 104, no. 2 (March 1989): 131–140.

———. "Western Truth Claims in the Context of the Modern and Postmodern Latin American Novel." *Readerly/Writerly Texts* 1, no. 1 (Fall–Winter 1993): 39–64.

———, ed. *The Novel in the Americas.* Boulder: University of Colorado Press, 1992.

Wood, Michael. "The New World and the Old Novel." *Inti* 5–6 (1977): 12.

Woodward, Geoffrey. *Philip II.* London: Longman, 1992.

Yates, Frances A. *The Art of Memory.* Chicago: University of Chicago Press, 1966.

Yúdice, George. "¿Puede hablarse de postmodernidad en América Latina?" *Revista de Crítica Literaria Latinoamericana* (Lima), no. 29 (1989): 105–128.